Modelling Household
Formation and Dissolution

Modelling Household Formation and Dissolution

EDITED BY

Nico Keilman

Anton Kuijsten

Ad Vossen

CLARENDON PRESS·OXFORD
1988

Oxford University Press, Walton Street, Oxford OX2 6DP

Oxford New York Toronto
Delhi Bombay Calcutta Madras Karachi
Kuala Lumpur Singapore Hong Kong Tokyo
Nairobi Dar es Salaam Cape Town
Melbourne Auckland
and associated companies in
Beirut Berlin Ibadan Nicosia

Oxford is a trade mark of Oxford University Press

Published in the United States
by Oxford University Press, New York

British Library Cataloguing in Publication Data
Modelling household formation and dissolution
1. Demography 2. Households
I. Keilman, Nico II. Kuijsten, Anton
III. Vossen, Ad
304.6   HB871
ISBN 0-19-829500-6

Library of Congress Cataloging in Publication Data
Data available

Set by Colset Private Ltd, Singapore
Printed and bound in Great Britain by
Biddles Ltd, Guildford and King's Lynn

Foreword

'THE days of the child-king are over,' wrote Ariës in his essay on the two successive motivations for the declining birth rate in the West. With the demise of the child-king the position of the family changed. It became an embattled institution. Demographers were slow to reassess the value of the traditional concept of marital status. Now they are undertaking this task and interest in living arrangements and household formation is growing rapidly.

In many Western countries, until the end of the 1950s, a person's living arrangements and the type of household in which he or she lived could be predicted reasonably well by looking at the individual's age and marital status. Most young adults who had never been married lived in the household of their parents. Married persons lived in a traditional family, the overwhelming majority of them having children. Females heading a one-parent family were usually separated, sometimes they had experienced a divorce.

But then, in the 1960s, the scene altered dramatically. Sexuality was increasingly separated from marriage and from procreation. Consensual unions gained acceptance and in most developed countries more liberal legislation led to increasing divorce rates. As a consequence of this, marital status became a less and less accurate predictor of living arrangements. Instead, interest in household processes grew rapidly.

And now, in the 1980s, both government officials and researchers are trying to gain insight into the formation and dissolution of one-parent families, non-family households, and the traditional family. These developments are of major importance to national and local policy makers because of their (profound) impact on social security (female headed one-parent families, child allowances, care for the aged), housing (one- and two-person households), sources of income, consumption, and so on.

In spite of its paramount political relevance, scientific knowledge of household demography is still limited, in particular regarding its modelling aspects. As opposed to the study of individuals, there is little agreement among researchers as to the approach best suited to study demographic aspects of households.

Discussions among demographers seem to focus on such points as:

- the most suitable definition of the household, based on sociological and economic theories about household formation and dissolution;
- the most suitable definition of the household for the purpose of data collection;
- the most suitable sources of household data: population censuses, vital registers, or special surveys?
- the problem whether the declining importance of the traditional family will

spread from Scandinavia, where the trend started quite some time ago, to other European countries and, if so, whether it will assume the same proportions;
• the most suitable methods of making household projections;
• the relationship between household studies and their practical use, for instance in the fields of housing policy, regional planning, and care for the aged;
• the most suitable unit of analysis and modelling: the individual or the household?

In order to contribute to the development of household demography, the Netherlands Interuniversity Demographic Institute (NIDI) organized, in co-operation with the University of Amsterdam, Tilburg University, and the Netherlands Demographic Society, and under the auspices of the European Association for Population Studies (EAPS), an international workshop on changing households, from 12 to 14 December 1984. In view of the fact that household demography is still in its infancy, the main purpose of the work-shop was to make an inventory of existing opinions and insights.

A selection of the papers presented at the workshop was made, and these underwent (major) revisions, in order to reflect the workshop discussions. Thus most of the chapters in this book originally stem from the workshop. Chapters 6 (Schwarz), 7 (Willekens), and 17 (Keilman and Keyfitz), however, were especially written for this volume.

I sincerely hope that this book may find its way to its perceived audience, and that it helps to clarify some of the issues raised above. At least, demo-graphers should try to understand the nature and causes of household pro-cesses, well before the household concept itself becomes obsolete!

DIRK J. VAN DE KAA
Director of the NIDI and
President of EAPS

September 1986

Acknowledgements

THE preparation of this volume was made possible by the generous institutional support of the Netherlands Interuniversity Demographic Institute (NIDI), the Department of Physical Planning and Demography of the University of Amsterdam, and the Department of Social Science of Tilburg University. The Netherlands Ministry of Education and Science supplied the NIDI with a grant to cover the costs of organizing the Workshop 'Modelling household formation and dissolution' in December 1984, and to cover part of the costs of producing this book.

Several persons contributed to this volume. Willemien Kneppelhout of the NIDI did the necessary translating and English-language editing of the text. We are deeply indebted to her for her suggestions for improving the text. The work of the secretarial staff of the NIDI is gratefully acknowledged. Tonny Nieuwstraten typed all the chapters, some of them more than once. Requests by us for yet another round of revisions were always received cheerfully. Jacqueline van der Helm and Joan Vrind assisted in the production of some chapters. Frans Willekens of the NIDI provided us with valuable advice during the course of the entire project. Finally, we would like to thank all publishers and individual authors for granting us permission to use material that was published earlier.

NICO KEILMAN
ANTON KUIJSTEN
AD VOSSEN

September 1986

Contents

ix

Contents

List of Tables

List of Illustrations

List of Contributors

J. BARTLEMA, Department of Social Science, Tilburg University, Tilburg, the Netherlands (Chapter 16).

J. BROUWER, AXON Systems Development and Research, Delft, the Netherlands (Chapter 15).

A. BROWN, Office of Population Censuses and Surveys, London, United Kingdom (Chapter 5).

D. COURGEAU, Institut National d'Études Démographiques, Paris, France (Chapter 11).

J. ERMISCH, National Institute of Economic and Social Research, London, United Kingdom (Chapter 3).

H. GALLER, Department of Economics, University of Bielefeld and Sonderforschungsbereich 3, University of Frankfurt, Federal Republic of Germany (Chapter 10).

F. KAMARÁS, Hungarian Central Statistical Office, Budapest, Hungary (Chapter 13).

N. KEILMAN, Netherlands Interuniversity Demographic Institute, The Hague, the Netherlands (Chapter 9, Chapter 17).

N. KEYFITZ, International Institute for Applied Systems Analysis, Laxenburg, Austria (Chapter 17).

F. KLIJZING, Netherlands Interuniversity Demographic Institute, The Hague, the Netherlands (Chapter 4).

A. KUIJSTEN, Department of Physical Planning and Demography, University of Amsterdam, Amsterdam, the Netherlands (Chapter 1, Chapter 12).

E. LELIÈVRE, Institut National d'Études Démographiques, Paris, France (Chapter 11).

W. LINKE, Bundesinstitut für Bevölkerungsforschung, Wiesbaden, Federal Republic of Germany (Chapter 8).

M. MURPHY, London School of Economics, London, United Kingdom (Chapter 5).

J. SCHMID, Chair of Population Sciences, University of Bamberg, Bamberg, Federal Republic of Germany (Chapter 2).

H. SCHOLTEN, National Physical Planning Agency, The Hague, the Netherlands (Chapter 14).

K. SCHWARZ, Wiesbaden, Federal Republic of Germany (Chapter 6).

List of Contributors

O. SULLIVAN, London School of Economics, London, United Kingdom (Chapter 5).

H. TER HEIDE, National Physical Planning Agency, The Hague, the Netherlands (Chapter 14).

A. VOSSEN, Department of Social Science, Tilburg University, Tilburg, the Netherlands (Chapter 1, Chapter 16).

F. WILLEKENS, Netherlands Interuniversity Demographic Institute, The Hague, the Netherlands (Chapter 7).

PART I

Preliminaries

1

Introduction

A. Kuijsten and A. Vossen

1.1. The relevance of household models

DEMOGRAPHY is the scientific study of human populations, primarily with respect to their size, their structure, and their development (United Nations, 1958, p. 3). Conventionally, populations are defined as sets of individuals with specific attributes defined and measured at the level of the individual population member. Population dynamics, that is, changes in the size and structure of populations, is modelled on the basis of the individual as the unit of observation and analysis. Population projections, being intelligent assessments of probable or imaginable future population dynamics, are modelled on the same basis. Data collection systems, whether civil registration systems or survey- or census-based data gathering systems, traditionally demonstrate the same individual-based tendency.

People have attributes that are indeed pure individual characteristics, sex and age being the most relevant ones in conventional demographic analysis. People also have attributes which can be defined and observed at the individual level, but which are essentially relational attributes, in the sense that they refer to membership of and/or position within primary groups such as families and households: marital status and household position are examples of this category.

The demography of households and families focuses on such primary groups, taking these as the units of analysis and prediction in studying changes in their number and composition. Since the types of primary groups are manifold, some organizing principles are expedient. In this respect, Ryder (1985) distinguishes three dimensions characterizing the family concept, proceeding from the least to the most complex dimension:

- the conjugal relationship, that is, the formation and dissolution of marital unions;
- the consanguineal relationship, that is, the relationship between parents and children; and
- the nuclear family, being the simplest residential combination of the conjugal and the consanguineal dimensions.

The household dimension, finally, refers to primary groups, both familial and non-familial, that are identified by co-residence.

3

This book deals with households, and with problems of modelling household dynamics in particular. Households are the most complex type of primary units, embracing aspects of all less complex dimensions of the above classification. Nuclear families as isolated co-resident groups are only one of the subsets of households, besides other subsets such as isolated co-resident conjugal units (childless couples), one-person households, and co-resident groups consisting of individuals not tied by conjugal and/or consanguineal bonds (non-family households). Several modelling problems (and their possible solutions) that stem from this asymmetrical relationship between the principle of co-residency implicit in the household concept and the principles of conjugality and consanguinity (the 'demographic' principles) implicit in the family concept will be dealt with in this volume.

For policy makers, the household is usually a much more relevant unit than the individual. First and foremost, the dimension of co-residency in the household concept automatically makes the household the perfect and essential unit of analysis and prediction underlying policy formulation in the field of (social) housing. Size and composition of a household are essential in evaluating its housing needs; sometimes, they determine whether or not the household is entitled to occupy a dwelling in the so-called social housing sector.

Moreover, size and composition of a household may be important determinants of its housing preferences. Since the satisfaction of specific demands with respect to type and size of a dwelling, as well as its location, often implies the necessity to move, the household is a relevant basic category for regional policies too. Besides being a co-residential unit, the household is the basic unit of consumption, especially as far as the procurement of consumer durables is concerned. Purchasing decisions as such, the choice from the multitude of types offered, and the way of using consumer durables depend on size and composition of the household unit. This relevance of the household unit for consumer behaviour is important for public services (energy provision, public transport, social security, and so on) as well as for services and commodities offered by private enterprises.

Changes in number and composition of households, then, are of paramount importance to policy makers, both in the public and in the private sector. Through constructing, testing, and applying household models, demographers can contribute to policy formulation.

1.2. A focus on household formation and dissolution processes

In demography, the family and the household have hitherto been treated in a stepmotherly fashion. The individual-based methods of analysis and the individual-based systems of data collection are understandable, if not completely satisfying, excuses. For too long, demographers have hesitated to draw the ultimate conclusion from what has been said above about the greater relevance of the primary group, and the household in particular, as a unit for policy concern in various fields and as a unit of consumption. There are some extenuating circumstances, of course, in defence of this neglect. The most important one is the scarcity of adequate data at the household level, especially the kind of data required for the analysis of the household's dynamic aspects. Indeed, a long tradition exists, in demography as well as in family sociology, in the analysis of qualitative aspects of the primary group, as well as with respect to the quantitative analysis of cross-sectional data. No such tradition exists with respect to the quantitative analysis of the dynamic processes involved. This is, of course, related to another circumstance: the relative paucity of methods of analysis and of modelling efforts focusing on primary group dynamics, the very topic to which this volume is devoted. Nevertheless, the excuses remain unconvincing. What is perhaps most puzzling in this respect is the ultimate theoretical consequence of the recognition not only that family and household are the basic decision-making units with regard to the aforementioned fields of housing, amenity use, consumption, and use of social security provisions, but that they are at the same time the basic decision-making units regarding most phenomena studied in conventional individual-based demography: fertility, nuptiality, divorce, and migration. A full-fledged elaboration of the consequences of this viewpoint for an alternative conceptualization of the basic demographic variables would lead us too far astray (see Ryder, 1983; Akkerman, 1982; and Willekens, 1985, for incentive pioneering explorations along this line of reasoning, with respect to the phenomena of fertility, household formation, and migration, respectively).

Small wonder, then, that this Cinderella position of household and family modelling efforts on the conduct-roll of conventional demography has thus far resulted in only one modelling strategy that has found world-wide application. This strategy, known as the headship rate method, rests on the principle of comparative statics. Based on observations taken from consecutive (census) counts, the development of households (or families) by number and type is described by the development of number and type of their heads, as being household or family 'markers' (Brass, 1983), on the basis of analysing trends in proportions of some broader defined population categories occupying the position of household or family head. Analysis as well as projection rely on data describing the situation at specific points in time. Thus, the headship rate method describes the results of dynamic processes between the time points in terms of changing headship rates, these dynamic processes themselves remaining a black box. Like the labour force participation rate in labour force studies, the headship rate is not a rate in the demographic ('occurrence/exposure') sense, and its analytical use reflects a focus on changes in stocks rather than on flows. This disadvantage may be compensated for, from a practical point of view, by the quick and easy applicability and the modest data demand of the method. From a methodological point of view, the headship rate model is rudimentary, as compared to all kinds of really dynamic models, if only because it is the dynamic processes that really cause the changes in the cross-sectionally observed stock numbers of households, and not the other way around. 'This mode of analysis presents the problem of structural transformation in terms of the processes that shape and reshape the structure. Thus, it is attuned to the tendency of present-day science to regard events rather than things, processes rather than states, as the ultimate components of the world of reality' (Ryder, 1964, p. 450). Though we do not neglect the static headship rate models below, we intend to focus the substantive part of this volume on efforts of dynamic household modelling, that is to say, on models that in one way or another emphasize a description and projection of processes of household formation and dissolution.

1.3. A classification of household models

Household models can, of course, be classified in many ways. We propose a classification based on two dimensions: the static/dynamic dichotomy on the one hand, and a dimension relating to the explanatory level on the other hand. This classification contains a relatively broad group of models, in comparison with the classification recently proposed by Bongaarts (1983, p. 32), who considers purely demographic models only. Models containing relationships between household characteristics and socio-economic, cultural, psychological, and so on determinants are omitted by Bongaarts. Our classification, shown in Table 1.1, results in six classes of household models.

TABLE 1.1. A classification of household models

	Econometric	Microdemographic	Macrodemographic
Static	1	3	5
Dynamic	2	4	6

Models belonging to class 1 may be typified as 'equilibrium models' which are extensively discussed in economic literature. Dynamic econometric models (class 2) include those of the IMPACT-project in Australia (Sams and Williams, 1982), the Cornell model in the USA (Caldwell *et al.*, 1979), the model developed at the Policy Studies Institute in Great Britain (Ermisch, 1983), and surely many others.

Static microdemographic models (class 3) are probably non-existent. Dynamic microdemographic models (class 4) have flourished in the past decade; in Galler's contribution (chapter 10) a specimen of this class is described.

Headship rate models are the typical representatives of class 5 models, the static macrodemographic models: two contributions in this volume are devoted to them (chapter 8 by Linke and chapter 13 by Kamaràs).

Dynamic macrodemographic models (class 6), finally, provide the body of this book. Most chapters deal with one or more representatives of this class of household models. Together, they reflect the recent world-wide surge of modelling efforts in the field of household and family dynamics.

1.4. Purpose and scope of this book

The purpose of this book is to trace trends in the most relevant aspects of household modelling. In this way, the authors wish to present a 'state of the art' of this sub-field of demography that might be denoted as 'household demometrics'. On the basis of such an overview, we could, in a later stage, try to formulate a research strategy which should ultimately lead to an improved quality of household models. In this book, especially in the sections in which current practice is reviewed, a few such attempts have already been made.

The structure of the book is basically the same as that of the workshop 'Modelling household formation and dissolution'. It is based on the usual sequence of events found in the philosophy of science, namely a step-wise description of the process, from a prototypical concept to a practicable model. Let us pin-point a few prominent stages in this process. As mentioned above, the starting-point is a conceptual framework, composed of a priori ideas regarding delimitation, definition, structure, and dynamics of the system which is to be modelled. In the model-building stage, we try to operationalize the results of the first stage. Data input is necessary to validate the model and—later—to draw up a theory, unless, of course, the researcher's findings demand that he review the initial conceptual framework, in which case the process should be started anew. The last stage of the process is the practical application of the theory, aimed at solving social issues. The process is visualized in Figure 1.1.

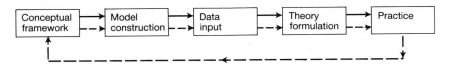

FIG 1.1. The model-building cycle.

It hardly needs saying that, in practice, this scientific process does not exactly follow the above ideal-typical model. For example, when the scientist is not pretentious and merely wants to find an *ad hoc* solution to a practical problem rather than substantially develop or refine a scientific method. Or else, theory and practice may fail to coincide due to a lack of (good-quality) data. The return on the total sum of investments is not maximal since there is no world-wide network which co-ordinates and regulates research efforts. Duplications and lacunae are unavoidable.

The structure of this book is a compromise between the ideal-typical process and a cross-section of the products of more or less completed scientific research arising from current issues. Part I comprises a number of pre-liminaries, part II contains a combination of data and trends, part III treats aspects of modelling, part IV looks at a number of applications of household models, and part V contains a few critical remarks as well as general conclusions on modelling household formation and dissolution. We will now summarize the individual chapters.

Part I continues with chapter 2, entitled 'Principles emerging from sociology for definitions and typologies of household structures', in which Josef Schmid tackles the problem of defining the concepts of the household and the family. A comparative analysis by place and time is difficult because of the large variety of definitions and criteria. Consequently, we are faced with typological problems. In the concluding paragraph, Schmid describes how the historical development of different types of household is linked to the complex of general social trends. He looks at the constantly declining household size, the increasing number of non-family households, one-parent families, one-person households, and unmarried cohabitation.

Following this sociological approach to household formation, John Ermisch approaches the subject, in chapter 3, from an economic point of view. His contribution is entitled 'An economic perspective on household modelling', as reflected his definition of a household: 'a unit which combines the time of its members and purchased goods and services into the production of "outputs", at least some of which are shared by its members'. He then gives a concise overview of several economic theories which try to explain demographic trends related to family and household formation. Ermisch introduces the concept of 'minimal household unit' to describe the relationship between the economic connotation of a household and the underlying demographic processes. These so-called MHUs are the central units of analysis in the model developed by the author as a basis for an economic explanation of household trends.

Part II, entitled 'Data and trends', comprises three contributions. In chapter 4 on 'Household data from surveys containing information for individuals', Erik Klijzing states that data systems based on censuses should only be used in static macromodels (generally called headship rate models) and that they are not suited to describing processes of household formation and dissolution. Dynamic models, based on individual transitions between household states, can do away with some of the drawbacks of static models. Such an approach needs flow data taken from special sample surveys. Klijzing assesses the merits of three types of surveys which could be used for this purpose. Finally, the author presents some results of the Dutch ORIN-survey which provides data for the execution of dynamic household models.

In their contribution entitled 'Sources of data for modelling household change with special reference to the OPCS 1% Longitudinal Study' (chapter 5), Michael Murphy, Oriel Sullivan, and Audrey Brown indicate how the data produced during a longitudinal sample survey in Great Britain can be used. The data allow the study of changes in household states between 1971 and 1981. With the aid of vital statistics registration, a 1 per cent sample of the 1971 census was 'followed' until the 1981 census. This yielded a fairly precise picture of the changes which had taken place during that decade and of the regional variations therein. The introductory paragraph gives an overview of the advantages and drawbacks of various data systems providing input for household models.

Karl Schwarz took on the difficult task of presenting a brief description and analysis of 'Household trends in Europe after World War II' (chapter 6). The author first treats the determinants of trends in household structure. He distinguishes demographic and non-demographic factors. He then compares the development of specific household categories in various European countries (one-parent families, consensual unions, one-person households). It is clear that substantial household trends are supranational, although the speed with which they spread and their repercussions differ.

Part III, which looks at the modelling aspect of households, comprises five chapters.

Chapter 7 by Frans Willekens is entitled 'A life course perspective on household dynamics'. The author treats the basic principles of household modelling. The key issue is the level of household models: should they be approached on the individual level, or on the household level? Willekens argues in favour of the individual level. He presents the life history analysis as a promising analytical framework for household modelling. Life courses of individuals and those of relationships induce changes in household size and composition.

There are two types of macrodemographic household models: static and dynamic ones. In 'The headship rate approach in modelling households' (chapter 8), Wilfried Linke reviews the former category. He analyses various modifications of the so-called classical headship rate method, in which the headship rates are specified by the number of family members and their age structure. In addition, Linke introduces a substitute for the headship rate: a new variable which could be described as an age-specific household membership rate according to the given household size. To conclude, he applies the different methods to the West German situation.

In chapter 9 called 'Dynamic household models', Nico Keilman gives an overview of five dynamic macrodemographic household models from four different countries (Canada, Federal Republic of Germany, Sweden and two from the Netherlands). The conclusion derived from the comparative analysis is that it is the behaviour of individuals, rather than that of households, which should be modelled. This conclusion supports the recommendations made by Willekens. Moreover, Keilman is of the opinion that the multidimensional method is a promising approach to household modelling. To conclude, he points to a few methodical problems related to the application of macrodynamic household models, such as the availability of data, inconsistencies related to the treatment of the two-sex problem, and the vast number of household states if one aims at a detailed decomposition.

In chapter 10 on 'Microsimulation of household formation and dissolution', Heinz Galler describes a microsimulation model which is being developed in West Germany. In this model, households are simultaneously generated by demographic and non-demographic processes, as individuals are subjected to transition probabilities. At the moment, these probabilities are derived from cross-sectional data. The author believes that the results will improve as soon as certain longitudinal data become available. The model is designed to construct projections for population, family, and household structures.

Dynamic household models can only exist if transition probabilities or transition rates are available. In their contribution entitled 'Estimation of transition rates in dynamic household models' (chapter 11), Daniël Courgeau and Eva Lelièvre discuss the estimation of such rates. They review three analysing techniques: nonparametric, semiparametric, and parametric. On the basis of a French retrospective life history survey (1981), bivariate and multivariate issues are dealt with. To conclude, the authors put forward four proposals for further research in this field.

In Part IV, four chapters examine the practical applications of household models.

In chapter 12, entitled 'Application of household models in studying the family life cycle', Anton Kuijsten describes the construction of so-called family life cycle tables with which he overcomes some shortcomings of the family life cycle concept, which he lists in an earlier paragraph. Kuijsten also discusses topics such as the impact of data availability on both modelling strategy and the specification of assumptions, and the analytical possibilities offered by these family life cycle tables.

This part of the volume contains an East European contribution. Ferenc Kamaràs uses the headship rate method to analyse the future household situation of the aged in Hungary. In chapter 13, entitled 'Some issues in modelling household behaviour of the aged in Hungary', he tries to trace the determinants of the changing household situation of the aged in the period 1970–80. He then examines how the household situation of the aged might change in the future, using a known population projection, and assuming constant values for the 1980 headship rates. Although the forecasting value of such a projection is deemed limited, it does show the extent to which the age and sex structure of the population influences household trends.

Henk ter Heide and Henk Scholten discuss in chapter 14 the role played by household trends in regional planning. In their contribution, entitled 'Application of household models in regional planning', they show that regional planners, in order to be able to prepare forecasts and assess policy impacts, require recursive models showing the interdependency of population redistribution (migration) and household formation and dissolution. They support their claim with the aid of an analysis of models which have been developed in the Netherlands and which, according to the authors, have several shortcomings. To conclude, they present proposals for further research aimed at gaining more insight into the relationship between household trends and population distribution and migration.

The last chapter in part IV is entitled 'Application of household models in housing policy' (chapter 15). The author, Jan Brouwer, describes the application of a dynamic macromodel used to construct household projections in the Netherlands. This model is evaluated in chapter 9 by Keilman. The projection's main assumption is that the process of individualization will continue in the coming years. Consequently, the number of households in the Netherlands will increase by another 1.5 per cent a year until 1990, and by 0.8 per cent after 1990; in the 1970s the rate of increase was 2.4 per cent.

Part V contains two contributions. 'Reflections on household modelling' by Jan Bartlema and Ad Vossen (chapter 16) is a critical analysis of the subject. In their brief evaluation, they point to the limited predictability of demographic determinants of household formation and dissolution. The main reason for this, according to the authors, is that the concepts used are outdated. In other words, the models are based on a 'statistical' reality which has a clear time-lag. In a sociological interlude, this idea is supported with the aid of the concept of the de-institutionalizing society. In their final paragraph, the authors point to the implications for household modelling of named processes of social changes.

Finally, chapter 17 presents a number of methodological problems related to dynamic household models. Nico Keilman and Nathan Keyfitz have selected seven subjects which played an important role in the foregoing chapters: the concept of the household itself; recent trends in household formation and dissolution; the relationship between household theories, modelling household trends, and forecasting them; micromodels and macromodels; modelling household dynamics; the individual versus the household as unit of analysis and model-building; and prospects for data collection and parameter estimation techniques.

Their overview reveals that a large number of theories exist to explain household trends; however, these theories can probably only contribute qualitatively to model-building and forecasting. Keilman and Keyfitz also conclude that insights gained from theories on stochastic processes could further the improvement of microsimulation models, in particular when dealing with competing risks. For methodological reasons, the authors give preference to the individual as the unit of analysis and modelling. They argue in favour of the application of indirect and mathematical–statistical estimation techniques in those models that have insufficient data for the direct determination of model parameters.

References

AKKERMAN, A. (1982). *Demographic Input to Regional Planning: Towards a Household Analysis of Regional Population Growth* (Demosystems, Edmonton).

BONGAARTS, J. (1983). The formal demography of families and households: an overview, *IUSSP Newsletter* 17, 27–42.

BRASS, W. (1983). The formal demography of the family: an overview of the proximate determinants, in: The family: Proceedings of the British Society for Population Studies Conference, 1983, Office of Population Censuses and Surveys Occasional Paper no. 31 (OPCS, London), 37–49.

CALDWELL, S. B., W. GREENE, T. MOUNT, AND S. SALTZMAN (1979). A macro/micro model of regional energy demand, *Papers of the Regional Science Association* (1979).

ERMISCH, J. (1983). Changing demographic patterns and the housing market, with special reference to Great Britain, Paper presented at the IUSSP/IIASA Seminar on Economic Consequences of Population Composition in Developed Countries, 12–14 December 1983, Laxenburg (Austria).

RYDER, N. B. (1964). Notes on the concept of a population, *The American Journal of Sociology* 69 (1964) 5, 447–63.

—— (1983). Fertility and family structure, *Population Bulletin of the United Nations* 15 (1983), 15–34.

—— (1985). Recent developments in the formal demography of the family, in: *International Population Conference, Florence 1985*, vol. 3 (IUSSP, Liège), 207–20.

SAMS, D. AND P. WILLIAMS (1982). Some projections of Australian population and labour force, 1980 to 2001, IMPACT Research Centre (University of Melbourne, Melbourne).

UNITED NATIONS (1958). Multilingual demographic dictionary, Population Studies no. 29 (United Nations, New York).

WILLEKENS, F. (1985). Migration and development: a micro-perspective, Working Paper no. 62 (Netherlands Interuniversity Demographic Institute, Voorburg).

2

Principles emerging from sociology for definitions and typologies of household structures

J. Schmid

ABSTRACT

In this contribution we will first look into a number of definitional problems of the terms household and family. It will be shown that comparative analysis across space and time is difficult because of the large variety of definitions and criteria. We subsequently point to classification problems. In the final section it is indicated how the historical development of various types of households is embedded in an intricate network of social trends. We will deal with matters such as the average household size, the growing number of non-family households, one-parent families, one-person households, and consensual unions.

2.1. Introduction

HOUSEHOLD is a very sober term for what is actually a basic human need. However, this concept, indispensable for social demographic analysis, says hardly anything about real life, just as the birth rate reveals nothing about the feeling of parenthood. This chapter attempts to meet a need: to clarify behavioural decisions of men and their consequences for the structuring of household types. Sociological insight into recent trends of family life and life course concepts form the background to the following analysis.

Definitions and typologies commonly in use to distinguish the many forms of households can be given easily and fast. Difficulties arise when the researcher wishes to detect the forces behind the household structures and their changes over time. Family sociology analyses, by tradition, the streams of influence on household structures. It deals foremost with the quality of human relationships in households which, after having come under pressure from the economic and social superstructure, change their scope, frequency, and intensity. Regional and historical differences in economic and social growth lead to variations in family size and household structures.

With the creation of the modern state, about two hundred years ago, another realm of influence affecting population processes came into being, namely legislation and state interference. They interfere with both the biosocial and the migratory movements and divert them from an originally detected—and prospected—path.

Because of the fact that family and residence are institutions shaped by special laws regularly adjusted by virtue of changing needs, formation, settling down, and dissolution of the family are not only the results of the immediate 'natural' behaviour and preferences of men but are also 'streamlined' by legal rules. This will further complicate the analysis of the structural change of households and the search for comparable examples in Europe, on purely sociological grounds.

Legislation, in particular administration practice, determines data collection. Demographic knowledge on the subject is limited to what the questionnaires tell us, and depends on the available investigation facilities. So, work on household structures has to take into account both the sociology of industrial development regarding the fate of the family, and laws and regulations regarding family life and housing. This chapter, however, will focus only on the social processes behind household structures.

2.2. Definitions: What is a household?

A 'household' refers, firstly, to a determinable residence or dwelling of people bound together to achieve given social goals. 'A number of persons under the same roof' seems to be the common denominator found in all existing definitions of a household.

A definition encompassing all possible items which may form a household is used in the U.S. Population Census (U.S. Bureau of the Census, 1964, p. lv):

A household consists of all the persons who occupy a housing unit. A house, an apartment or other group of rooms, or a single room, is regarded as a housing unit when it is occupied or intended for occupancy as separate living quarters. Separate living quarters are those in which the occupants do not live and eat with any other persons in the structure and in which there is either . . . direct access from the outside or through a common hall, or . . . a kitchen or cooking equipment for the exclusive use of the occupants.

The British define a household as a 'living arrangement'. A household is therefore always what a census is able or willing to record. The power exerted on statistical surveys by administration and legislation has obvious repercussions for the definitions used. Even slight differences in definitions of a household will yield different data. Definitions influence the collecting of household data and vice versa.

At first glance, the following are important components of household definitions:

(*a*) the use of a household, indicated, for example, by the presence of cooking equipment;

(*b*) the privacy of a household, usually expressed by a separate entrance; and

(*c*) the number of related and non-related persons present.

The last point exerts a considerable influence on the enumeration of people in households (see Kobrin, 1976, p. 127). Although 'household' is, first of all, an administrative category, more 'cultural', that is, sociological, definitions also exist. The German 'Handwörterbuch der Sozialwissenschaften' defines a household as a unit which is aimed at making arrangements to secure the satisfaction of common needs of a group of persons.

A household never exists in isolation, and is never detached from the community whose needs it has to meet. Households have both an economic and a biological base, and they function as permanent institutions (Egner, 1956, p. 66).

2.3. Typologies: Which types of households can be distinguished?

For reasons of clarity, the term 'family', and its definition, has not been used until now. But when it comes to ranking and classifying household types, the term 'family' and its various forms can no longer be avoided.

The analysis of structures of households, however, means delving into a very complex picture of 'co-resident domestic groups'. Some categories closely resemble family structure, and some classifications actually use family features, for example, family households and non-family households. A *family household* consists of a married couple, with or without children, or a man or woman with child(ren), or any other combination of relatives living together. A *non-family household* consists of an individual living alone or sharing living quarters with one or more unrelated persons.

The use of the term family for the classification of households entails a specification and an evaluation of the status of co-resident persons, because family is defined as 'those members of the household . . . who are related, to a specific degree, through blood, adoption or marriage' (United Nations, 1973).

The interdependence of household and family is illustrated by the following: a couple and their child, two related married couples, or any other group of two or more persons related to each other is considered a family if the members occupy the same living quarters and eat together.

The interconnectedness of family and the household is revealed by the following examples: single persons do not form a family but they do have to maintain a household because they live by themselves. The common features of a household, such as location, shared activity, and kinship do not necessarily have to be present at the same time. For example, living together of non-relatives, including consensual unions or communal living arrangements of unmarried persons, denotes shared location and activity, but not kinship.

A household, therefore, proves to be the more comprehensive term because it is valid irrespective of the relationships of the persons involved. Families are always (except when separated) households, but members of a household do not necessarily form a family (by blood or by marriage). By virtue of the fact that—to this day—the bulk of households are families, the term *family household* can be used for the sake of classification and analysis. Following the work of Laslett (1972, p. 23) on family history in Europe, we discern the well-known *nuclear family*, commonly called *conjugal family unit*, and the *extended family household*, which consists of a conjugal family unit with the addition of one or more relatives other than offspring, the whole group living together on its own or with servants (Laslett, 1972, p. 29), and finally the *multiple family household* which comprises all forms of domestic groups, including two or more conjugal family units connected by blood (kinship) or by law (marriage).

This specification, very familiar to historical demographers and to 'family reconstitutionists' in particular, will not be pursued in detail here, because this chapter forms the basis for a discussion on the most recent trends. Therefore, non-familial households deserve special attention, in particular cohabitation of non-relatives and single-person households.

Official registration uses ten types of households, denoted in Table 2.1. Households under A embrace typical family households, that is, spouses with or without children and even grandparents. In types A4 and B1 three generations live together. Households under C include extended families and non-relatives such as servants and helping hands. It may be assumed that it is a

TABLE 2.1. Types of household

A1	Households consisting of spouses without children (one-generation households)
A2	Households consisting of parents and unmarried children (two-generation households)
A3	Households consisting of parents and married children (without grandchildren) and, possibly, unmarried children (without grandchildren)
A4	Households of type A3 including grandparents, parents, and children or grandchildren (three-generation households)
B1	Households from A1 to A4 including relatives by blood or by law
B2	Households of type B1 including relatives other than lineal ones
C1	Households of types A1 to B1 including non-relatives
C2	Households of type B2 including non-relatives
D	Households consisting only of non-relatives
E	One-person households

housing community where living and working coincide. D and E comprise the so-called *non-familial households*.

As stated above, family ties are a precondition for the formation of a household, but they are not the only condition: we increasingly find co-resident non-relatives who form marriage-like heterosexual unions, or communities of people sharing the necessary chores to maintain a common dwelling. Such communes usually include consensual unions.

The group of non-familial households also encompasses the significantly growing number of *one-person households* (type E). An attempt to explain these trends will be given in the following section.

2.4. Influences from family sociology

After having denoted household classifications, we must be aware that such classifications are not at all fixed but that they change with time, even under our very own eyes. We witness a steady shift in the structure of households with regard to the preponderance of certain household types, and we also see how some household types gradually disappear.

Family sociology may be able to explain recent trends in household formation. At least, sociology should offer insights which go beyond mere registration of structural items and changes therein. Representative titles on contemporary family sociology are Adams (1980), Coleman (1984), Golanty *et al*. (1982), Strong *et al*. (1983), Van den Berghe (1979), and Yorburg (1983).

Previous sections have roughly pointed out household structures and household trends found in the past few decades. If these trends had only been locally restricted phenomena, they would never have been given so much attention by social scientists and demographers. Taking Europe as an example, we can demonstrate how new demographic events result in changes in household structures.

Taking into account that demographic changes are consequences of new behavioural patterns concerning marriage, reproduction, and parenthood, then social analysis reveals steps of influence, ranging from the social and economic structure to the behavioural consequences in the demographic structure. Structures as such are determined by social relations, that is, more or less patterned behaviour. So we can, as a first step, interpret present social and economic structures as well as demographic structures in terms of some sort of mass behaviour behind these structures. In doing so, we gain a deeper insight into the question how contemporary household structures come into existence.

The broader social and economic settings in the West lead to changes of behaviour and attitudes characterized by:

(*a*) delayed marriage;

(*b*) declining parenthood motivation; and

(*c*) a growing search for individual standing.

These behavioural changes have an impact on family size and the individual life course. As a consequence, they bring about:

(*d*) birth decline;

(*e*) a decline in family size;

(*f*) a growing number of personally moulded living arrangements;

(*g*) a rising divorce rate.

We must take for granted that characteristics (*a*) to (*g*) together form the present state of household formation and dissolution. The most recent household trends which deserve attention and further investigation include the following:

1. a continuous decline in the average size of households;
2. the growing number of non-familial households; and
3. the mounting importance of the one-person household coupled with growing numbers of one-parent family households and 'living together' arrangements.

The 'three-step flow of influence' framework which is described above can be presented as in Figure 2.1.

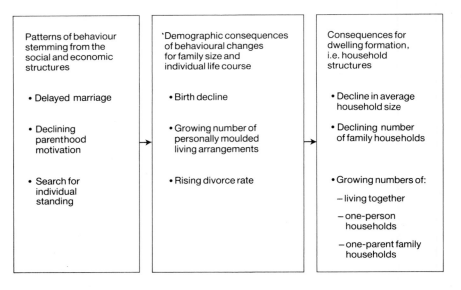

FIG. 2.1. The 'three-step flow of influence' framework

2.4.1. The continuous decline in average household size

The decline of the peasantry and the absorption of the masses (originally living in modest agrarian communities) by new agglomerations and new housing conditions in the centres of industrial production and commerce exerted much more pressure on family size than had been customary in the agrarian way of life. There is no need here to describe the reorientation of the economy from agriculture to industry and mass production, but it should be kept in mind that the processes set in motion by the Industrial Revolution strongly affected family life and household structure and have not yet come to a halt. Limited space, the fear of dropping below the generally accepted consumption levels, and the growing concern about the social standing and economic success of children have resulted in a continuous *decline in marital fertility*. In most Western European countries the number of children in marriages, which was between 4 and 8 around the turn of the century, has dropped to below 2, on average.

Another cause contributing to declining household size is that married children increasingly move out of the parental home, leaving behind a 'nuclear family'. Official statistics do not indicate the physical distance between generations living separately. It is an informed guess that in many cases the parents or grandparents live very near the nuclear family household, sometimes 'just around the corner', or even in the same house with a separate entrance. The generations themselves see this as some sort of 'living together'.

Another reason for the decreasing household size is the wish by younger generations to live an independent and free life. They leave the parental home at a much earlier age than in the past and give the parents the feeling that they are living in an 'empty nest'. Unfortunately, official statistics are very meagre and do not give us an exact picture of the amount of time children spend with their parents.

For convenience's sake (taxation, car dues, and so on) young people officially say they live in their parents' household, even when they have actually left it. The possibility of having more than one official residence, at least in West Germany, distorts the situation described by official statistics.

The trend toward smaller households, furthermore, is reinforced by the considerable number of *one-parent families*. They constitute between 10 and 20 per cent of all families in the West and result from situations such as death of a spouse, divorce, separation, desertion, the adoption of a child by a single person, or the birth of a child to an unmarried woman. Only in the two last-mentioned cases is this situation often chosen deliberately and voluntarily, and one may assume that such parents are usually satisfied with the fact that they are unmarried. In all other cases, the phenomenon is created by the compelling circumstances of a broken relationship.

2.4.2. The growing number of non-familial households

The family as the lifelong 'natural' setting of mankind is increasingly being replaced by non-marital alternatives, such as consensual unions (living together), communes (communal living), and singlehood. Because of its overwhelming importance, singlehood will be treated separately. Cohabitation means living together in a sexual relationship when not legally married. This has, in the past decades, been very common among widowed people because remarriage would entail the loss of the old-age pension of either one of the co-residents. The interest of society, however, has focused more on cohabitation among the young, before and after having reached the average age at marriage. In the meantime, particularly in the past decade, cohabitation or 'living together' has become such a widespread phenomenon, found throughout all age groups and social strata, that it has ceased to be shocking or immoral. Today it is hardly even worth noting, at least for the public. This is, of course, not the case for demographers.

We have to distinguish between cohabitators who see their situation as a pre-marital one (as a modern substitute for becoming engaged) and those who are not willing to get married at all. For example, two-career partners who postpone marriage and childrearing up to the point where it seems too late for both.

As the general experience in the West (excluding perhaps Sweden and Denmark) shows, cohabitors very seldom have children. Their growth in number does not only reduce the proportion of family households but they also contribute to a further lowering of the aggregate fertility level of the population concerned.

Researchers and registration authorities have problems finding out the magnitude of this phenomenon in society. In the past, it existed in a murky, subcultural sphere which was very difficult to penetrate by social science. A questionnaire contains, in the best of cases, indications on how many non-relatives—and of what age—live together in a household. So it reveals only the quantity of cohabitations. Empirical projects must be aware of the fact that cohabitation is the final state of a gradual shift from being single into a relatively stable 'free' partnership (Cole, 1977, p. 70):

Research . . . suggests that most couples do not make a conscious decision to live together but rather tend to gradually drift together as a result of spending increasing amounts of time together. The pattern usually starts with the partners spending one night a week together, moves on to their adding a second and then a third night a week, until one of them gradually finds it more convenient to move more clothes and personal items over to the other's room or apartment, and ends with their moving in and living together . . . They must now redefine their social situation to account for the fact that they are cohabiting. This redefinition frequently is accompanied by a reassessment of their feelings toward their partner as well as their own self-concept. If the partners perceive that cohabiting provides them with a favourable reward–cost ratio, they will likely continue to live together.

Cohabitation, as a very common choice, produces significant 'secondary consequences' for society and population trends in particular: it delays marriage and (as, among others, the German experience shows) fertility as well.

It remains to be seen whether cohabitation, thanks to a trial-and-error experience in partnership, will increase the quality and stability of marital unions. Communes, as a form of non-familial households, consist of more than two persons living together. The fact that they very often call themselves a family suggests a common spirit which holds them together and goes beyond a mere living arrangement. The term commune applies to a living arrangement in which the members share responsibilities for work and their personal property and establish a sense of family, regardless of whether they share sexual partners or not. In most cases people join communes after having been dissatisfied or disillusioned by society as a whole or by the social group they used to live in. So there is an obvious propensity to undergo quasi-religious rules.

2.4.3. Upsurge of one-person households

A growing number of one-person households is the reason for the following observed tendencies: the declining average household size, the rise of non-familial households, and the declining birth rate. During the last decade, most Western countries experienced a doubling of the number of one-person households.

The population of one-person households includes those who have never been married, the widowed, and the divorced. The status and goals in life of single persons are so diverse that their only common denominator is their unmarried status. There are singles who are unmarried by choice and intend to remain so. Others feel they are in a transitory stage from single to married or between marriage and remarriage. It is wise to distinguish singlehood by choice from its compulsory forms. Voluntary abstention from marriage is growing among young people of marriageable age. This can be deduced from the proportion married in the age cohort 20 to 30 years. The percentage of married persons in this age group declines significantly for both sexes.

Another cause of singlehood is the divorce rate which is on the rise in Western countries. Divorce means a major change in an individual's life and it is not always immediately followed by remarriage, partly because of a certain reluctance to enter a new relationship, but also because of difficulties in finding another partner. If a new partner is already present, and reluctance to remarry exists because of a bad experience in a former relationship, the solution will be found in a consensual union. Remarriage will also be delayed, if not wholly prevented, where family law prescribes severe regulations for a spouse's support following divorce. So a rising divorce rate produces, unquestionably, one-parent family households and one-person households.

2.5. Conclusions

It may be too much to speak of a new pattern of households reflecting the changes brought by our modern economy and civilization. It would also be rash to say that the trends are progressing linearly, for example, towards the point where single-person households would be the norm. As a matter of fact, the factors responsible for the growing proportion of single persons will not cease to have effect, but, at the same time, the growing diversity of lifestyles will produce an ever more complex picture. The empirical reality of households will offer classification problems, as is already the case for social stratification. Conventional criteria which held good until the 1960s are no longer valid and will therefore raise problems of statistical registration and of reasonable ordering—a challenging task for future social scientists.

One may assume that the exclusive application of—on the one hand—pure economy such as cost–benefit analyses and neoclassical modelling, and, on the other hand, pure psychology such as the psychology of matchmaking, will fail to grasp the new household types. What we need is a more balanced utilitarian view of the subject and categories focusing on life cycle-linked likes and dislikes, necessities, and options.

References

ADAMS, B. N. (1980). *The Family: A Sociological Interpretation* (Houghton Mifflin Co., Boston etc.), 2nd ed.

COLE, C. (1977). Cohabitation in social context, in: R. W. Libby and R. N. Whitehurst (eds.), *Marriage and Alternatives: Exploring Intimate Relationships* (Glenview, Illinois).

COLEMAN, J. C. (1984). *Intimate Relationships, Marriage and Family* (Bobbs–Merrill, Indianapolis).

EGNER, E. (1956). Haushalt, in: R. König (ed.), *Handwörterbuch der Sozialwissenschaften*, vol. 5 (Tübingen).

GOLANTY, E. AND B. HARRIS (1982). *Marriage and Family Life* (Houghton Mifflin Co., Boston etc.).

KOBRIN, F. E. (1976). The fall in household size and the rise of the primary individual in the United States, *Demography* 13 (1).

LASLETT, P. (1972). Introduction, in: P. Laslett and R. Wall (eds.), *Household and Family in Past Time* (Cambridge University Press, Cambridge).

STRONG, B., CHR. DE VAULT, M. SUID, AND R. REYNOLDS (1983). *The Marriage and Family Experience* (West Publishing, St. Paul, Minn.), 2nd ed.

UNITED NATIONS (1973). *Methods of Projecting Households and Families*, Population Studies no. 54 (United Nations, New York).

U.S. BUREAU OF THE CENSUS (1964). *U.S. Census of Population: 1960*, vol. 1: characteristics of the population, part I: United States summary (US Government Printing Office, Washington, DC).

VAN DEN BERGHE, P. L. (1979). *Human Family Systems: An Evolutionary View* (Elsevier, New York).

YORBURG, B. (1983). *Families and Societies: Survival or Extinction?* (Columbia University Press, New York).

3

An economic perspective on household modelling

J. Ermisch

ABSTRACT

On the basis of an economic theory of household formation, this chapter discusses an appropriate definition of a household and the desirable units for the analysis of household formation. It is proposed that analysis be divided between two levels: one of demographic transitions between types of 'minimal household unit', and one of household formation from combinations of these units. Previous economic analysis has concentrated on the first level, and the relevant economic theories are 'discussed. A new economic model applicable to the second level is presented. The two levels are brought together in an integrated analysis to conclude the chapter.

3.1. What is a household?

THE economic theory of household formation described later in this chapter provides the basis for a definition of a household. This theory is based on the so-called 'household production' approach, which has become common in investigating the economics of household behaviour, including consumption, labour force participation, and fertility.

A household is a unit which combines the time of its members and purchased goods and services into the production of 'outputs', at least some of which are shared among its members. In general terms, these 'outputs' are the characteristics of consumption activities yielding personal satisfaction. Some examples are shelter, meals, and home entertainment.

Although expressed differently, this definition of a household is essentially the same as earlier definitions. For example, Hajnal (1982) defines a household as a housekeeping or consumption unit, the defining characteristic being 'shared consumption'. A definition of this type is used in most modern censuses. The sharing of meals is often taken as an indicator, but this is not essential. For instance, in the 1981 British Census 'a household is either one person living alone or a group of people (who may or may not be related) living, or staying temporarily, at the same address with common housekeeping. Enumerators were told to treat a group of people as a household if there was any regular arrangement to share at least one meal a day, breakfast

23

counting as a meal, or if occupants shared a common living or sitting room'. The last criterion was not applied in the 1971 Census, but tests prior to the 1981 Census indicated that, without the prompting of an enumerator, respondents had identified themselves as households solely on the basis of this criterion; thus it may have been used in practice earlier, although not consistently. The broader set of criteria is more consistent with the definition derived from the economic theory of household formation and used here.

Hajnal (1982) has argued that the 'shared consumption' concept of a household has quite a general application across societies and over time. This finding is important because it means that the definition of household employed here is useful for a wide range of empirical studies.

3.2. Units for analysis of household formation

Economists are interested in how various economic constraints affect people's choices, who to live with being one of those choices. In order to do such analysis the basic unit should be an economic decision-making unit. At the same time, the units should represent the 'building blocks' from which households are formed. Individuals are obviously the most basic building blocks, but economic decisions are often made by a larger unit—a couple or a family—and housing choices are put into effect by this larger unit. One of these choices could be to set up a household with persons from outside the unit. Thus married couples constitute a single unit because they make joint decisions about whether to live as a separate household, or whom to live with, and joint housing choices. Parents and their children are also a single unit since parents make decisions for their dependent children.

Analysis is easier if the units are such that demographic influences on household formation and composition can be separated from economic influences. In particular, it would be helpful to separate instances of *family* formation and dissolution from *household* formation and dissolution.

The 'minimal household unit' suggested by Ermisch and Overton (1984, 1985) satisfies these requirements. A minimal household unit (MHU) is the smallest group of persons within a household that can be considered to constitute a *demographically* definable entity. It is definable in purely demographic terms in the sense that an individual, over his lifetime, moves from one type of MHU to another by means of a simple demographic transition or event, as is illustrated in Figure 3.1. The four basic MHU types are:

1. childless, non-married adults;
2. lone parents with their dependent children;
3. childless married couples;
4. married couples with dependent children.

Individuals are considered, at least potentially, capable of making their

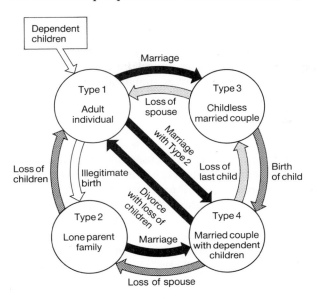

Source: Population Trends 35 (by permission of the Controller of Her Majesty's Stationery Office).

FIG. 3.1. The Minimum Household Unit family life cycle

own decisions as soon as they are able to leave school and earn their own living. All childless adults over the minimum school-leaving age who are not married are thus an MHU of type 1. Other ages of 'maturity' could be used; the important point is that young persons reach an age when some are in the position to make their own housing choices, which include continuing to live in their parents' household. Type 1 could be further subdivided into never-married and ever-married while Type 3 could be broken down into those ever or never having had children, but this is not essential.

An MHU corresponds to a narrow definition of a family. They are the smallest familiar elements within households. The number of MHUs in the population is the maximum number of households that could be formed from the population. These units are the foundation for the analysis which follows. Demographic transitions are defined in terms of them, and households are viewed as being formed from combinations of them (including one on its own).

Thus demographic processes, particularly those of family formation and dissolution, indirectly affect the number and composition of households by affecting the number and composition of MHUs. The grouping of MHUs into households is viewed as a set of economic choices made by MHUs. This two-level conception of household formation and dissolution does not deny that economic factors may influence the demographic processes as well. In fact, as the next section shows, the main focus of economic analysis has been on family formation and dissolution. But because the decision-makers and the nature of economic effects on household formation may be different at the two levels, the separation proves analytically helpful.

3.3. Economic perspectives

Most economic theories relevant to household formation have concentrated on economic influences on demographic transitions rather than on the grouping of families and individuals into households. Their focus has been on family formation and dissolution. Since different types of MHU have different probabilities of living alone as a separate household, family formation and dissolution indirectly affect household formation, but little explicit attention has been given to decisions concerning the household group.

For instance, Easterlin's (1980) relative income theory has been applied to the timing of marriage and childbearing and the likelihood of divorce. According to the theory, people's material aspirations are shaped by the economic circumstances that they have experienced. When earnings prospects are high relative to aspirations, early marriage and childbearing will be encouraged, but when earnings are insufficient to support one's aspirations, marriage and childbearing will be postponed. At least in America and some other industrialized countries, these aspirations have generally included a separate household for a married couple. Thus, changes in income prospects relative to aspirations or 'relative income' indirectly affect household formation, but one sort of adaptation to low relative income would be to marry but live in a household with others (for example, parents). Relative income could thereby directly influence household formation while its influence on marriage would be moderated.

Easterlin (1980) has also suggested that difficulties in role fulfilment have an important influence on marital breakdown and that these are affected by relative income. If a husband's income is insufficient to achieve the couple's aspirations, then his wife will find it more difficult to give up her job. As a consequence, the husband may feel that he is an inadequate provider, and his wife may feel resentful that she must face a conflict between the need for her earnings and her role in caring for her children. He is not able to fulfil the role of a 'good provider', and she is not able to fulfil the role of a 'good mother'. The failures put strains on the marriage. In contrast, when the husband's income is high relative to aspirations, these roles can be fulfilled since aspirations can be achieved without his wife working during periods when children need more parental time. This view of roles may be a typically American one, but the theory does suggest a reason why the incidence of divorce may vary inversely with a couple's relative income.

The theories of marriage, fertility, and divorce associated with the 'new home economics' derive somewhat different economic influences on family formation and dissolution (see, for example, Becker, 1981). In these theories, the raising of children, mutual love, and companionship are important sources of a couple's well-being. These cannot be purchased nor provided by oneself. Thus, in economic terms, the man's and woman's inputs in providing them are complementary. This complementarity is the prime source of the net benefits from marriage. A couple also combines their time and purchased goods and services to produce other 'output' for home consumption, like meals. In these activities as well, complementarity enhances the benefits from the marriage partnership since it increases the advantage of a division of labour between the spouses, particularly between work in the home and paid employment. The benefits from the division of labour increase with the disparity in the spouses' earning opportunities. A smaller diference between men's and women's earning capacities tends, therefore, to decrease the benefits from marriage and diminish the incentive to marry. A stronger attachment to paid employment by women would also reduce the benefits from marriage associated with the division of labour since it would be practised to a lesser extent.

Holding the relative wages of men and women constant, higher real income would tend to produce a greater demand for the characteristics associated with married life (for example, love, companionship, and the raising of children). If it is the norm for married couples to set up a separate household, higher income would also help couples finance this big step.

Since children are an important reason for marrying, the timing of marriage is likely to be strongly related to the timing of childbearing. The new home economics also has something to say about the latter. In particular, because of the large input of a mother's time in the care of young children, higher women's earning opportunities raise the cost of childbearing and encourage the postponement of motherhood. A strong attachment by women to paid employment has a similar effect. In contrast, higher men's earnings tend to bring births forward in time (see De Cooman *et al.*, 1985).

Thus, for a number of reasons, these theories predict that higher women's wages relative to men's and stronger attachment by women to paid employment are associated with later marriage and childbearing. From a feminine point of view, a similar prediction emerges. This is associated with a higher cost of accepting the traditional marital division of labour, thereby lowering the attractiveness of marriage for women.

A scarcity of unmarried members of the opposite sex in the preferred age range reduces the benefits from marriage since there would be a smaller probability of finding a partner with the desired qualities, and it would also increase the (time) cost of searching for a suitable partner. This is the so-called 'marriage squeeze' phenomenon.

The new home economics' view of divorce is a logical extension of its view of marriage (see Becker *et al.*, 1977). Divorces occur because the benefits from marriage to a particular partner do not materialize, or disappear. Given the variation in outcome, this is more likely the lower the expected benefits are. Thus, those economic factors influencing the benefits of marriage affect the likelihood of divorce in the opposite direction. Disappointed expectations and perhaps difficulties of role fulfilment probably lie behind the tendency for couples in which the husband experiences unemployment to be more inclined to divorce, and behind the tendency for divorce to be higher in communities and periods in which the unemployment rate is higher (see Bishop, 1980; and South, 1985). At least in America, the characteristics of social transfer programmes also affect the likelihood of divorce (Bishop, 1980).

But this analysis has been concerned with economic influences on family formation and dissolution—demographic transitions in the jargon of this chapter—rather than household formation decisions *per se*. In the latter case, economics has had fairly naïve models. They generally view 'privacy' for a family or unmarried person as a normal good, more of which is desired at higher levels of income. Thus the likelihood of forming a separate household would rise with income. Since privacy in a separate household generally means consuming more housing, the probability of forming one tends to fall as the price of housing increases (see, for example, Hickman, 1974). The economic model developed later in this chapter brings in additional aspects to the household formation decision, and from it testable hypotheses are derived.

In sum, previous economic analyses of family formation and dissolution show how economic variables can influence household formation indirectly by influencing the composition of MHUs. This is the first level of analysis. The second concerns the combination of MHUs into households, and there is little economic analysis of this behaviour. This split is not made because people necessarily go through these two stages, but it is made for analytical reasons. It is difficult to develop tractable models yielding predictions of economic effects when the two levels of analysis are combined. First, the people involved in the decision may differ at the two levels. A person may decide to marry, but the decision whether to live alone, with one's parents, or with others would probably be made jointly by the couple. Second, the nature of the direct economic effect on household formation can differ from the indirect effect through family formation. For example, the new home economics suggests that a woman with a higher earning capacity would be less likely to marry at a young age (marriage usually involving formation of a separate household with her husband), but she would be more likely to form a household on her own. Furthermore, if the two levels were combined and the analysis were based on individuals, the combination of MHU types and household group types (for example, household size) would produce a very large number of different family/household groups for modelling and empirical analysis. Thus, for analytical convenience the analysis is broken down into these two levels.

3.4. Analysis: Demographic transitions

In the analytical framework proposed here, a demographic transition is a movement by an individual from one MHU type to another. Thus the definition of demographic transitions is individually based while, as shall become clearer later on, the analysis of household formation is based on MHUs. Since transitions between MHU types other than through childbearing tend to be based on individual decisions (marriage and divorce) or events affecting individuals (ageing and death), while household formation decisions are based on decisions by an MHU, there is some intuitive appeal to this 'split-level' analysis of how people end up in households of varying compositions. Childbearing does, of course, involve two people, and, in addition, when one's last child reaches 'maturity', in the sense of being an MHU in its own right, there is a transition of an individual between MHU types (that is, from type 4 to 3, or 2 to 1) without any decision by, or demographic event affecting, the parent. In any case, transitions between MHU types are taken as the demographic transitions in this framework.

The previous section has shown that these transitions may be dependent on certain economic characteristics of an individual and, in some cases, his/her spouse. Some of these characteristics may be the same as those affecting the type of household in which the person lives, as derived in the economic theory of household formation described below, but it is instructive to isolate the channel of influence.

In a fairly general formulation, the probability that an adult individual moves from MHU type i to type j in a small interval of time can be expressed as:

$$h_{ij}(d,X), \ i \neq 0 \ \text{ and } \ \sum_{j=0}^{4} h_{ij}(d,X) = 1;$$

where d is the duration in type i; X is a vector of characteristics of the individual (and of the spouse when $i = 3$ or $i = 4$), including age and sex; $j = 0$ represents death; and $i = 1, 2, 3, 4$ are the respective MHU types listed above. A new MHU type 1 is 'created' with probability one when a young person reaches the age of 'maturity' (16 in the application below). Figure 3.1 illustrates the various transitions (note that $h_{23} = h_{32} = 0$).

As formulated, the demographic transitions are represented by a multi-state, semi-Markov process (that is, the transition probabilities are dependent on duration in the state of origin) which is conditioned by measured characteristics of an individual. Courgeau and Lelièvre (chapter 11) discuss the estimation of models like this, and Moore and Pyke (1968) consider the estimation of this type of model in the absence of conditioning explanatory variables. Even if such variables are important, estimation ignoring them (or at least those other than age and sex) could provide useful estimates of transition probabilities for the population as a whole. Estimation could be further simplified if we assumed a simple Markov process (no duration dependence). A variation on the multi-state analysis of Willekens *et al.* (1982) would then be applicable. In all of these cases, data on transitions between MHU types is needed. Conventional marriage, divorce, birth, and death statistics generally produce rates by age and sex, sometimes by marital status, but rarely by family status. Rates which are broken down according to all of these characteristics would be needed to estimate the MHU type transitions. Special surveys may be able to fill this gap in some countries if they have a longitudinal dimension. In Britain, the OPCS 1% Longitudinal Study (see chapter 5 by Murphy, Sullivan, and Brown) is a promising source for data which could be used to estimate the probabilities of transition between MHU types.

It is, however, beyond the scope of this chapter to discuss methods of estimating the transition probabilities $h_{ij}(d, X)$. My primary intention for introducing the subject is to show how the two levels of analysis suggested here fit together. The $h_{ij}(d, X)$ functions represent a fairly general formulation of the demographic transitions. Given these relationships and an initial population of MHUs, the subsequent population of MHUs is determined. For instance, among the 12,000 households in the 1976 General Household Survey (see chapter 4 by Klijzing) in Great Britain, Ermisch and Overton (1984) estimate that there were about 7,270 MHUs of type 1, 500 of type 2, 4,160 of type 3, and 4,160 of type 4. The household formation level of analysis considers how these MHUs combine into households.

3.5. Analysis: Household formation

The analysis focuses on five basic 'household contexts' or 'household groupings' within which an MHU may live:

1. alone;
2. with parents (perhaps others as well, but no adult children of a parent in the MHU);
3. with adult children (no others);
4. with other non-married adults only;
5. other combinations.

While these are empirically important and interesting groupings in Britain, there is nothing sacrosanct about them. Other societies may find different combinations more interesting and important. For the purpose of using this analytical framework to investigate how economic and demographic factors influence the number of households and their size distribution, it is more helpful to specify household context in terms of 'household size' expressed in terms of the number of MHUs in the household or the number of adults in the household. The latter specification is also conducive to testing some of the predictions of the economic model described in the next section.

In general terms, the probability of an MHU of type i being in household context k is denoted as:

$$P_{ik}(Z), \sum_k P_{ik}(Z) = 1;$$

where Z is a vector of characteristics of the MHU (for example, ages and sexes of its members, their economic characteristics, and so on). The economic model which is used as a basis for the estimation of the $P_{ik}(Z)$ functions is now described.

3.6. Economics of household formation

This section summarizes an economic model which is quite stylized in many respects, but which is an improvement on earlier, less explicit models of household formation decisions and which can be developed further.

Individuals or family units (MHUs) make choices concerning their optimal household grouping (or 'household context'). There appear to be three important aspects of household groups which are relevant to this choice. First, most individuals or families desire privacy, and the larger the number of household members the less privacy there is likely to be for each individual member. On the other hand, all household members can conceivably contribute to the work which arises around the home, such as cooking, repairs, and cleaning. The time spent doing these chores obviously has a cost in that leisure and time which could be spent in paid employment must be renounced. Additional household members could substitute for an individual's own time. Thirdly, there are economies of scale associated with housing and some other consumer durables in that the service given by a given quantity of these goods does not decline proportionately with an increase in the number of consumers of the service. Thus, the per caput cost of the services from housing and other consumer durables falls with additional household members, at least up to a point.

In this model, time and the services from purchased goods and services are inputs into the production of outputs, which are the 'satisfaction-yielding' objects, rather than objects of choice directly yielding satisfaction. This is the so-called 'household production' approach, which has become common in investigating the economics of the household (see Ermisch, 1981, for a formal exposition of the model). Household members other than those in the MHU can aid in this household production by contributing their time. As noted above, the per caput cost of the services of some purchased goods also declines with the number of household members.

For some individuals, the desire for companionship may mean that an additional household member is initially preferable, all else being equal, but eventually the desire for privacy becomes paramount. These ideas are introduced by presuming that an MHU has a preference ranking over combinations of home-produced outputs and the household grouping which can be represented by an ordinal utility function. The marginal utility of an additional household member may, then, be initially positive for some individuals, but eventually it is negative for all MHUs.

It is assumed that an MHU chooses the household grouping, its labour supply, and the purchases of goods and services which maximize this utility function subject to its budget constraint, the household production relationship, and the degree of economies of scale associated with certain goods. The household grouping which solves this maximization problem is the optimal one for the MHU. For the moment, consider this grouping to be characterized by the number of *adult* household members. The optimal size of household group for an MHU is achieved when the gains from additional members arising from aid in home-related work and economies of scale just offset the loss of well-being arising from a reduction in privacy. In particular, a separate household is formed when those gains cannot offset the perceived loss of privacy from any additional members of the household. The outcome depends upon the tastes of the members of an MHU, particularly their desire for privacy relative to material goods, their abilities in the various home-related tasks, the earning capacities (real wage) of members of the unit, and the non-earned income available to the unit.

It is possible to decompose the effect on optimal household size of a change or difference in a real wage rate into an 'income effect' and a 'substitution effect'. The former is equal to the product of the effect of an additional point of non-earned income and the number of hours worked while the latter is equivalent to the effect of a change in the real wage rate if the individual were 'compensated' (in either direction) by changes in non-earned income so as to attain the same level of utility as prior to the change in wage rate.

In general, the directions of both the income and substitution effects on household size are ambiguous. But if we focus on non-married individuals (with or without children), and assume that other household members are a substitute for an individual's own time in household production while purchased goods and services are complementary with time *and* that there are no scale economies, then the substitution effect is such that a higher wage rate *increases* the desired number of household members. Under these household production assumptions the existence of economies of scale is, therefore, a *necessary* condition for a *negative* substitution effect. Econometric analysis of the variation in household size among MHUs found strong evidence of a negative substitution effect (Ermisch, 1981), thereby suggesting that household economies of scale are a very important factor in household formation

decisions. That is, whereas higher earning capacity makes time more valuable, the larger resources it makes available create more privacy which
compensates for the scale economies lost. But this inference depends upon
the validity of the household production assumptions, which some may
question.

A change or difference in the prices of housing and consumer durables has
income and substitution effects on optimal household size similar to earning
capacity, although opposite in direction. Their strength will depend upon the
proportion of an MHU's income which is spent on them. Since expenditures
on housing generally represent a large share of an MHU's budget, increases
in the cost of a dwelling unit will generally increase optimal household size
significantly only if increases in real wages have a net depressing effect on
household size. Variation in the constraints on access to housing in the public
sector would clearly also affect the household size an MHU chooses, since
the constraint on the amount of housing the MHU could consume at the subsidized public sector rents would be directly affected. A tighter constraint
would have an effect similar to a rent increase.

Another proposition which flows from the model is that labour force participation rates and hours worked by members of the MHU, and therefore
total income of the MHU, are mutually dependent variables with household
size/grouping. Use of labour force participation or total income as an
explanatory variable in an ordinary least squares regression would therefore
be improper, producing biased estimates of the effects of all variables on
household size or the probability of living in a particular household context.
The model also predicts that if the population of MHUs of a given type is
split into those with labour force participants and those without, the effect of
non-earned income will differ between the two groups. Econometric analyses
of household size by Ermisch and Overton (1984) give support to this
hypothesis. The theoretical model suggests that a non-working couple is
more likely to form a separate household than an individual not in employment with the same economic and social characteristics (for example, age,
location).

Finally, the extension of the theoretical model to include children suggests
that their presence has an important independent influence on decisions concerning household grouping. Children are likely to enhance the value of
privacy to the MHU, and since they also increase 'congestion' in the use
of housing and consumer durable goods, the reduction in the per caput cost
of services from such durable goods associated with an additional household
member tends to be smaller, the larger the number of children. Moreover,
older children may help in the household, so the increment added by an additional household member to 'household production' is reduced. All of these
impacts of children tend to make the optimal household size for an MHU
with children lower, and the probability of forming a separate household
higher than for an otherwise identical MHU without children. The number

and ages of children could also influence optimal household size and the probability of living in a particular household context.

It is reasonable to suppose that tastes and abilities in home-related work may vary in the course of life and between the sexes. Also, because of the impact of experience and custom on tastes and efficiency in home-related work, these may differ between persons previously married and bachelors/ spinsters. Thus age, sex, and marital status variables should be considered as factors influencing optimal household size and household context.

The theoretical model has suggested a number of economic and demographic variables which may have an important influence on decisions concerning the household group in which to live. That is, it suggests the variables which should be included in the vector Z in the probability relations $P_{ik}(Z)$. It has also provided some hypotheses about the effects of some of these explanatory variables, and it has indicated which are truly independent variables and which are mutually dependent. The latter distinction is a guide to the proper statistical techniques for estimating these effects. Two particular hypotheses that emerged from the theoretical model were that, all else being equal, MHUs containing a couple are more likely to form a separate household than MHUs containing one adult, and that MHUs containing children are more likely to form a separate household than otherwise identical MHUs without children. There is, therefore, good reason to suppose that each type of MHU has a different set of probability relations $P_{ik}(Z)$, making it necessary to estimate the relations separately for each MHU type.

3.7. Econometric analysis of household context

Ermisch and Overton (1984; 1985) show how the economic theory of household formation can be applied to estimate probability relations. This analysis supports the hypothesis predicted by the theoretical model that non-employed couples are more likely to form a separate household than non-employed individuals with the same income and of the same age. It also supports the hypothesis that the presence of a child in an MHU enhances the probability that an MHU lives alone (based on comparisons of one-parent MHUs and individuals with identical characteristics).

In this analysis, the income available to an MHU consistently proves to be an important constraint on its ability to form a separate household, although there is considerable variability in the strength of the effect of economic constraints on the probability of the MHU living alone. The effect is highest for MHUs containing a young single person, but economic sensitivity is progressively lower for the following groups of MHUs: older, non-married persons below pensionable age without children, one-parent MHUs, non-married persons of pensionable age, and retired couples. MHUs of types 3 and 4 with a head below pensionable age were not analysed because such a large propor-

TABLE 3.1. Percentages of women without a home of their own after marriage

	When married				
	1955 or earlier[a]	1956–60	1961–5	1966–70	1971–5
Marriage below age 20					
At marriage	65	47	50	46	45
6 months later	61	43	35	35	34
1 year later	56	37	28	28	30
2 years later	45	33	20	19	16
5 years later	22	17	12	12	—
Marriage at 20 or over					
At marriage	50	38	26	21	21
6 months later	45	33	21	15	14
1 year later	40	28	17	12	10
2 years later	33	22	13	9	7
5 years later	16	12	7	5	—

[a] Two-thirds were married in 1951–5 and one-third earlier. Because the sample comprised women aged under 50 in 1976, women marrying at age 25 or over are under-represented among the sample married in 1951–5, and some marrying at ages 20 and over are under-represented among the sample married before 1951.

Source: Holmans (1981).

tion were separate households. With the possible exception of young couples, the sensitivity of their separate household decisions to economic constraints is probably even weaker than that found among retired couples.

While the vast majority of married couples in Britain set up as a separate household there are still a surprisingly large proportion of newly married couples who do not do so. As Table 3.1 shows, this proportion has fallen substantially over the post-war period, reflecting the alleviation of the acute post-war housing shortage and real income growth, but 14 per cent of women married during the period 1971–5 did not have a home of their own (either rented or owned) six months after marriage, if they married at age 20 or older; this proportion was as much as one-third if they married as teenagers. It would appear that income and borrowing constraints play a major role in the lower probability of forming a separate household by couples marrying as teenagers, but they would also appear to be more sensitive to housing market constraints—house price, rents, and the queues for subsidized public housing—than persons marrying later in their lives. Table 3.1 also indicates that age at marriage has quite long-lasting effects on the likelihood of a couple having a home of their own. There appears still to be scope for income and housing market factors to affect the propensity of young couples to form separate households.

The analysis of one-parent MHUs and married couples (types 2, 3, and 4) containing parents in their 'middle ages' (late thirties to early sixties) raises an issue concerning the 'real' difference between household contexts 1 and 3. When a child reaches maturity, he becomes an MHU in his own right, and the parental MHU 'moves' into household context 3—living with adult children. Other than their child ageing, nothing has changed for these parental MHUs. In particular, no different *choice* concerning household context has been made. It would not, therefore, be very meaningful to treat contexts 1 and 3 as being distinct in analyses of socio-economic influences on household contexts like those above. For example, in their analysis of one-parent MHUs, Ermisch and Overton (1985) analysed the probability of being in either context 1 or context 3 $(P_{21} + P_{23})$. At the same time, the analysis of single-person MHUs, some of whom are the 'adult children' living at home in the analysis of MHU types 2, 3, and 4, assumes that such persons can make choices about household context, and those remaining at home are put in household context 2 ('with parents').

This weak sort of asymmetric treatment of parents and their adult children is fully justifiable in the analysis of socio-economic influences on the likelihood of living in a particular household context when the five household contexts defined earlier are used. But if we define household context in terms of 'household size', defined in terms of the number of MHUs in the household or the number of adults in the household, parents and their adult children must be treated symmetrically. That is, each MHU in a particular household must be assigned the same household size. For instance, a couple living with their son aged 18 would constitute two MHUs, each of which lives in a household of 2 MHUs and 3 adults. A household size definition of household context can be used to derive the number and size distribution of households.

The econometric analysis described so far has focused on the factors influencing the probability that an MHU sets up as a separate household, with all the other household contexts being grouped together in the analysis. Table 3.2 shows that the propensity to live alone has increased in a number of European countries. More evidence on this phenomenon can be found in chapter 6 by Schwarz, and some of its backgrounds are discussed by Schmid in chapter 2. A focus on the probability of being a separate household, particularly among non-married persons, is justifiable on these grounds, but the analysis can be more general.

The more general analysis considers whether the economic and demographic variables used earlier in analysing the probability of being a separate household can help classify MHUs according to their household context. The classification power of the variables for MHUs of type 1 was tested using discriminant analysis in Ermisch and Overton (1984). Being single, being young, and the size of an MHU's earning capacity were found strongly to affect the household context within which an MHU lives.

TABLE 3.2. One-person households in European countries

(a) Percentage living alone at two dates

	Men		Women	
	1st date	2nd date	1st date	2nd date
Single				
Federal Republic of Germany				
(1972, 1981)	15.1	17.8	22.9	21.5
France (1975, 1981)	12.4	14.0	15.1	18.4
Switzerland (1970, 1980)	10.0	14.3	17.8	26.1
Divorced[a]				
Federal Republic of Germany	47.6	60.7	42.7	47.2
France	41.5	35.5	34.4	32.8
Switzerland	39.7	50.4	39.1	42.4

(b) One-person households as a percentage of all households

	Dates				Reference to dates			
	1	2	3	4	1	2	3	4
Federal Republic of Germany	12	20	25	30	1946	1961	1970	1981
Austria	17	20	25	27	1951	1961	1971	1981
France	19	20	22	24	1946	1962	1975	1981
Great Britain	11	11	18	22	1951	1961	1971	1981
Netherlands	9	12	17	18	1950	1960	1971	1978
Sweden	—	20	25	33		1960	1970	1980
Switzerland	—	14	20	29		1961	1971	1980

[a] Dates as before.

Source: Roussel (1983), Tables 4 and 9.

A more direct approach (although computation is costly for a large sample) to estimating the effect of economic and demographic variables on the probability $P_{ik}(Z)$ that an MHU lives in a particular household context is an application of 'multinomial logit' or 'multinomial probit' (see, for example, McFadden, 1976). The result would be direct estimates of each of the $P_{ik}(Z)$ relations. Given a value for Z, the probability of being in household context k would be determined. As suggested earlier, an interesting application would be to define the context in terms of a measure of household size. While perhaps providing less understanding about the influences on household formation than the five contexts used above, it would be useful for exploring the sensitivity of the number and size distribution of households to economic and other variables.

3.8. Household formation and dissolution: Integrated analysis

In the framework outlined above, the number of households of a given type k depends upon the demographic transitions which produce the number of MHUs of type i and upon the probability that an MHU of type i lives in household context k. Economic factors (for example, earning capacities of MHU members) and demographic states (age, sex, and marital status) operate at both levels of analysis, appearing in the X and Z vectors, which appear in the demographic transition functions $h_{ij}(d, X)$ and $P_{ik}(Z)$, respectively. Demographic trends such as the rising divorce rate alter the composition of MHUs in the population (through demographic transitions), and may also alter the mean probability that an MHU of a given type i lives in a particular household context k. The composition of households in the population can, therefore, be changed through both channels. An economic change could effect demographic transitions and P_{ik}, only the former, or only the latter.

The changes in the proportion of one-person households in European populations shown in Table 3.2 have come about through changes at both levels of analysis. Rising divorce, wider sex differences in mortality, later marriage (in the 1970s) have changed the demographic transition probabilities $h_{ij}(d, X)$, perhaps shifting the whole function, and the composition of MHUs in the population has changed as a result. These changes alone would have altered the number and composition of households, but in addition, because of economic growth, housing market developments, and other factors, the household context probabilities P_{ik} changed, the probability that MHUs of type 1 live alone rising in particular.

The terms household formation and dissolution are often used to refer to a dynamic process in which particular households are created, for instance by a young couple marrying, or a young person leaving home to set up on his own, or two persons coming together to share a flat, and dissolved by divorce, or a young person leaving home, or two (unrelated) persons each deciding to get a flat of their own. In terms of the framework suggested here, the first examples of creation and dissolution respectively come about through demographic transitions, affecting household formation through changing the composition of MHUs in the population. The other examples involve the household formation level of analysis: the probability that an MHU of a given type lives in a particular household context. In my view, the largest part of household formation and dissolution in this sense comes about through the demographic transitions—the first level of analysis. The economic analysis used in this chapter has concentrated on the second level of analysis; much more analysis needs to be done on the first level. That is, analysis of the $h_{ij}(d, X)$ functions with given $P_{ik}(Z)$ relations.

It is the contention of this chapter that analysis is clearer if these two levels are separated. For instance, a child leaving home is an important part of the dynamics of household formation and dissolution. But leaving home to marry and leaving home to set up a household on his own are quite different decisions, at least in terms of the economic aspects of the two decisions. Modelling is made easier by making the suggested distinction.

Acknowledgements

The concept of a 'minimal household unit' was originally suggested by Elizabeth Overton, and it was developed jointly with her. Many ideas that have made their way into this chapter arose from discussions with her, for which I am grateful.

References

BECKER, G. S. (1981). *A Treatise on the Family* (Harvard University Press, Cambridge, Mass.).
—— E. M. LANDES, AND R. T. MICHAEL (1977). An economic analysis of marital instability, *Journal of Political Economy* 85(6), 1141–87.
BISHOP, J. (1980). Jobs, cash transfers and marital instability: a review and synthesis of the evidence, *The Journal of Human Resources* 15, 301–34.
DE COOMAN, E., J. ERMISCH, AND H. JOSHI (1985). The next birth and the labour market: a dynamic model of births in England and Wales, Centre for Economic Policy Research, Discussion Paper no. 37, London.
EASTERLIN, R. A. (1980). *Birth and Fortune: The Impact of Numbers on Personal Welfare* (Grant McIntyre, London).
ERMISCH, J. (1981). An economic theory of household formation, *Scottish Journal of Political Economy* 28, 1–19.
—— AND E. OVERTON (1984). Minimal household units: a new perspective in the demographic and economic analysis of household formation, Policy Studies Institute Research Report, London.
—— —— (1985). Minimal household units: a new approach to the analysis of household formation, *Population Studies* 39, 33–54.
HAJNAL, J. (1982). Two kinds of preindustrial household formation system, *Population and Development Review* 8, 449–94.
HICKMAN, B. G. (1974). What became of the building cycle? In: P. David and M. Reder (eds.), *Nations and Households in Economic Growth: Essays in Honour of Moses Abramovitz* (Academic Press, London), 291–314.
HOLMANS, A. (1981). 'Housing careers of recently married couples, Population Trends 24, 10–14.
MCFADDEN, D. (1976). Quantal choice analysis: a survey, *Annals of Economic and Social Measurement* 5, 363–90.
MOORE, E. AND R. PYKE (1968). Estimation of the transition distributions of a Markov renewal process, *Annals of the Institute of Statistical Mathematics* (Tokyo) 20, 411–24.
ROUSSEL, L. (1983). Les ménages d'une personne: l'évolution récente, *Population* 38, 996–1016.
SOUTH, S. (1985). Economic conditions and the divorce rate: a time series analysis of

the postwar United States, *Journal of Marriage and the Family* 47, 31–41.
WILLEKENS, F. J., I. SHAH, J. M. SHAH, AND P. RAMACHANDRAN (1982). Multi-state analysis of marital status life tables: theory and application, *Population Studies* 36, 129–44.

PART II

Data and trends

4

Household data from surveys containing information for individuals

F. Klijzing

ABSTRACT

Input for many macromodels of household headship is the kind of stock data that censuses provide. The level of disaggregation required by micromodels of individual household status transitions is better served by sample surveys of special design. Sample surveys that produce flow data can be broadly divided into three groups: single-round retrospective interview surveys, multi-round retrospective interview surveys, and multi-round prospective surveys or panel studies. One example for each of these three ideal types of sample surveys is discussed, all from the European scene. The chapter concludes with a presentation of some of the results of a Dutch survey on alternative living arrangements that combines various aspects of the survey methodologies discussed.

4.1. Introduction

TWO typical sources of household data are population censuses and sample surveys. In either case, the information collected for each individual can sometimes be quite personal (Bulmer, 1979). In order to ensure co-operation from the public, anonymity is explicitly guaranteed. In many countries of the Western hemisphere, protection of private life against outside intrusion is a much debated issue nowadays. Public willingness to take part in large-scale information gathering projects seems to be diminishing. The Netherlands is no exception to this rule, as is illustrated by the indefinite postponement of the 1981 population census. Non-response from the pilot census turned out to be discouragingly high.

Such continent-wide developments tend to increase the significance of sample surveys as a source of household data, as compared to population counts. Non-response is bothersome to sample surveys too, but in many cases some sort of control is possible. What is even more important, sample surveys—especially small-scale ones—are more flexible in that they allow for various types of designs. That is, a sample survey may be either cross-sectional (census taking)—single-round or multi-round (repeat survey)—or longitudinal (a panel study). There is also the possibility of retrospective

43

questioning on items of particular interest, thus permitting a wider time span to be covered. Census questionnaires, on the other hand, contain at most a few questions on, for instance, place of residence one and/or five years ago. Another reason for the rising popularity of sample surveys as suppliers of household data has to do with the accessibility of their data. Requests for particular tabulations of census materials not yet published may always be sent to the Statistical Office of the country in question, but direct access to the data files themselves will hardly ever be granted. Even sample tapes of census results are not always made available for individual analysis. This, once again, has to do with the issue of confidentiality mentioned before (Flaherty, 1978). The final destination of many sample survey data, on the other hand, is frequently some sort of public archives or data bank (like the Steinmetz archives in the Netherlands), where they are stored for further inspection by whomsoever wishes. Admittedly, it may take some years before the data set is thus released, but once deposited, even individual records may be scrutinized. Absence of name and address makes personal identification virtually impossible.

Due to this particular combination of relative advantages of sample surveys over population censuses as providers of household data, survey data are more widely applied to various household models. It is the objective of this paper to illustrate this point with the aid of a description of recent or ongoing research projects in the realm of household demography. The emphasis is on the European scene only. We do not, in any way, claim to be exhaustive. We will discuss the kind of individual data especially suited for testing dynamic models: multi-round prospective surveys, multi-round retrospective surveys, and single-round retrospective surveys. To conclude, some results from a 1984 household survey in the Netherlands are presented to illustrate the kind of flow data that only sample surveys can provide. Implications for household modelling are indicated.

4.2. Household data disaggregated

As indicated in the Introduction, one of the methodological advantages of sample surveys is that they allow for various designs, including the cross-sectional snapshot view that census taking permits. But since a synchronic picture does not embody the kind of flow data that are at stake here, such stock-data collecting sample surveys will not be dealt with any further. The remaining sample survey study designs that do provide a more diachronic household perspective fall into three broad categories. We will briefly review them all, presenting one European example for each of them. The examples chosen are rather arbitrary and should not be seen as the best representation of each ideal type of sample survey.

Generally speaking, flow data on household structure can be produced through (1) single-round retrospective interview surveys, (2) multi-round retrospective interview surveys, or (3) multi-round prospective surveys. The latter ideal type of course is just another term for a longitudinal or panel investigation. The information it gathers is called 'prospective' because of the progressive way in which it monitors processes. The step-by-step picture of change that is built up is not complete until the last round is over. This is not to say that multi-round prospective sample surveys do not contain retrospective questions. Quite to the contrary, particular transformations between round t and $t + 1$ may be further highlighted by retrospective questions at $t + 1$ on the responsible mechanisms. In fact, it is analytically useful to subdivide ideal type (3) into those multi-round prospective sample surveys that carry retrospective check items (3*a*), and those that do not (3*b*). In practice, however, most panel investigations have both. Changes in attitudes, for instance, can only be measured 'prospectively', whereas historical events are perhaps better retrieved retrospectively. Panel research methodology, especially as it relates to household demometrics, is presently receiving widespread international attention through workshops, seminars, and special conferences. We will now leave this issue for what it is and proceed to present the ongoing research project at the University of Bielefeld, West Germany, as one example of a multi-round prospective sample survey.

4.2.1. Multi-round prospective surveys

As was the case in preceding panel investigations in the Federal Republic of Germany on 'generatives Verhalten' (and in Austria for that matter) the longitudinal research project on 'generatives Verhalten in Nordrhein-Westfalen' of the University of Bielefeld refers in its project title to fertility rather than to household structure. At a conceptual level, this probably illustrates that it is not so much the issue of household composition *per se* that inspired this and many other similar sample surveys, but rather the study of fertility and nuptiality as its proximate or intermediate determinants (Bongaarts, 1983). At a more practical level the reference to 'generatives Verhalten' probably also reflects some concern with fertility levels that are far below replacement, as well as with changing norms and patterns of family formation in West Germany. The same applies to many other similar surveys carried out in Europe: they all furnish badly needed data on individual household status transitions, whereas in actual fact, they were set up for a different purpose.

In any case, the Bielefeld project aims to study the determinants and consequences of changing fertility, parenthood, and family formation, both as behavioural patterns and as valuation complexes (Kaufmann *et al.*, 1982). The survey held its first round of interviews in late 1981/early 1982, its second in late 1983/early 1984; a third round was planned for 1986. Thus, the rounds are approximately two years apart. The interplay between the phasing of rounds, the analysis of results per round, and the presentation of findings is

always a major bottleneck in longitudinal research (Keilman, 1985). At the
time of this writing, no published results of the Bielefeld study had yet been
encountered in the literature so that we will restrict ourselves to a summary
description of the sample design and the questionnaire.

In the first round, 2,620 women aged 18 to 30 years were interviewed, all
of German nationality and all-time residents of Cologne, Herne, Gütersloh,
or Kleve in Nordrhein-Westfalen. Their distribution according to living
arrangement at the time of the first interview was as follows:

1. without a partner   27.5%
2. living apart together (LAT) 20.5%
3. cohabitational union   8.8%
4. marital union   43.0%
5. not classified   0.2%

Of the 720 females without a partner (1), 66.2 per cent were still living at
home with their parent(s), 24.6 per cent were heading a one-person household, and the remaining ones were members of other types of living arrangements such as flat sharing, communes, and the like. Comparable percentages
apply to women who had a so-called LAT relationship at the time of the first
interview (2). Respondents in marital or non-marital unions, apart from
themselves being interviewed, were given a separate questionnaire to be completed by their partner. At the end of the interview all respondents were asked
whether they would be willing to participate in a follow-up study some two
years later. The addresses of those who responded favourably ($N = 2,160$ or
82.4 per cent) were kept on record. At the time the second round was held,
however, for various reasons (change of residence, refusal, respondent not at
home, interview not successful) only 1,472 panel respondents remained. This
is the final sample population for which results between rounds 1 and 2 can be
compared. As said before, no such trend studies are available yet, but it may
be interesting to list a few of the psychological items that figured on both
schedules.[1] In order not to affect the exact wording of the questions by the
process of translation, they are given in their original language:

• in einer guten Partnerschaft darf es zu keinen Konflikten kommen;
• Kinder zu haben, ist das wichtigste im Leben einer Frau;
• wenn man einen Partner gefunden hat, mit dem man zusammenbleiben
  will, dann sollte man selbstverständlich heiraten;
• auch wenn die Frau berufstätig ist, sollte die Hausarbeit vor allem ihre
  Aufgabe sein.

These and similar statements had to be rated on a 5-point scale running
from 'fully agree' to 'fully disagree'. It will be interesting to know, in due
time: (a) how opinions as expressed at the first round came out the second
time; (b) whether attitudinal changes thus measured can be related to particular historical events that occurred during this interval; and (c) which role
they play in the way people subsequently reorganize their lives. In any case,

dynamic transition rates derived from the flow of events between the first two rounds of the Bielefeld project can be entered again as parameters to run a microsimulation model predicting the distribution of households by type at some future time. Indeed, the sequencing of rounds in panel research opens up interesting possibilities for validating the prognostic value of micro-simulation models (see class 4 of household models in the Introduction).

4.2.2. Multi-round retrospective surveys[2]

There are numerous cross-sectional sample surveys repeated on a regular basis that routinely collect past and present household information. Again, as with panel investigations, they are often of the 'fertility' variety, probing into reproductive behaviour and/or attitudinal aspects. But it is rather rare to find trend studies attempting to link up the differences in household com-position, as observed from one round to the next. Part of the problem of course is that, from round to round, sample definitions are frequently adapted to changing research objectives. A good but arbitrarily chosen example is the NEGO series of four fertility surveys in Belgium. What started as a fertility survey among married women only in 1966 turned gradually into a fertility and family development survey among women of all marital states, as illustrated by the latest round in 1982 (Cliquet and Debusschere, 1984). Furthermore, the first two rounds covered Belgium as a whole, the other two were limited to the Dutch-speaking population. Such modifications in sample design make comparison of the results from the dif-ferent rounds extremely difficult. Nevertheless, it is not exaggerated to say, perhaps, that household data from multi-round cross-sectional sample surveys tend to be underutilized. A clear exception to this rule is the General Household Survey (GHS) tradition in Great Britain which was established in 1971.

With a standard sample size of around 15,000 private households each year, GHS is a multi-purpose undertaking without a dominant theme. The main areas covered are demography, housing, employment, education, health, and income but there are many annually rotating subsidiary topics too (Barnes, 1979). Originally, GHS primarily produced stock data on household composition, but since 1979 questions on family formation were included as well in a special Family Information section which in that year applied to 6,082 women aged 18 to 49 years, of all marital states. Their distri-bution according to marital status at that time was as follows:

single	17.9%
married	69.0%
remarried	5.0%
widowed	1.0%
divorced	4.3%
separated	2.8%

Of all these 6,082 women, 3 per cent ($N = 162$) indicated that they were cohabiting. Although Brown and Kiernan (1981) estimate from this that the total number of cohabiting women aged under 50 in 1979 was about one third of a million, their share was still low by international standards. GHS statistics also indicate that cohabitation is more prevalent among separated and divorced women (16 and 20 per cent, respectively) than among single women (8 per cent). In addition to the question on current cohabitation and length of cohabitation, the survey also contained questions on pre-marital cohabitation for all currently married women as well as for those currently widowed, divorced, or separated. The results suggest an increasing incidence of pre-marital cohabitation, particularly during the 1970s. Whereas only 1 per cent of the pre-1961 marriages had been preceded by cohabitation with the same partner, for the 1977–9 marriage cohort this figure had risen to 19 per cent. Women who said they had cohabited pre-maritally were further asked how long they had lived together as man and wife before getting married. The mean or median of this interval is significantly shorter for first marriages than for remarriages.

These are but a few of the findings from one particular round of the GHS; somewhat less has been published on other rounds. Sometimes, GHS results are compared with census returns so as to analyse intercensal trends in household composition. From one such comparison (OPCS, 1982) it is evident that non-family households are on the increase in Great Britain while family households are losing ground. The increase of the former is due especially to the rise in the number of one-person households, whereas the decline of the latter is due, among other things, to the shrinking number of households with dependent children.

4.2.3. Single-round retrospective surveys

As part of the World Fertility Survey (WFS) project, a single-round retrospective interview survey was launched in Norway in 1977 in which complete marriage, pregnancy, and cohabitation histories were reconstructed for 4,137 women aged 18 to 44 years, of all marital states. Apart from these retrospective sections, the questionnaire also contained items on residence and household, migration, sexual intercourse, infecundity, contraception, preferences for children, childcare, attitudes on abortion, politics, and religion, income, occupational activity, education, and family origin. For the last three topics, the female respondents were interrogated about their partners as well. Preliminary analyses of these survey results have been presented by Brunborg (1979) and by Noack and Østby (1979). Here we will concentrate on a few findings of the cohabitation and marriage histories of that survey (Blanc, 1984).

Overall, it appears that couple formation in Norway—whether through marriage or cohabitation—is starting at an increasingly early age. Employing

TABLE 4.1. Probabilities of couple formation and dissolution, females, Norway

	Birth cohort		
	1933–1942	1943–1952	1953–1959
Probability of			
• marriage as the first union			
(cumulated until age 24)	0.69	0.62	0.38
• cohabitation as the first union			
(cumulated until age 24)	0.09	0.22	0.44
• legalization of cohabitation within			
one year	>0.50	>0.50	0.31
• dissolution of cohabitation within			
one year	0.06	0.10	0.17
• first marriage dissolution within			
five years	0.03	0.04	0.12

the double-decrement life table analysis (non-parametric analysis, see Courgeau and Lelièvre, chapter 11), Blanc computed the competing risks of entering marriage as the first union or entering a consensual union as the first union, both by age 24, for three birth cohorts: those born between 1953 and 1959 (aged 18 to 24 at the time of the interview), those born between 1943 and 1952 (aged 25 to 34 years), and those born between 1933 and 1942 (aged 35 to 44 years). Using the same technique, she also derived probabilities of legalization and separation within a period of one year for women whose first union was a consensual union (Table 4.1).

These figures point to an increase over time in the propensity to enter a consensual union rather than marriage as the first union, in addition to the earlier age at first union. While marriages are still more stable than consensual unions, they have become less so over time, as shown by the rising probability of first marriage dissolution after five years. For women who entered a consensual union as their first union, recent cohorts are less likely to marry the first man they live with and more likely to separate from him than women in earlier cohorts. Blanc interprets this as indicating that non-marital cohabitation has come to be viewed less as a prelude to marriage and more as a convenient household arrangement which can be abandoned relatively easily. The probability of legalizing an existing consensual union rises dramatically, however, when a pregnancy occurs that is brought to term. Then, the cumulative probability of legal marriage within one year following the beginning of the union is 0.66 for women who do get pregnant and 0.35 for those who do not. Corresponding probabilities for legalization within two years are 0.85 and 0.52, respectively. Even with the increase in the prevalence of non-marital cohabitation and non-marital fertility, the large majority of Norwegian births still take place within a legal context. Nevertheless, the question arises as to the precise impact of these changing patterns of family formation on reproductive behaviour in general, and long-term population change in particular. As an example of a macrodynamic household model (class 6, see Introduction), Blanc's life table analysis goes a long way towards highlighting the behavioural aspects of this complex issue, but single-round retrospective interview surveys are probably not the best instrument to measure its attitudinal components. For that purpose, as we have seen before, one would need a longitudinal design.

4.3. The Dutch ORIN survey

Concluding this overview of the various ways of producing flow data on household formation and dissolution, we would like to present some provisional figures from a Dutch study (ORIN). As part of a research project on alternative living arrangements in the Netherlands, in early 1984, about 1,600 males and females aged 18 to 54 years, of all marital states, were retrospectively interviewed about their household histories of the past seven years (1977–83).[3] The sample frame for this survey was provided by a microcensus conducted in late 1983 which comprised some 20,000 household units from all over the country. From all household members thus enumerated, 1,600 were selected to be re-interviewed according to age, sex, marital status, household type, and position within the household. Because the ORIN study is based on a sample of a sample, more than the usual precautions were taken to ensure national representation. No details are given here but due account will be rendered in the first project report which is to appear soon.

The main objective of ORIN was to trace the origins of the present household situation of each respondent as far back as 1 January 1977, reconstructing all changes in marital status, household composition, living arrangement, and so on that had occurred since then. To this end, a transition matrix was used of the (simplified) form set out in Table 4.2.

TABLE 4.2. ORIN-transition matrix with four household classes

	TO			
	F1	F2	N1	N2
FROM				
F1	X			
F2		X		
N1			X	
N2				X

where F1 = Family household type 1
       F2 = Family household type 2
       N1 = Non-family household type 1
       N2 = Non-family household type 2

For F1, three different groups of respondents were selected from the microcensus sample frame: (*a*) children aged 18 to 34 years still living at home, with both parents present; (*b*) males or females living together with their first marital partner; and (*c*) males or females living together with their second (or third) marital partner. By definition, type (*a*) respondents have not yet started their own independent household history. From a cohort perspective, they provide the entries for the above transition matrix. For F2, there are two different groups of respondents: (*d*) children aged 18 to 34 years still living at home, with one parent present; and (*e*) lone parents, with or without a non-marital partner. Non-family household type 1 refers to: (*f*) persons living on their own, exclusively; whereas type 2 includes: (*g*) non-marital partners in a consensual union without dependent children living with them; and (*h*) any group of two or more persons living together neither in a marital, nor in a consensual, union. The difference between N1 and N2, of course, is that between one-person and multi-person non-family households. In the case of F1(*b*) and F1(*c*), both marital partners are present, whether or not they have dependent children at home, whereas F2(*e*) denotes the absence of either one of them. Again, all child respondents are aged 18 to 34, all others 18 to 54 years.

All these subtypes combined would result in a 8 × 8 matrix, the 'leaving-home behaviour' of (*a*) and (*d*) providing the point of departure for each individual household history. For purposes of presentation, however, subtypes (*a*) and (*d*) on the one hand, and subtypes (*b*) and (*c*) on the other hand, will be aggregated so as to produce a 6 × 6 transition matrix, of the form expressed in Table 4.3.

TABLE 4.3. ORIN-transition matrix with six household classes

	TO					
	F1(*a*) + F2(*d*)	F1(*b*) + F1(*c*)	F2(*e*)	N1(*f*)	N2(*g*)	N2(*h*)
FROM						
F1(*a*) + F2(*d*)	X					
F1(*b*) + F1(*c*)	X	X				
F2(*e*)	X		X			
N1(*f*)	X			X		
N2(*g*)	X				X	
N2(*h*)	X					X

Table 4.4 gives details on the individual household status transitions observed between 1 January 1977 and early 1984, in an unweighted form. Because the ORIN sample is highly stratified, with an over-representation of alternative living arrangements at the expense of marital unions, these figures

TABLE 4.4. Individual household status transitions between 1 January 1977 (horizontally) and early 1984 (vertically), unweighted figures from the ORIN survey

	F1(a) + F2(d)	F1(b) + F1(c)	F2(e)	N1(f)	N2(g)	N2(h)
F1(a) + F2(d)	144	102	32	152	105	49
F1(b) + F1(c)	1	310	154	78	23	2
F2(e)	0	16	62	17	12	0
N1(f)	4	21	8	132	29	7
N2(g)	2	10	11	16	29	1
N2(h)	0	1	3	21	8	39
Total	151	460	270	416	206	98

F1(a) + F2(d) = children aged 18 to 34 years in one- or two-parent families
F1(b) + F1(c) = married persons aged 18 to 54 living together with marital partner
F2(e) = parents in one-parent households
N1(f) = persons aged 18 to 54 years living alone in a one-person household
N2(g) = non-marital partners in a cohabitational union without children
N2(h) = members of a non-family household living together neither in a marital, nor in a consensual, union.

do not properly reflect the population distribution by age, sex, and household type in 1984. Weighted figures appear in Table 4.5, but discussion will be limited to unweighted results only.

Arranged diagonally are those cases where no change in household status took place during the previous seven years. All in all, 885 individuals did change their household status, not counting those that changed twice or more, such that their 1984 position was once again the same as in 1977. The least stable are the single-parent families, the one-person households, and those formed by non-marital cohabitants without children, showing retention probabilities of only 23, 32, and 14 per cent, respectively. Hence these three household types together account for the major part of all household formations observed. Of those living in a consensual union at the time of the ORIN survey, 51 per cent had been living with their parents 7 years earlier. For persons living on their own, the corresponding figure is 36 per cent. Only 2 per cent of the marital unions had been non-marital in 1977. Finally, nearly all respondents living with their parent(s) at the time of the survey had done so in 1977 (95 per cent). There is not much difference between males and females in the frequency with which they change their household status. According to age, however, it is clear that inter-household mobility is highest among the younger age groups, tapering off rapidly thereafter.

These figures provide a first basis for the derivation of occurrence/exposure rates or transition probabilities. To that end, one would ideally need closed intervals not truncated at either side. In the ORIN data set there

TABLE 4.5. The relative distribution in the sample ($N = 1{,}601$) of individual household members[a] aged 18 to 54 years on 1 January 1984, according to age, sex, and household category (weighted figures)

	F1(a) + F2(d)	F1(b) + F1(c)	F2(e)	N1(f)	N2(g)	N2(h)	Total Rel.	Total Abs.
FEMALES								
18–24 years	34.1	4.1	2.8	15.4	22.5	18.5	11.4	182
25–34 years	3.6	17.5	20.1	17.5	19.0	9.4	15.0	241
35–44 years		17.1	31.6	7.5	3.3	5.3	12.8	205
45–54 years		12.6	29.8	8.1	2.6	6.1	9.9	158
MALES								
18–24 years	50.4	1.5	0.4	12.5	13.1	21.6	11.8	190
25–34 years	11.9	15.5	3.5	21.4	28.7	17.5	15.7	251
35–44 years		18.0	5.6	10.1	7.7	11.7	13.3	213
45–54 years		13.7	6.2	7.5	3.1	9.9	10.1	161
TOTAL	100.0	100.0	100.0	100.0	100.0	100.0	100.0	1,601
	($N = 274$)	($N = 1{,}036$)	($N = 43$)	($N = 124$)	($N = 76$)	($N = 48$)		

[a] Excluding children older than 34 years still living at home.

F1(a) + F2(d) = children aged 18 to 34 years in one- or two-parent families
F1(b) + F1(c) = married persons aged 18 to 54 living together with marital partner
F2(e) = parents in one-parent households
N1(f) = persons living alone in one-person households
N2(g) = non-marital partners in a cohabitational union without children
N2(h) = members of a non-family household living together neither in a marital nor in a consensual union.

are many intervals that fulfil this condition. These not only involve changes in household status *per se* but also changes in birth order, labour force participation status, migration status, and so on. Unravelling the interrelationships between these various event histories constitutes a major analytic goal of the ORIN research project as a whole. In this respect there is a close affinity with the French '3B' survey reconstructing three biographies: family, profession, and migration. The event histories collected in both surveys permit the testing of various macrodynamic household models (see also chapter 11 by Courgeau and Lelièvre). A comparison of the results of the two surveys, especially with respect to fertility–migration interactions, is planned.

4.4. Summary

In summary, then, more and more governments in Europe appear to have difficulties in keeping up their long-standing census traditions. In part, this is due to the trends towards individuation and privatization, which are characteristic of modern society. This gradual loss of whole counts of population numbers entails that survey research is becoming increasingly important. This is true for information in general, and for household data in particular. Concurrent with these developments, there is a trend in household demography to drift away from macromodels of household headship based on aggregate stock data towards micromodels of individual household behaviour based on flow data. Only special types of sample surveys are able to provide this latter kind of information. They can be classified into three broad categories. One example of each of them, taken from the European scene, is discussed. The paper concludes with a presentation of some results of a single-round retrospective interview survey on alternative living arrangements in the Netherlands.

Notes

1. Published after the workshop: 'Familienentwicklung in Nordrhein-Westfalen; Generatives Verhalten im sozialen und regionalen Kontext', no. 47, Publication Series of the Prime Minister of the Federal State of Nordrhein-Westfalen. Düsseldorf, Mar. 1985.
2. The material in this section quoted from Barnes (1979), Brown and Kiernan (1981), and OPCS (1982) is Crown copyright. The Office of Population Censuses and Surveys gave permission to reproduce the statistics, which is gratefully acknowledged.
3. The ORIN project is carried out by the Netherlands Interuniversity Demographic Institute (NIDI) in collaboration with the Universities of Amsterdam, Tilburg, and Wageningen. Its members are: D. J. van de Kaa (project director), F. K. H.

Klijzing (project co-ordinator), N. W. Keilman, G. H. Moors, A. C. Kuijsten, L. Th. van Leeuwen, C. J. Weeda, and P. A. M. van den Akker. The project is funded by the National Programme of Demographic Research.

References

BARNES, B. (1979). Household surveys in the United Kingdom, *Population Trends* 16, 12–16.

BLANC, A. K. (1984). The impact of changing family patterns on reproductive behaviour: nonmarital cohabitation and fertility in Norway. Paper presented at the Annual Meeting of the Population Association of America, Minneapolis, May 2–5.

BONGAARTS, J. (1983). The formal demography of families and households: an overview, *IUSSP Newsletter* 17, 27–42.

BROWN, A. AND K. KIERNAN (1981). Cohabitation in Great Britain: evidence from the General Household Survey, *Population Trends* 25, 4–10.

BRUNBORG, H. (1979). Cohabitation without marriage in Norway, Article 116, Central Bureau of Statistics, Oslo.

BULMER, M. (ed.) (1979). *Censuses, Surveys and Privacy* (Holmes and Meier, New York).

CLIQUET, R. L. AND R. DEBUSSCHERE (eds.) (1984). Relationeel en reproductief gedrag in Vlaanderen. Eerste resultaten van de Nationale Enquête Gezinsontwikkeling 1982–1983—NEGO IV (Relations and reproductive behaviour in Flanders. First results of the National Survey of Family Growth 1982–1983—NEGO IV), Monograph no. 1, Centrum voor Bevolkings- en Gezinsstudiën, Brussels (in Dutch).

FLAHERTY, D. H. (1978). Respect de la vie privée et accès des chercheurs aux données individuelles; compte rendu de la conférence de Bellagio (Italie)—Août 1977, *Economie et statistique* 108, 64–9.

KAUFMANN, F.-X., A. HERLTH, J. QUITMANN, R. SIMM, AND K.-P. STROHMEIER (1982). Familienentwicklung: generatives Verhalten im familialen Kontext, *Zeitschrift für Bevölkerungswissenschaft* 8(4), 523–45.

KEILMAN, N. W. (1985). De opzet van een longitudinale relatie- en gezinsvormingssurvey (Organizing a longitudinal survey on living arrangements and family formation), Internal Report no. 39, Netherlands Interuniversity Demographic Institute, Voorburg, The Netherlands (in Dutch).

NOACK, T. AND L. ØSTBY (1979). Some results from the Norwegian fertility survey—1977, in: H. Brunborg and K. Sørensen (eds.), *The Fifth Scandinavian Demographic Symposium* (Scandinavian Demographic Society, Oslo), 211–25.

OFFICE OF POPULATION CENSUSES AND SURVEYS (1982). Family and household statistics from the 1981 Census, *Population Trends* 27, 14–17.

5

Sources of data for modelling household change with special reference to the OPCS 1% Longitudinal Study

M. Murphy, O. Sullivan, and A. Brown

ABSTRACT

The Office of Population Censuses and Surveys Longitudinal Study (LS) is described, and some illustrations of its potential for household modelling are discussed. The large sample size (one per cent of the population) and the linkage of individuals and their households in two censuses permits more detailed analysis of the dynamics of household change than has hitherto been possible in Britain. The comprehensive coverage of the LS permits investigation of possibly numerically small, but important subgroups in the population by looking at household circumstances at various levels of aggregation and at two points in time, giving both a spatial and a temporal dimension. Consistency with the full census of population, the principal source of data for planning, should further enhance the usefulness of this data source.

5.1. Sources of data for models of household change

MODELS of household and family change are based on the analysis of transitions between states. In many cases, suitable data for the direct estimation of such rates do not exist and ingenious methods have had to be derived to infer them (Preston and Coale, 1982). In other instances, for renewable events, even when data exist for the direct estimation of transition rates, there are problems associated with the difference between 'movement'- and 'transition'-based approaches (Ledent, 1980). In many cases, such transition rates and/or probabilities are derived from vital statistics data (Willekens *et al.*, 1982) or from sample surveys (Murphy, 1983). Klijzing (chapter 4), Willekens (chapter 7), and Courgeau and Lelièvre (chapter 11) discuss these aspects in more detail.

The disadvantage of vital statistics data for such models is that they refer to *de jure* rather than *de facto* circumstances and they are therefore particularly poor at estimating the informal counterparts of formal events: cohabitation as opposed to marriage and marital separation as opposed to divorce. This is especially unfortunate as it is precisely in these areas that the most rapid changes are taking place. Furthermore, these data usually lack contextual data on the social, economic, and demographic circumstances of the indi-

TABLE 5.1. Educational characteristics of young people aged 20–29 and living arrangements, Great Britain, 1980 (%)

	Position in household				
	Head of household (ever-married) or spouse	Head of household (single) or unrelated to head of household	Child (or child-in-law) of head of household	Other relation to head of household	Sample size (= 100%)
School-leaving age					
16 or under	61	6	31	2	2,935
17	46	15	38	2	467
18 and over	43	23	32	2	626

Source: Murphy (1983), Table 5.

viduals concerned, and thus make the analysis of homogeneous groups impossible. These differentials may be substantial. For example, Table 5.1 shows the living arrangements of young people by educational level. The better educated are much less likely to be living in a family household, and similar results apply for other variables such as social class.

Sample social surveys can provide information on background characteristics for use with household models. However, they also have a number of disadvantages. The two main designs for the collection of data in such surveys are longitudinal and retrospective cross-sectional. Large-scale longitudinal surveys are often confined to a particular birth cohort, and in Britain this is almost exclusively the case, with the principal surveys being based on samples of births occurring in 1946, 1958, and 1970. These studies refer only to the experience of a specialized group and, in particular, permit analysis only up to the age at which the last cohort sweep took place, which is likely to be at a relatively young age. Moreover, attrition from such studies, although not substantial, tends to increase with time, making them less representative of the original birth cohort; in particular, lack of success in tracing individuals might be expected to be associated with household movement. In addition, such samples will become less representative of the appropriate resident age group because they are typically not 'topped-up' with immigrants.

On the other hand, cross-sectional surveys generally cover the whole age range, and permit the construction and analysis of synthetic cohort data. Retrospective event-history data collected in such studies have usually been confined to demographic events such as marital and fertility histories, with the occasional collection of relevant histories in other areas such as employment (Martin and Roberts, 1984) and housing (Murphy, 1984). Although there is considerable scope for enlarging the retrospective component in cross-sectional studies, resource constraints and the fact that the whole age range is generally covered means that the numbers in particular age bands tend to be small, leading to sample-size problems in modelling. Moreover, these data generally refer to resident survivors in private households, whose experience is not fully representative of the population as a whole.

While conventional longitudinal and retrospective cross-sectional studies have some benefits for analysing household change, there are also considerable disadvantages. The purpose of this paper is to describe a unique source of data which may be used, among other things, for the analysis of household change.

5.2. The OPCS 1% Longitudinal Study

The Office of Population Censuses and Surveys 1% Longitudinal Study (henceforth referred to as the LS) contains longitudinal data on a 1 per cent sample of the population of England and Wales. This sample was initially selected from the 1971 Census, and comprised all people born on four selected birth dates. The characteristics of the sample members, of other people enumerated in the same household, and of the housing unit were obtained from the 1971 Census schedules, and certain registered vital events (in particular deaths and births) occurring to sample members in the period 1971–81 were linked to this information. 1981 Census information for original sample members, additional sample members, and the other members of their households has recently been added, and permission has been given for the incorporation of registered vital events to sample members

TABLE 5.2. 1% OPCS Longitudinal Study: Population covered 1971–1981

	000s
Sample members selected from 1971 Census and traced[a] at NHSCR	513
Additions to the Study 1971–1981:	
Births in Great Britain to mothers usually resident in England and Wales	71
Immigrants and re-entrants registering with the NHSCR	28
Deletions from the Study 1971–1981:	
Deaths	60
Emigrants[b] surrendering their NHS cards	14

[a] Only those persons who have been traced in the National Health Service Central Register (NHSCR) are included in the sample for the analysis of events in the period 1971–81.

[b] The recording of emigrants at NHSCR is known to be deficient (Immigration and emigration are known to have been roughly in balance during the period 1971–81).

Source: Brown and Fox (1984).

TABLE 5.3. Events occurring to sample members 1971–1981

	000s
Live and still births to sample women	61
Live and still births to sample men (1971–1981)	45
Deaths of infants under one year of age	2
Deaths of spouse of sample member	22
Cancer registrations (1971–1975)	9

Source: Brown and Fox (1984).

subsequent to 1981. Table 5.2 shows the population covered in 1971 and 1981 and Table 5.3 the vital events occurring to sample members in the intercensal period (Brown and Fox, 1984).

Table 5.2 illustrates one of the unique aspects of the LS; whereas in most longitudinal surveys attrition of survey members leads to progressively smaller sample sizes, in the LS the addition of new births and of immigrants with the selected birth dates should balance losses from the study as a result of deaths and emigration, so that the sample continues to represent about 1 per cent of the population. It can be seen that over the first 10 years of the study, 60,000 sample members died and 14,000 are known to have left the country. Of these, about 69,000 were original sample members (the others were additions) so that, of the 513,000 with 1971 Census information, up to 444,000 may have been alive and resident in Great Britain in 1981. A 91 per cent success rate is claimed for tracing these members in the 1981 Censuses of England, Wales, and Scotland. On the accretion side, there were 71,000 births and 28,000 immigrants and re-entrants with the selected birth dates registered at NHSCR during 1971–81. About 90 per cent of these children and 50 per cent of the immigrants have been found in the 1981 Census.

The composition of the 36,000 'lost' members of the original sample is currently being investigated, in order to assess the extent of bias introduced by their loss to follow-up.

Table 5.3 shows the number of registered vital events occurring to sample members between 1971 and 1981. As well as deaths, immigrations, and emigrations (shown in Table 5.2), these events comprise:

    (i) live and still births to sample members;
    (ii) deaths of children under one year of age;
    (iii) deaths of spouse; and
    (iv) cancer registrations.

Consideration is also being given to the possibility of adding marriages and divorces to this list.

Among the major advantages of the LS for the purposes of modelling household structures are then, that:

    (i) it comprises two samples from consecutive censuses, which are very large by comparison to most retrospective cross-sectional surveys;

(ii) study members span the whole age range, in contrast to many longitudinal surveys which are constrained to a single age cohort;

(iii) additions and deletions to the study are located through registration information, so that attrition to follow-up is reduced and the sample continues to represent one per cent of the population;

(iv) it allows greater flexibility of use of census variables, including the opportunity to derive new classifications and different definitions from those used in published tables;

(v) its prospective element is, at least in theory, infinitely extendable; and, last but not least;

(vi) since most of the information is processed anyway, either as part of the census or through various registration systems, only relatively small costs are involved in the final linkage of data.

Work on the LS to date has included an analysis of mortality for the period 1971–5, examining the relationship between mortality and a range of factors identified in the 1971 Census (Fox and Goldblatt, 1982), a number of studies of cancer incidence and mortality (for example, Leon and Adelstein, 1983; Jones, Goldblatt and Leon, 1984), an analysis of social mobility (Fox, 1985), and a study of sociodemographic factors in migration, using information about sample members in 1971 to investigate the propensity to move around various demographic events (Grundy and Fox, 1985). However, the inclusion of the 1981 Census data, enabling the measurement of transition between states from 1971 to 1981, provides an unparalleled basis for the formal modelling of changes in a number of areas, including mortality, migration, and household structure.

5.3. Uses of the LS for analysis of household change

One of the most important aspects of the LS for investigating household change is that information is available not only on the sample member but also on all other people in the same household at census. In contrast, then, to most cross-sectional surveys where the individual is the unit of analysis, it is also possible to analyse changes in the household or family group of the LS member through time (which must be regarded as the appropriage units of analysis for any study of household structures; see Willekens, chapter 7).

This is illustrated in Table 5.4, which shows how individuals move between various household and family states at different ages, by use of the linked data for 1971 and 1981. The first four categories used are essentially those of minimal household units (MHUs) discussed in some detail by Ermisch (chapter 3). Table 5.4 shows that although between 10 and 20 per cent of European families with dependent children are lone-parent families (Schmid, chapter 2), in Britain at least this will usually be a temporary phenomenon.

TABLE 5.4. Household status of selected age groups in 1981 by status in 1971, England and Wales

Age in 1971	Status in 1971	Status in 1981 (%)					
		One person	Lone parent	Married couple without dependent children	Married couple with dependent children	Other	Sample size (=100%)
20–24	One person	26	3	16	54	2	14,671
	Lone parent	10	27	2	60	1	502
	Married couple, no d.c.	5	3	11	80	1	7,163
	Married couple with d.c.	5	8	2	84	1	8,716
	Other	19	4	16	54	6	2,921
40–44	One person	77	1	15	5	3	3,027
	Lone parent	55	13	19	11	2	729
	Married couple, no d.c.	8	0	87	3	2	5,196
	Married couple with d.c.	7	2	64	26	1	18,053
	Other	21	2	50	15	14	906
60–64	One person	90	0	4	0	5	5,196
	Lone parent	78	—	14	4	4	51
	Married couple, no d.c.	24	0	72	0	3	14,012
	Married couple with d.c.	14	2	75	5	4	623
	Other	42	0	36	0	21	735

The first four household categories are MHUs 1 to 4 (Ermisch, chapter 3). The 'other' category comprises visitors and those in communal establishments.

Source: OPCS 1% LS.

Among 20- to 24-year-old lone parents in 1971, only one-quarter were still lone parents in 1981; nearly two-thirds had married, and the rest did not have dependent children present. This emphasizes that lone parenthood is likely to be experienced by much greater proportions of parents and children at some stage in the future than the figure obtained from current status cross-section data (in 1981, 13 per cent of dependent children were in lone-parent families). However, a much lower proportion of older lone parents, for example, about one-third of those aged 40 to 44 in 1971, were married 10 years later, whereas over half, 55 per cent, formed a one-person MHU. At this age, the largest number of transitions are associated with the onset of the 'empty nest' phase as parents cease to have dependent children in the household. At later ages, the most important transitions are from married-couple MHUs to one-person MHUs.

Changes in household circumstances can, of course, involve both changes of structure and changes of location. These two processes are likely to be associated (for example, a housing move may be made after the birth of a child), and neither is independent of the social and economic context in which it occurs. The structure of the LS permits not only the analysis of the characteristics of individuals, families, and households, but also, since the census enumeration district of evidençe is known, the linkage of areal environmental data to household and individual data. This has considerable ramifications for the study of changes in household structure on the micro- as well as on the macrolevel, since it allows analysis of the effects of particular areal characteristics on household structures and/or the implications of changes in household composition for specific areas (although, of course, the direction of these effects are not easily disentangled). For example, inner-city areas tend to contain a disproportionate number of the socially disadvantaged members of the community, such as one-parent families, the separated and divorced, the elderly, and ethnic minority groups. The LS provides a means to monitoring changes in the composition of households in inner-city areas, which has obvious implications both for urban planning and for the allocation of welfare resources.

Such considerations not only give insights into social processes at work, but are also necessary if household models are to be applied at the subnational level, since geographic mobility and 'life cycle' mobility—essentially household structure change—are very closely associated.

In terms of future potential, the LS offers the prospect of a decade-by-decade source of information for modelling household structure at a relatively small cost. Over time, this would increasingly begin to resemble a true cohort approach, with the vital registration element providing not only a useful cross-check on intercensal numbers but also offering the opportunity to construct full fertility histories, compensating for the omission of these from the 1981 Census and possibly from all future British censuses. Such histories, linked to census information, may be important, for example, in helping to identify the characteristics of groups who are most likely to be recipients of welfare benefits. Changes in these characteristics are therefore of immediate relevance to social policy makers.

In the short term, linkage of 1971 and 1981 data will permit analysis not only of changes in the states of individuals, but also of some aspects of intergenerational continuities by, for example, exploring the relationship between the circumstances of young adolescents in their parents' home in 1971 and in their own homes when they are in their early twenties in 1981 (an examination of fertility in the intercensal period with reference to the childhood circumstances of young people has recently been undertaken—see Werner, 1984). For household modelling such continuities are relevant, because, for example, those who were born to young parents are themselves on average likely to start the process of family formation earlier, with consequent implications for housing demand. Such considerations are also relevant to the types of housing provided.

For example, Table 5.5 shows that those who were brought up in rented accommodation are more likely to be in the rented sector after leaving home themselves, with the reverse being the case for those from an owner-occupier background. In addition, the local authority sector contains much higher

TABLE 5.5. Housing tenure and household status in 1981 by housing tenure in 1971: People aged 10 to 14 in 1971, England and Wales

Tenure and household status in 1981	Tenure in 1971 (%)		
	Owner-occupier	Local authority renter	Other tenures
Owner-occupier			
1-person	52	10	19
lone parent	0	0	0
married couple, no d.c.	13	10	10
married couple with d.c.	6	7	6
Other	2	1	1
Local authority renter			
1-person	3	39	14
lone parent	1	3	2
married couple, no d.c.	1	4	2
married couple with d.c.	3	12	7
Other	0	1	0
Other tenures			
1-person	7	5	25
lone parent	0	0	1
married couple, no d.c.	3	3	4
married couple with d.c.	2	2	3
Other	6	3	5
Sample size = 100%	16,136	16,675	3,680

Source: OPCS 1% LS.

proportions of couples with children, emphasizing the role of supply factors for understanding household formation. In the longer term, if the linkage is continued for successive censuses, the ability to examine such generational continuities will be greatly enhanced.

While household formation often tends to receive the greatest attention, of course this process is considerably balanced by household dissolutions at older ages, and such events for many purposes are of comparable interest. Since the elderly are not generally included in longitudinal surveys, the benefits of the L S and other similar surveys become particularly evident.

Among the elderly, changes in living arrangements will often involve movements between the private household sector and institutions (which are not usually covered in household surveys) and much of the interest in these changes is concerned with aspects such as kin support, which is not available from vital registration data. Table 5.4, for example, showed that those aged 60 to 64 without a spouse were much more likely to have entered an institution 10 years later than were those with a partner. Mortality rates by household status have also been estimated (Fox and Goldblatt, 1982; chapter 4).

5.4. Uses of linked data for household modelling

Although some inferences about household structure in the intercensal period are possible, the primary use of sources such as the L S for modelling household change is concerned with the analysis of 'square tables' (Upton, 1977, chapter 10); that is, the classification of the same individuals by their statuses on the same variables at two points in time, as in Table 5.4. The natural analytical approaches to such data include multistate life tables and similar techniques and especially log-linear models. These have often been used in the analysis of specific processes, such as 'mover–stayer' models in both occupational and geographical mobility studies (Bishop *et al.*, 1975). Such models have recently become associated with the problem of the incorporation of recognized and unrecognized heterogeneity in models of social processes (Heckman and Singer, 1982). (This is not, of course, to imply that life tables and generalized linear models are truly distinct, but only that different terminologies and emphases are used). The large sample size and the various levels of aggregation for different variables available in the L S, in conjunction with generalized linear models, provide a useful complement to models of household change based on more widely used data sources.

The L S 10-year perspective, by definition linked to the decennial census periodicity, and the resulting compatibility with all census variables and classifications, makes models based on this source particularly useful both for simulation and for policy analysis. For example, in Britain, as in most countries, household projections are made by the headship method which uses age categories and household types: future headship rates are mechanistically projected by use of mathematical curve-fitting over censuses. In contrast, a model of household change should be able to incorporate the results of differing assumptions about the future propensity of various groups (preferably groups which may be treated as homogeneous in behaviour for the purposes of projection) to form particular types of households.

Keilman (chapter 9) states that for most dynamic household models appropriate data are difficult to obtain. The sorts of data available from linked census records can overcome some of these data deficiencies.

LS-type data may be used to construct the household accommodation matrices of Akkerman (1980) and the household-membership–accommodation matrices of Pitkin and Masnick (1986); moreover the sample size is adequate for the construction of large matrices, which would not usually be the case for most household surveys. In addition, longitudinal data permit more 'dynamic' models than these since achievement of headship (or some equivalent generalized marker concept) may be modelled explicitly, thus overcoming a major objection to the 'headship rate' approach which is that it describes a state rather than elucidating a process.

Such data may also be used to construct the transition probabilities for individuals moving between different household types over the 10-year reference period, and thus provide partial information of the sort required for models based on such transitions as the Swedish model (Keilman, chapter 9; Holmberg, 1986). Moreover, linkage of births and deaths permits estimation of some changes in household structure in the intervening period. However, without further assumptions, it does not permit calculation of, for example, rates of leaving home, such as those by age. Consequently, LS-type data would more naturally fit into the class of projection models based on a fixed-interval Leslie matrix-type formulation.

Acknowledgements

This chapter is published with permission from the Controller of Her Majesty's Stationary Office. © Crown copyright.

We would like to take the opportunity of thanking Professor John Fox (City University) for his comments, and the Economic and Social Research Council (ESRC) for financial support under grant number D00250012 to M. Murphy and O. Sullivan.

References

AKKERMAN, A. (1980). On the relationship between household composition and population age distribution, *Population Studies* 34(3), 525–34.

BISHOP, Y. M., S. E. FIENBERG, AND P. W. HOLLAND (1975). *Discrete Multivariate Analysis: Theory and Practice* (MIT Press, Cambridge, Massachusetts).

BROWN, A. AND A. J. FOX (1984). OPCS Longitudinal Study: 10 years on, *Population Trends* 37 (HMSO, London), 20-2.

FOX, A. J. (1985). Social class and occupational mobility 1971-1977 Office of Population Censuses and Surveys Monitor Series LS no. 2 (HMSO, London).

—— AND P. O. GOLDBLATT (1982). Longitudinal Study: socio-economic mortality differentials, Office of Population Censuses and Surveys Monitor Series LS no. 1 (HMSO, London).

GRUNDY, E. M. D. AND A. J. FOX (1985). Migration during early married life, *European Journal of Population* 1(2/3), 237-63.

HECKMAN, J. J. AND B. SINGER (1982). Population heterogeneity in population models, in: K. C. Land and A. Rogers (eds.), *Multidimensional Mathematical Demography* (Academic Press, New York) 567-99.

HOLMBERG, I. (1986). Household and housing forecasting models, in: J. Bongaarts, T. K. Burch, and K. W. Wachter (eds.), *Family Demography: Methods and their Application* (Oxford University Press, Oxford).

JONES, D. R., P. O. GOLDBLATT, AND D. A. LEON (1984). Bereavement and cancer: some data on deaths of spouses from the Office of Population Censuses and Surveys Longitudinal Study, *British Medical Journal* 289, 461-4.

LEDENT, J. (1980). Multistate life tables: movement versus transition approaches, *Environment and Planning A* 12, 533-62.

LEON, D. A. AND A. M. ADELSTEIN (1983). Cause of death amongst people registered with cancer 1971-75, SSRU Working Paper 5, Social Statistics Research Unit, City University, London.

MARTIN, J. AND C. ROBERTS (1984). *Women and Work: A Lifetime Perspective* (HMSO, London).

MURPHY, M. J. (1983). The life course of individuals in families: describing static and dynamic aspects of the contemporary family, in: The family: Proceedings of the British Society for Population Studies Conference, 1983, Office of Population Censuses and Surveys Occasional Paper no. 31 (OPCS, London), 50-70.

—— (1984). The influence of fertility, early housing career and socio-economic factors on tenure determination in contemporary Britain, *Environment and Planning A* 16, 1303-18.

PITKIN, J. R. AND G. MASNICK (1986). The relationship between heads and non-heads in the household population: an extension of the headship rate method, in: J. Bongaarts, T. K. Burch, and K. W. Wachter (eds.), *Family Demography: Methods and their Application* (Oxford University Press, Oxford).

PRESTON, S. H. AND A. J. COALE (1982). Age structure, growth, attrition and accession: a new synthesis, *Population Index* 48(2), 217-59.

UPTON, G. J. G. (1977). *The Analysis of Cross-tabulated Data* (John Wiley, Chichester, Sussex).

WERNER, B. (1984). Fertility and family background: some illustrations from the OPCS Longitudinal Study, *Population Trends* 35 (HMSO, London), 5-10.

WILLEKENS, F. J., I. SHAH, J. M. SHAH, AND P. RAMACHANDRAN (1982). Multi-state analysis of marital status life tables: theory and application, *Population Studies* 36, 129-44.

6

Household trends in Europe after World War II

K. Schwarz

ABSTRACT

In this chapter we summarize the most important recent household trends in Europe. Demographic and non-demographic determinants of these trends are discussed. A comparison is given of specific household categories in various European countries: one-parent families, consensual unions, and one-person households. Substantial household trends are supranational; but the speed with which they spread differs between regions.

6.1. Introduction

STRICTLY speaking, it is impossible to describe European household structures and trends within the space of a few pages, but it is certainly a challenge. The difficulty lies in the following.

First of all, despite continued—and in no way fruitless—efforts by the United Nations, a uniform definition of a household and of the—closely related—family has not yet been found in Europe, let alone in the rest of the world. Moreover, the concept of a household has changed with time. Consider, for example, the disparate criteria used for the classification of people who have more than one house or other type of dwelling, the classification of lodgers such as subtenants or company employees, or criteria for the determination of heads of household, for which no laws exist.

Second, the table designs vary from one country to the next and—within one and the same country—from one period to the next. An important reason for this is that, in the past, household (and family) statistics were neglected.

So much of demography is focused on the study of individuals, that the study of groups is comparatively neglected, [though] it is through the family, that each generation is replaced by the next generation. Through the family (in Europe in most cases identical with the household) children are brought into the world and cared for until they can assume their own responsibilities in society. It is also through the family that each generation fulfils a major proportion of its responsibilities to the ill, the dependent, and the aged of the preceeding generations. (United Nations, 1973.)

In this context, it is worth mentioning that it is easier to differentiate by demographic and socio-economic characteristics of individuals, rather than of groups, however small they may be.

Third, there are two approaches to studying household trends and structures. The traditional approach defines household types on the basis of numbers, size, and composition of households, depending on the kind of relationships among the household members and on the characteristics of the heads of household. But one can also take the household members themselves as the basis for analysis and, from there, ask in which type of household people of a given sex, age, family, and so on, with or without children, living with or without other household members, related or not related, and so on, live. For many purposes, this latter approach is more appropriate. Yet we believe that it has been neglected up till now. For the above reasons, it is difficult to obtain a reliable picture of the type of households people live in in Europe.

Finally, it should be said that a thorough analysis of the structure and trends of households in Europe requires a prior examination of the social and economic situation in the various countries. Such a study cannot be carried out here.

As a result, we will have to restrict ourselves to a small number of observations, and to a limited number of countries. Hence, we will give examples which have been partly taken from the papers by Klijzing, Wall, Link, and Berge and Bugge, prepared for the Workshop 'Modelling household formation and dissolution'.

6.2. Population trends and numbers of households

For decades, population trends have not kept pace with the growing number of households. The number of households increased at a much faster pace, in particular in highly industrialized European countries. Logically, household size decreased.

The reasons for this trend are primarily demographic. Children and youngsters live with adults, usually their parents, at least until they are 15 years old, but often beyond this age. If the number of children in a population decreases, so will the number of persons per household. On the other hand, a growing number of old people leads to an increasing number of households, because elderly people often live with their spouse only; if their spouse dies, they usually remain living alone for the rest of their lives, or else they move into a nursing home. The changing age structure of Europe's population in the past few decades, which was characterized by a declining proportion of young people on the one hand and a sharp increase in the proportion of elderly on the other hand, significantly influenced the number of households and the number of persons per household.

In addition, the increase in the number of households is caused by a growing trend toward a more independent, individual life-style. It is clear that people are more prepared than they were in the past to pay the price of lone-liness in return for greater independence. The following developments played an important part:

- the improved health of the elderly, as a result of which the elderly do not depend on their family for care and nursing until they have reached a very advanced age. One may assume that, in most of Europe, real nursing is usually not necessary before the age of 75;
- the improved material situation of youngsters who have not yet completed their education and, in particular, of the retired elderly population, thanks to improved welfare for the aged;
- the changing economic structure. For example, households nowadays hardly ever have servants living in, or employees of a business living in the home. An important reason for this is that employment opportunities in the agricultural sector have fallen drastically;
- the process of urbanization is closely related to the above point. Housing conditions in the cities are generally not suitable for households of more than one generation. In many countries, moreover, older people have very little to do in the urban households of their children.

Against this background, we will now consider a few household trends which we believe will become increasingly significant in the near future. Many, if not all, the influences named are still valid. Table 6.1 shows some household developments for 19 European countries over a period starting around 1960 and ending around 1980. Some patterns are worth mentioning. Scandinavian countries had small households, both in the 1960s and the 1980s, Finland showing a remarkable decrease. Contrary to these homo-geneous countries with respect to average household size, Western Europe and Eastern Europe show a much greater diversity. The patterns of the F R G, England, and Wales are very similar to the Scandinavian pattern. Ireland, with its relatively high fertility and strong outmigration of single persons and small households, displays an average household size which is very much like that in Southern Europe. The Soviet Union is the outlier of Eastern Europe: its high (and, in fact, increasing) average household size is due to the growing share of its high-fertility Asian population. The figures imply that the average household size for family households containing at least five persons rose from six to about eight persons per household.

Focusing on changes in average household size, it should be noted that Finland, the Netherlands, Bulgaria, and Portugal show the largest decreases (0.033, 0.035, 0.031, and 0.051 persons per household per year, respectively). In Ireland and Greece the average household size diminished only very slowly.

The disproportional increase in the number of households was linked to important changes in household size. In this respect the sharp increase in the number of one-person households and the decreasing proportion of house-holds of five or more members deserves mention.

K. Schwarz

TABLE 6.1. Private households by size, selected European countries, around 1960 and 1980

Country	Year	Population in private households (000s)	Private households (000s)	Average size of private households	Size distribution of private households (%)				
					1	2	3	4	5+
Northern Europe									
Norway	1960	3,525	1,139	3.1	18	24	21	19	19
	1980	4,046	1,524	2.7	28	26	16	18	12
Sweden	1960	7,341	2,582	2.8	20	27	22	18	13
	1980	8,132	3,498	2.3	33	31	15	15	6
Finland	1960	4,396	1,315	3.3	22	19	18	16	25
	1980	4,780	1,782	2.7	27	26	19	18	10
Denmark	1960	4,483	1,544	2.9	20	27	20	18	15
	1981	4,951	2,029	2.4	29	31	16	16	8
Western Europe									
Ireland	1966	2,754	687	4.0	13	20	17	14	36
	1977	3,270	841	3.9	16	22	15	15	32
England and	1966	45,750	15,360	3.0	15	31	21	18	15
Wales	1981	47,806	17,706	2.7	22	32	17	18	11
The Netherlands	1960	11,199	3,130	3.6	12	24	19	18	27
	1979	14,030	4,803	2.9	21	29	16	21	13
Federal Republic	1961	56,012	19,460	2.9	21	26	23	16	14
of Germany	1980	61,481	24,811	2.5	30	29	18	15	8
France	1962	45,287	14,562	3.1	20	27	19	15	20
	1975	51,151	17,745	2.9	22	28	19	15	15
Austria	1951	6,857	2,205	3.1	18	27	22	15	18
	1980	7,410	2,669	2.8	26	26	17	16	14
Eastern Europe									
Poland	1960	28,799	8,253	3.5	16	19	19	20	27
	1978	34,095	10,948	3.1	17	22	23	21	17
Czechoslovakia	1961	13,638	4,398	3.1	14	27	22	20	17
	1980	15,199	5,376	2.8	22	——66[a]——			12
Hungary	1960	9,583	3,079	3.1	15	26	24	19	17
	1980	10,377	3,719	2.8	20	28	22	19	11
Bulgaria	1956	7,315	1,965	3.7	6	18	23	24	28
	1975	8,609	2,755	3.1	17	23	21	21	18
Soviet Union[b]	1959	186,881	50,333	3.7	—	26	26	22	26
	1979	262,436	66,307	4.0	—	30	29	23	19
Southern Europe									
Portugal	1960	8,777	2,233	3.9	8	19	22	19	32
	1981	9,794	3,427	2.9	—	—	—	—	—

TABLE 6.1. *Continued*

Country	Year	Population in private households (000s)	Private households (000s)	Average size of private households	Size distribution of private households (%)				
					1	2	3	4	5+
Italy	1961	49,861	13,682	3.6	—	—	—	—	—
	1977	53,490	15,981	3.3	13	22	22	21	22
Yugoslavia	1961ᶜ	18,549	4,649	4.0	14	15	17	19	35
	1971	20,492	5,375	3.8	13	16	19	21	31
Greece	1951	7,309	1,778	4.1	9	16	18	19	39
	1979	9,450	2,492	3.8	11	21	21	24	22

[a] This figure comprises 2-, 3-, and 4-person households.
[b] Data refer to family households only.
[c] All households.
Source: U N Demographic Yearbook, various years.

One demographic cause of the fall in the average household size is the ageing of the population, as mentioned before. Therefore, to permit comparison over time and space, one should standardize for the age distribution of the population. This is done by the index of overall headship, as proposed by Burch (1980). This index is comparable to Coale's index of overall fertility in that it is based on the ratio of observed to expected numbers (of households) that would result if certain maximum ('natural headship') rates were to apply to the population. It serves as an inverse measure of household complexity (the propensity of adults to double up rather than to head their own household): the higher the index of overall headship, the smaller the average number of adults per household. The selection of standard rates itself is rather arbitrary. The advantage of the index over traditional headship rates is that no relationship data are required, only age–sex specific population numbers and total household counts. Data requirements are thus much less prohibitive. Nevertheless, the fit reported by Burch with headship rates calculated in the classical way for some 30 countries all over the world around 1960 is quite good ($r = -0.92$). His 1960/61 values of the index for some European countries are reproduced in the first column of Table 6.2. Other European countries not listed by Burch were added as well. In addition, using the same standard rates, index values for the two following population counts appear in the second and the third columns, respectively. A few patterns should be noted.

First of all, many countries show a systematic increase in the index of overall headship over time. No doubt the rise in one-person households is partly responsible for these trends, although wide differences exist in the way this, and other household types are being defined. Nevertheless, the pattern emerging from these figures is consistent. Some countries experienced a

K. Schwarz

TABLE 6.2. Overall headship rates for selected European countries at three
consecutive census dates

	1960s		1970s		1980s	
Northern Europe						
Norway	(1960)	0.77	(1970)	0.81	(1980)	0.87
Sweden	(1960)	0.82	(1970)	0.86	(1975)	0.91
Finland	(1960)	0.83	(1970)	0.87	(1975)	0.86
Denmark	(1960)	0.84	(1970)	0.91	(1981)	0.93
Western Europe						
England and Wales	(1961)	0.75	(1971)	0.81	(1981)	0.85
The Netherlands	(1960)	0.75	(1971)	0.81	—	—
Federal Republic of Germany	(1961)	0.83	(1970)	0.87	(1981)	0.92
France	(1962)	0.77	(1975)	0.81	(1981)	0.85
Austria	(1961)	0.79	(1971)	0.84	(1981)	0.85
Eastern Europe						
Poland	(1960)	0.84	(1970)	0.79	(1978)	0.81
Czechoslovakia	(1961)	0.83	(1970)	0.81	(1980)	0.87
Hungary	(1963)	0.79	(1970)	0.78	(1980)	0.82
Bulgaria	(1965)	0.76	(1975)	0.75	—	—
Southern Europe						
Italy	(1961)	0.68	(1971)	0.73	(1981)	0.79
Yugoslavia	(1961)	0.74	(1971)	0.72	—	—

Source: compiled by Klijzing (1984).

higher rate of headship change than others, which explains why ranking positions at the latest census are no longer the same as at the first.

Secondly, point estimates for Eastern European countries suggest, on the
other hand, that here quite the opposite took place, at least during the first
intercensal period. Remarkably, these countries are all situated to the right of
Hajnal's dividing line from Leningrad to Trieste separating 'European' from
'Eastern European' marriage patterns (Hajnal, 1965). Standardizing the
index for differences in marital status as well would probably further enhance
comparability of results.

Thirdly, all values in Table 6.2 are based on population counts, either
whole counts or microcensuses. Such figures can, of course, also be derived
from sample surveys, provided national representation is guaranteed.
Member states of the European Economic Community are required to conduct a biennial labour force survey, in conjunction with which household
statistics are collected. Thus, the index for the Netherlands according to the
1981 labour force survey is 0.88, continuing the trend observed between the
1960 and 1971 censuses.

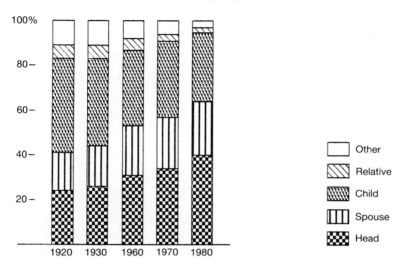

Source: Wall (1984).

FIG. 6.1. Percentage distribution of household members by their relationship to household head, Switzerland

6.3. Characteristics of changes in household structures

6.3.1. Household composition

The household composition in Switzerland, for which we have information dating back to 1920, is shown in Figure 6.1. In Swiss households, the share of relatives (for example, aunts, uncles, cousins, brothers-, and sisters-in-law) as well as that of non-relatives (for example, servants) has diminished. Moreover, from 1920 to 1960, and from 1970 to 1980, the proportion of children in Swiss households decreased. In view of the declining birth rates following World War I, and again after 1965, this trend is quite plausible. However, the fact that children leave the parental home at an earlier age than in the past certainly also plays a role. See, for example, the situation in West Germany between 1961 and 1982. As shown in Table 6.3, the proportion of single persons leaving the parental home increased considerably between 1961 and 1982; 20 to 29-year-old women in particular left the parental home in great numbers. Women who are still single at that age live independently more frequently than do men of the same age. This was not yet the case 20 years ago. The above trend clearly reflects the growing independence of unmarried women.

Male/female differences in home-leaving behaviour are documented for

TABLE 6.3. Proportion of single persons living with their parents, by sex and age, Federal Republic of Germany (%)

	1961		1982	
	Men	Women	Men	Women
15–19	95	96	98	95
20–24	95	96	77	63
25–29	89	81	51	38
30–34	72	60	43	36
35–39	56	22	41	37

Source: Schwarz (1984), Table 10.

ten European countries by the results of the Commission of the European Communities Survey, December 1982 (quoted by Kiernan, 1984). Figure 6.2 shows that, in 1982, about half of the women aged 23–4 years in the countries of the European Community and nearly a quarter of the men of the same age were married.

The declining proportion of 'relatives' in Swiss households indicates that single women, widows, and divorcees are no longer as dependent on the support of their parents or brothers and sisters as they were in the past. They are either employed, or else they are entitled to social welfare (or alimony) or a pension.

The number of three or even four-generation households has dropped drastically. In 1961, there were still over one million such households in West Germany; in 1972 only about 770,000, and by 1982 the number had dropped to some 500,000. No more than 5 per cent of all West German children grow up in households in which they live with both their parents and their grandparents. If the grandparents are very old, it is more common that they live with their (adult) children. In such cases, the grandchildren have generally already left the parental home. Similar situations in other European countries are unknown to us, but Priest (1985) reports on the situation in Canada: between 1971 and 1981 the share of one-generation households in all private households rose from 38 per cent to 47 per cent, whereas households with three generations fell slightly from 4 per cent to $2\frac{1}{2}$ per cent. Expressed in absolute numbers, there was an increase from 2.3 million to 3.9 million one-generation households in the period 1971–81, and the number of three-generation households decreased from 243,000 to 218,000 in those years.

As for the cohabitation of several generations, or with relatives and in-laws, regional differences are considerable, both within one and the same country, and between the different countries of Europe. In the largest cities of Germany, three-generation households no longer exist. In Swiss households, the percentage of 'relatives' in households was only 3 per cent in 1970

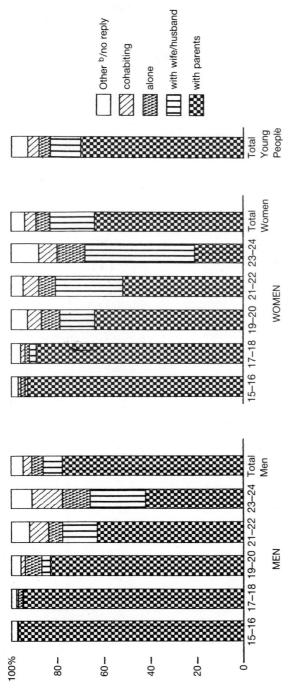

FIG. 6.2. Living arrangements of young people in Europe[a] by age, 1982

Source: 'The Young Europeans': Commission of the European Communities Survey, December 1982, quoted by Kiernan (1982).

[a] Belgium, Denmark, France, Germany, Greece, Ireland, Italy, Luxemburg, the Netherlands and the United Kingdom.

[b] 'Other' refers to sharing accommodation with another person or persons.

and 2 per cent in 1980; in Italian households it was 8 per cent in 1971, and in Greece 12 per cent in 1964.

In the past, non-relatives included such people as maids, servants, pupils, apprentices, and so on. In Germany, records dating back to 1910 are at hand. In 1910, 17 per cent of all households lodged non-relatives; in the upper classes this was even the rule. Such households have almost disappeared. A new type of household has taken its place, in which the members could, *de jure*, be called non-relatives, but who *de facto* live together as married couples. We will deal with this matter later.

6.3.2. One-parent households

By one-parent households, we mean households in which single, widowed, or divorced men and women, but also married persons with single children who no longer live with their spouse, share the same household. We took Switzerland (CH)—1970 and 1980—as an example (see Table 6.4) and, for the sake of comparison, added data for Czechoslovakia (Czech Republic—CSR—only).

Here, as elsewhere, unmarried lone parents and separated married parents living with their child(ren) are primarily women. In 1980, the number of lone mothers with children under the age of 18 years in Switzerland was six times as big as the number of lone fathers. Whereas the number of widowed fathers and mothers is declining steadily, the proportion of households consisting of divorced fathers and mothers with children is rising sharply. This is the result

TABLE 6.4. One-parent families by marital status of head, Switzerland (CH) and Czechoslovakia (CSR) (%)

	Men				Women			
	1970		1980		1970		1980	
	CH	CSR	CH	CSR	CH	CSR	CH	CSR
Marital status:								
single	—	3	—	3	5	9	7	7
married, living apart	14	27	17	37	10	24	12	25
widowed	73	40	57	30	62	26	46	22
divorced	14	29	26	29	23	40	36	46
TOTAL (000s)[a]	12	16[b]	15	23[b]	69	11[b]	94	181[b]

[a] Absolute numbers = 100%.
[b] Including marital status unknown. Switzerland: with children under 18 years of age; Czechoslovakia: with children under 15 years of age.

Sources: Blanc, O.; Les Ménages en Suisse; Population 1985/4–5; pp. 657 ff.; Pavlík, Z., and K. Kalibová: One-parent families in Czechoslovakia; Paper for the Seminar on One-parent families in Brussels, Oct. 1985.

of a combination of three factors: declining mortality as a result of which the number of widows and widowers (living) with young children (minors) is declining; the rising number of divorces due to which an increasing number of children grow up with either the mother or the father; and the declining marriage frequency among lone parents. Finally, it is becoming more common for children from broken families to live with their father.

Table 6.5 shows the extent to which children grow up in one-parent families in Sweden and in West Germany, from 1960. In 1960, the situations in Sweden and in the FRG were very similar; 92 per cent of all children grew up in households with married parents. In 1982, this proportion had dropped to 74 per cent in Sweden; in West Germany it was still 90 per cent. The developments in these countries were very different after 1960. They reflect the number of children born outside of marriage: in 1983, 44 per cent of all births in Sweden; in West Germany, no more than 9 per cent of all births. In general, however, the above figures do not reflect the whole range of cases in which children nowadays grow up without—or partly without—both their natural parents. Estimates for West Germany show that 24 per cent of all minors lived with only one of their parents for part of their life, and that of these 24 per cent, 11 per cent had lived with a stepfather or stepmother between the ages of 15 and 17. No doubt, such cases wil become more common if marriage frequencies fall even further, and if the tendency to get divorced continues to rise. And so it will become increasingly difficult to

TABLE 6.5. Children under 18 by type of household, Sweden and Federal Republic of Germany (%)

		Children under 18 living in a household of			
		both parents	the unmarried		Total[a] (000s)
			father	mother	
Sweden	1960	92	1	7	1,772
Federal Republic of Germany (FRG)	1961	92	1	7	13,567
Sweden	1970	88	1	11	1,980
FRG	1970	93	1	6	16,244
Sweden	1974	83	1	16	1,998
FRG	1974	93	1	6	16,142
Sweden	1982	74	2	24	1,913
FRG	1982	90	2	8	13,511

[a] Absolute numbers = 100%.

Sources: Federal Statistical Office, Fachserie 1 Reihe 3 and Nilsson, Th.: Les Ménages en Suède: Population 1985, no. 2,224–47.

determine the nature of the relationships between adults and children within households.

6.3.3. Households of men and women in consensual unions

Households of unmarried men and women, with and without children, living together as a married couple, have always existed. However, in the past they were so rare that little importance was attached to this phenomenon. Moreover, there were definitional problems, and it was difficult to study them at all because it was not yet a generally accepted life-style in the eyes of society. That is no longer the case. In Europe, most couples who get married nowadays have lived together before marriage. It is therefore no longer possible *not* to consider households of consensual unions when studing household structures and household types. Table 6.6 gives an indication of the importance of this phenomenon.

TABLE 6.6. Percentage consensual unions by age group, females

Country		Age			
		18–19	20–24	25–29	30–34
Denmark	1981	—	37	23	11
France	1981	—	8	5	2
The Netherlands	1982	3	16	10	4
Great Britain	1979	4	5	4	2
Norway	1977	6	12	5	2
Sweden	1981	—	44	31	14

Source: Netherlands Central Bureau of Statistics, Monthly Bulletin of Population Statistics 1984 (2), p. 12.

In Austria, 44 per cent of all women who got married for the first time in 1977 said they had lived with their husband before marriage (Haslinger, 1981). In the period 1972–82 consensual unions in West Germany increased fourfold. Age-specific differences, however, were large; namely, an eightfold increase among persons under 35 years, and only a very small increase among persons over 60 (Linke, 1985). In Germany, no more than 10 per cent of such households have children, only about a third of whom are the child of both parents (Schulz, 1984).

As far as we know, representative statistics of communal living arrangements in which several single persons and/or married couples together run a household do not exist. Is this type of household really so insignificant that it is actually not worth studying?

TABLE 6.7. Trends in one-person households since World War II

One-person households as a percentage of all households

	c. 1946	c. 1950	c. 1955	c. 1960	c. 1965	c. 1970	c. 1975	c. 1980
Western Europe								
Austria	16	18		20		25		26
Belgium	19			17		19		
France				20		22		25
Germany (FRG)	12	19	18	21		25	29	31
Ireland	11			13	13	14		16
Luxembourg	9			12	13	16		21
The Netherlands	9			12		17	19	22
Switzerland				14		20		29
United Kingdom								
England and Wales		11	12	15	18		22	
Northern Ireland		9		12	13	15		
Scotland		11		12	16	19		
Iceland and Scandinavia								
Denmark		14						31
Finland		18		22	17	24	26	27
Iceland		18		13				
Norway	18	15		18		21		
Sweden	25	21		20	22	25	30	33

K. Schwarz

TABLE 6.7. Continued

One-person households as a percentage of all households

	c. 1946	c. 1950	c. 1955	c. 1960	c. 1965	c. 1970	c. 1975	c. 1980
Southern Europe and Turkey								
Cyprus	12			11		11		
Gibraltar		5				11		
Greece		9		11	8	13		
Italy		10			12			10
Malta		10	11	11				
Portugal		8		12		10		13
Spain						8		
Turkey			4	4		3	3	6
Eastern Europe								
Albania			7					
Bulgaria			6		17			
Czechoslovakia	16			14		18		
Germany (GDR)					27	26		27
Hungary				14		18		20
Poland				16		16	16	17
Romania					14			
Yugoslavia	12		12	14		13		14

Source: Compiled by Wall (1984).

6.3.4. One-person households

We are well informed about the trends in one-person households because all national household statistics have always been subdivided by size. Table 6.7 shows trends in one-person households, as a percentage of all households, in European countries since World War II.

The increase in one-person households can only be partly attributed to a rise in the number of single adults, of members of married couples living apart, or of widows and divorced persons. The process of individualization has also played a significant role. For example, in the period 1961–82 the proportion of men and women in one-person households, as a percentage of persons not living with a marriage partner in West Germany, has changed depending on their marital status, as shown in Table 6.8. It is more common nowadays for single and widowed persons to live alone. Such single persons are generally young men and women who leave the parental home at an earlier age than in the past; widows and widowers are—understandably— mainly elderly persons.

TABLE 6.8. Persons in one-person households in the Federal Republic of Germany, as a proportion of persons not living with a marriage partner (%)

Marital Status	Men		Women	
	1961	1982	1961	1982
Single over 20 years	17	30	22	42
Married, living apart	55	66	25	42
Widowed	37	64	41	72
Divorced	59	61	36	47

Source: Schwarz (1983).

There are far more women than men living in one-person households, since everywhere the number of widows greatly exceeds the number of widowers. There is no doubt about it: female life expectancy is much higher than male life expectancy and so the number of years women spend living alone greatly exceeds that of men.

It would be rash to conclude that the sharply rising number of one-person households eventually leads to loneliness. Parents, children, or other close relatives often live in the same city, in the same neighbourhood, in the same street, or even in the same house.

Table 6.9 shows the number of years spent in one-person households by males and females in the Federal Republic of Germany. Our calculations are based on a life table for 1980/82, and age-specific proportions of men and women living alone in 1982.

The table shows that women 'pay' for their higher life expectancy with a

TABLE 6.9. Remaining life expectancy and remaining life expectancy to be spent in a one-person household, by sex and age, computed from period life table, Federal Republic of Germany, 1980/1982 (years)

	Men		Women	
Age	Total life expectancy	of which alone	Total life expectancy	of which alone
0	70.2	5.9	76.9	13.0
20	51.8	6.0	58.1	13.1
40	33.1	3.3	39.8	11.2
60	16.5	2.2	20.8	10.0
75	7.6	1.7	9.7	5.9

longer 'single' life. But we also know that, although relations between elderly parents and children are close, both sides prefer to live apart for as long as possible.

References

BERGE, E. AND L. S. BUGGE (1984). The structure of households in Scandinavia since 1950, paper presented at the workshop 'Modelling of household formation and dissolution', 12–14 December 1984, Voorburg, The Netherlands.

BURCH, TH. K. (1980). The index of overall headship: a simple measure of household complexity standardized for age and sex, Demography 17(1), 25–38.

HAJNAL, J. (1965). European marriage patterns in perspective, in: D. V. Glass and D. E. C. Eversley (eds.), Population in History (Edwards Arnold Publishers, London), 101–43.

HASLINGER, A. (1981). Ehe ohne Trauschein, Demographische Informationen 2/1981 (Institut für Demographie der Österreichischen Akademie der Wissenschaften, Vienna).

KIERNAN, K. E. (1984). The departure of children, paper presented at the IUSSP-seminar 'The demography of the later phases of the family life cycle', 3–7 September 1984, Berlin.

KLIJZING, F. K. H. (1984). Household data from surveys containing information for individuals, paper presented at the workshop 'Modelling of household formation and dissolution', 12–14 December 1984, Voorburg, The Netherlands.

LINK, K. (1984). Trends in household developments in Eastern Europe since World War II, paper presented at the workshop 'Modelling of household formation and dissolution', 12–14 December 1984, Voorburg, The Netherlands.

LINKE, W. (1985). Nichteheliche Lebensgemeinschaften in der Bundesrepublik Deutschland: Sonderauswertung von Mikrozensusdaten, revised by G. Clausen, Publication Series of the Federal Minister of Youth, Family, and Health, vol. 170.

PRIEST, G. E. (1985). Private households by number of generations present: new data from the census of Canada, Canadian Statistical Review 60(1), 6–10.

SCHULZ, R., in collaboration with M. FRANKE AND K. GÄRTNER (1984). Vorkommen und Probleme nichteheliche Lebensgemeinschaften, unpublished manuscript (Bundesinstitut für Bevölkerungsforschung, Wiesbaden).

SCHWARZ, K. (1982). Bericht 1982 über die demographische Lage in der Bundesrepublik Deutschland, *Zeitschrift für Bevölkerungswissenschaft* 8(2), 121–223.

—— (1983). Die Alleinlebenden, *Zeitschrift für Bevölkerungswissenschaft* 9(2), 241–57.

—— (1984). When do children leave the home of parents? An analysis of cohort data in the Federal Republic of Germany for the years 1972–1982, paper presented at the IUSSP-seminar 'The demography of the later phases of the family life cycle', 3–7 September 1984, Berlin.

UNITED NATIONS (1973). The determinants and consequences of population trends: new summary of findings on interaction of demographic, economic and social factors, vol. 1, Population Studies no. 50 (United Nations, New York).

WALL, R. (1984). The development of the European household since World War II, paper presented at the workshop 'Modelling of household formation and dissolution', 12–14 December 1984, Voorburg, The Netherlands.

PART III

Modelling

7

A life course perspective on household dynamics

F. Willekens

ABSTRACT

Changes in household size and structure are related to the life courses of the household members and of the relationships between the members. Life events, which constitute the structure of the life course, are concentrated in relatively short periods in a person's lifetime. They are the outcome of substantive (e.g. behavioural) and random processes. The chapter reviews substantive insights into the life course, mainly derived from psychological literature. Some results are used in developing a microdemographic model of household dynamics, in which events are the outcome of both chance (stochastic process) and choice (decision rule).

7.1. Introduction

FEW areas of demographic research can claim the scientific and policy relevance that is generally associated with household demography. Few areas, however, have received as little attention from the scholarly community as household demography. The complexity of the subject matter, the lack of adequate and comparable concepts and data, and the absence of household models are reasons frequently given (for example, Bongaarts, 1983, p. 27). The causes of the unsatisfactory state of affairs are sought in the subject matter, not in the discipline or the profession.

But demography is not well equipped to study households or any other group of persons which forms a unit either biologically, socially, or economically and which therefore should be treated as a unit. The unit of analysis in demography has traditionally been the individual. Birth, death, childbearing, migration, marriage, and other events are studied for individuals. When demographic events involve more than one person, such as marriage, consistency problems may arise (for example, the two-sex problem). In order to remove the consistency problem, the different persons who are affected by the same event must be studied simultaneously, that is, as a group.

The family, the household and any other identifiable group of persons consist of two components:

- members of the group, and
- relationships between members.

The study of group dynamics may be enhanced if the two components are identified. Family and household dynamics may therefore be represented as an outcome of changes occurring to the individual members and changes in the relationships, the latter affecting some or all members of the group. In other words, the life course of the group may be expressed in terms of the life courses of the members and the life courses of the relationships. The significance of the life courses of the individual members for the dynamics of family and household life has been discussed in psychology, economics and sociology. Elder (1978, pp. 29–30), for instance, views the family in terms of the interdependent life courses of the family members and stresses that the family life cycle cannot be understood without reference to the life cycles of the individual members, and vice versa.

In this chapter, the household dynamics are expressed in terms of the life courses of the household members and the life courses of the relationships between the members. If the family and household changes shape through the individual life cycle, as several authors believe, the study of household dynamics may start with an investigation of the individual life cycle. Consequently, the individual is chosen to be the unit of analysis. To describe the life course of relationships, one household member is selected as a reference person and the relationships between the household members is viewed from her/his perspective. Section 7.2 reviews a few concepts that are useful in the study of individual life courses. The life courses of relationships are covered in section 7.3. The purpose of the study of the life course in sections 7.2 and 7.3 is twofold: first, to summarize and integrate theoretical and conceptual insights from a number of disciplines that are considered to be helpful in developing a life course perspective on household dynamics; and second, to present a conceptual framework for the modelling of processes of household formation and dissolution. Sections 7.2 and 7.3 therefore contain more substantive information than is strictly needed in the presentation of the household model in section 7.4. The purpose of section 7.4 is to illustrate the implications for household modelling of the adoption of a life course perspective. The household size and structure at any one point in time are viewed as being caused by events separating consecutive stages in the life courses of individuals and/or relationships. These events are referred to as life events and transitions. The life events are assumed to be generated by underlying life course processes. The pattern of occurrence of the life events or transitions is fully determined once the process is specified and the values of the parameters of the process are fixed.

Substantive research on families and close relationships indicates the usefulness of the life course perspective for understanding the dynamics of the phenomena under study. Most family and household models we are familiar with adopt a different perspective. The model presented in section

7.4 is illustrative for models derived from the body of knowledge that might be denoted as life course theory. It combines elements of chance and elements of choice and relies heavily on the concept of developmental readiness. It should be viewed as a prototype. A number of methodological problems remain to be solved before a full integration of theory and modelling is realized.

7.2. The life course of an individual

As a person ages, she/he passes through a sequence of stages. Infancy, childhood, adolescence, young adult, adulthood, and mature age are examples of stages that are frequently distinguished in psychological literature (see, for example, Erikson, 1980). Each stage is associated with a particular developmental potential or developmental readiness, determined by biological, psychological, and social factors. Each stage may therefore be characterized by a set of attributes pertaining to the individual.

To describe the life course, it is convenient to consider an individual as a 'carrier' of attributes. At each age, a particular combination of attributes characterizes a person. Living status (alive/dead), marital status, health status, level of education, and region of residence are attributes used to characterize individuals. The values on each attribute are referred to as aspects, in concordance with the literature on decision processes (see, for example, Montgomery, 1983, p. 346). Frequently, the attributes are categorical variables, which can take on a finite number of values (levels). Age is not considered to be an attribute; it is a time variable measuring the time elapsed since a reference event (birth) or the duration of the developmental process. Whether or not age is viewed as an attribute is irrelevant for the life course analysis.

Some attributes may be fixed for the entire life span, while others vary. Gender, year of birth, and endowments are examples of invariant attributes; the value of the attribute does not change with age. Marital status and level of education may change as life progresses. A selection of attributes, the levels of which may change over age, may be used to characterize the life course; they are referred to as primary attributes. The attributes selected to describe the life course depend on the purpose of the study. In nuptiality analysis, for instance, marital status is a primary attribute, while in morbidity analysis, health status is a primary attribute and marital status may be of secondary importance, at most. Primary attributes are used to identify the stage occupied in the life course. Secondary attributes differentiate individuals in the same stage. Each combination of values of primary attributes (aspects) defines a state or status, and individuals with the same primary attributes are said to occupy the same state. Notice the distinction made between state and stage. Any combination of values of primary attributes specifies a state. A stage, sometimes also denoted as a spell, refers to a period in the life course. Because of our definition of primary attributes, a transition to a new stage of life implies a passage to a different state.

A life event is a change in the value of a primary attribute and a passage to a different state. Changes in values of secondary attributes do not imply a passage to another state but they may enhance or inhibit a passage because of their impact on the primary attributes. For instance, in household analysis, the transition from 'living alone' to 'living with a partner' may be affected by the onset and progression of a search process. The stage in the search process is a secondary attribute of individuals with the primary attribute 'living alone'. In the study of the search process, however, the stage of the process becomes of prime importance and the stage occupied will generally be upgraded to be a primary attribute of the individual(s) involved in a search.

Each primary attribute may be associated with a life event. For instance, the attribute 'marital status' may be associated with the event 'marital change'. The attribute 'region of residence' is associated with the event 'migration'. An event or change in the value of a primary attribute results in a new value of the attribute. The definition of life events, adopted in this chapter, is consistent with the psychologist's concept of a life event as a change in a person's social setting requiring major life adjustments (see, for example, Hultsch and Cornelius, 1981, p. 74). Demographic events, such as marriage, death of spouse, birth of child, and divorce, are among the most important life events. Psychological literature typically focuses on the identification of life events and on the adjustment process (for a review, see, for example, Paykel, 1983). In demographic literature, the focus is on the pattern of occurrence and determinants of the life events.

Events may be characterized by the primary attribute variable with which they are associated. Events may also be distinguished on the basis of other criteria, such as their frequency and their relationships to other events. Events that occur at most once in a lifetime are nonrepeatable events. Repeatable events can occur more than once. Some of the nonrepeatable events result in an attrition from the population, for example death and emigration. Events may also be characterized by their relationship to other events. The sequence and timing of events is sometimes restricted by biological, social, or other reasons. Events may prohibit or inhibit the occurrence of other events; or may make the occurrence of other events feasible or they may bring on their occurrence (see Courgeau and Lelièvre, ch. 11). For instance, a divorce can occur only after a marriage. Childbirth can occur independently of marriage although, in most societies, childbirth out of wedlock is socially unacceptable.

The sequence of events of the same type constitutes a career. Each primary attribute that is not invariant over a person's lifetime may therefore be associated with a career or pattern of change of the attribute. Invariant attributes, such as gender, do not exhibit a career. The life course is composed of many careers, such as the marital, educational, professional, employment, medical, maternal, and residential careers. Most careers are active simultaneously; they are parallel careers. Some careers can start only when other careers are completed; they are sequential or serial careers. The onset of the professional career, for instance, generally follows the termination of the educational career. The onset of a career coincides with an event, called event-origin. For instance, first marriage may be used as the event-origin of the marital career; the entry into the labour market is the onset of the employment career, while graduation from school signifies the start of the professional career. The location of the onset of a career is frequently not a simple task. One may argue that the marital career does not start with first marriage, but with the onset of the search for a partner.

Each career is characterized by the frequency, sequence, and timing of a particular life event. Life events are not equally distributed over the life span, but are generally concentrated in relatively narrow periods of life. The location of these periods is influenced by biological, psychological, and social factors. In sociological literature, for instance, the patterning of life events and the resulting structuring of life is viewed as an important instrument of social control and a stabilizing factor in social structure (Elchardus, 1984). Careers and the life course are therefore composed of transition periods of limited duration and stable periods of extended duration (Levinson *et al.*, 1978, p. 19; Reinke *et al.*, 1985). The stable periods are generally referred to as stages.

Life events and the combination of life events in careers are viewed as the outcome of substantive and random processes. Substantive processes are biological, psychological, or social processes preceding life events. Decision-making (mental) processes are examples of substantive processes. The explanation of life events in terms of the substantive processes causing the events to occur remains a major challenge in life course analysis. In this chapter, simple decision processes are used to explain the departure from the parental home and the beginning of a partner relationship.

To study the timing of life events, we must introduce a time scale. Time can be measured in various time scales, such as the historical (calendar) time or the time elapsed since a given previous event. Each time scale may be viewed as a different clock which started to run at a given historical time. In this chapter, age is used to measure time; it is the time elapsed since the event of birth which characterizes the start of the life course. It is sometimes also referred to as developmental time. It will be assumed that the status of the life course process at a given point in time only depends on developmental time (age) and related factors and is independent of historical time. The life course parameters therefore depend on age only.

7.3. The life course of a relationship

In order to understand household dynamics we must understand the dynamics of relationships among people. People are said to be involved in a relationship if they are affected by, or influence, each other. In this chapter, we focus on relationships between two people (dyadic relationships). In particular, we address partner relationships and parent–child relationships. The presence of a relationship between two people implies that their activities (behaviour) are causally interconnected and that a status change of one person frequently causes a change in the other (Berscheid, 1985, pp. 146–7). To characterize a relationship, it is necessary to identify the activities of each person that affect and are affected by the activities of the other, and to specify the nature of the impact. In this way, financial, economic, emotional, sexual, intellectual, and residential relationships may be distinguished. An economic relationship may result in common housekeeping and a residential relationship in co-residence. Co-residence is, however, not the only form of residential relationship. Instead of sharing the same dwelling, people may live in the same neighbourhood. Some relationships are of a composite nature, such as the conjugal relationship.

Relationships may also be characterized by the properties of the interaction pattern. A particularly relevant type of relationship is a close relationship. Berscheid (1985, p. 147) states that a relationship between two people is close if the relationship is enduring, the interaction is frequent, and the impact is strong and diverse. Relationships considered in family and household demography are close relationships.

Clark (1985) distinguishes two types of close relationships based on the rules governing the interaction. In communal relationships, the persons feel obliged, and usually want, to be especially responsive to each other's needs. There is an implicit agreement to be concerned for each other, and the partners are emotionally involved. These relationships are often exemplified by relationships with kin, romantic partners, and friends. Members of a communal relationship are often perceived as a 'unit' by outsiders and attributes of one person reflect upon the other. In exchange relationships, the interaction is governed by the expectation that a beneficial action results in a comparable benefit in return. There is no special responsibility for the well-being of the other. Exchange relationships are exemplified by relationships with strangers, acquaintances, and business partners. The extent to which either communal or exchange relationships help the members fulfil their own needs is referred to as compatibility.

Both communal and exchange relationships may vary in certainty and endurance. The feeling of certainty that a relationship actually exists and the endurance of the relationship may be enhanced by an agreement or contract. Contracts provide security to the members of the relationship by regulating the structure, content, and continuity of the relationship. The character of a contract may vary from a simple agreement (implicit contract) to an explicit and legalized contract. It is interesting to note that the legalization of social contracts has always been important when property was involved. The first marriage contracts regulated the transfer of property between generations. Even today, cohabitating people generally draw up some type of explicit contract when property is involved (for example, joint house-ownership).

Relationships have a life course of their own. The onset of a close relationship initiates a process of mutual identity confirmation (Erikson, 1980; Knudson, 1985). According to Combrink–Graham (1985), the process involves periods of attachment and bonding (centripetal periods) and periods of disengagement and individuation (centrifugal periods). Erikson (1982, p. 16) refers to communality and individuality. The interplay between communality (emphasis on 'we') and individuality (emphasis on 'I') provides the tension that is necessary for relationship development. In recent decades, with the emphasis on the individual, close relationships are increasingly being viewed as experiences, as elements of an exploring, growing self, and no longer as roles and status positions that are associated with publicly acknowledged social structures (Held, 1986, p. 162). A consequence is an avoidance of lifelong commitments and rigid structures preventing the changes that may be necessary for the growth of the self. The deinstitutionalization of social relationships, *in casu* marriage, illustrates this trend. The marriage *institution* is losing its importance as a regulator of partner relationships for several, all simultaneously interconnected, reasons. First, the security it used to offer to the weakest partner in the dyadic relationship has been undermined by relaxations in the marriage law. Second, alternative legal means are available to regulate the transfer of property between generations. Third, the growing economic independence of women and social security offered by the state reduces the need for security arrangements through marriage. Fourth, increasing individualism results in weaker social ties. Fifth, changes in the social norms governing cohabitation have weakened the position of marriage as an organizing principle. To regulate partnerships, implicit contracts or other types of explicit contracts are substituted for explicit marriage contracts.

This discussion has some important implications for household modelling. The position of marriage as an organizing principle is weakening. In addition to the marriage contract, new types of explicit and implicit contracts govern relationships between cohabitating people. Insight into these contracts is needed to describe and understand the process of household formation and dissolution. Household models should take the existence of alternatives to the marriage contract into account (compare section 9.1). In section 7.4 we omit any reference to the marriage institution and the marriage contract, although it will be assumed, for the sake of simplicity, that partners remain together until the union is dissolved by death.

The distinction of different types of social contracts governing dyadic relationships leads to a new perspective on household typology. It enables us to separate living arrangements from partnership arrangements (social contracts). The following types of living arrangements are independent of the partnership arrangements:

- one-person household;
- cohabitating group of people with or without children, and with or without a co-residence contract;
- lone parent with children

The following types of conjugal relationships are distinguished:

- single;
- consensual union with
  - marriage contract;
  - other type of explicit contract, legalized or not;
  - implicit contract;
- union dissolved, either voluntary or involuntary.

The typology encompasses the traditional marital states. The cross-classification of types of living arrangements and partnership types provides a typology, based on two status variables. Note that the cohabitating group of people is generally a couple, but it can also be a commune or a collective household (group of individual persons without implicit partnership contract).

The previous discussion has implications not only for household modelling but also for the definition of the family. Traditionally, the family concept has been closely linked to marriage. The substitution of new partnership contracts for the marriage contract calls for an enlargement of the family concept; unmarried couples with another type of explicit contract are *de facto* families. A family is therefore redefined as a group of people related through an explicit partnership contract or through birth or adoption. This definition is consistent with the perspective of a family as a form of companionship instead of an institution.

7.4. A microdemographic model of household dynamics

The life course of a household may be expressed as a set of interrelated life courses of the individual household members. Each life course consists of a sequence of life events. The nature of the life events and their timing (spacing) fully describes the life course. Because of the interdependence among individual life courses, the nature and timing of life events occurring to an individual is affected by, and affects, the life events experienced by other individuals. The interdependence may be represented by the life course of relationships.

In this section, a model of household dynamics is presented and illustrated with hypothetical data. Since the purpose of the model is to illustrate the representation of the household life course as a set of interrelated life courses of individuals rather than to approach reality in its complexity, several simplifying assumptions are made. The following life events are considered in the household model: birth, death, leaving the parental home, beginning of a partner relationship, birth of a child, and the departure of the children from the home. The lifespan of an individual is decomposed into five stages. Each stage is associated with a particular developmental potential or developmental readiness. The first stage is childhood and is assumed to last exactly 18 years for both males and females. In the second stage of young adulthood, the person leaves the parental home and may form a partner relationship. It is assumed that the partner is of the opposite gender and that the relationship involves co-residence. The initiation of a relationship is constrained by the availability of partners, that is, by the presence of partners of the opposite gender who are willing to start a relationship. The existence of a partner relationship is assumed to be a prerequisite for childbearing. The second stage lasts until the birth of the first child. The childrearing period constitutes the third stage of the life course. The onset of the third period does not coincide with a given age but with first childbirth. The reproductive period is assumed to be terminated at age 40. At that age, the attention of the family shifts from childrearing to the departure of the children from home. This departure-from-home process is assumed to be completed at age 65. Beyond that age, the focus is increasingly on the completion of the life course. Childless couples skip the third and fourth stages and their life course is said to be incomplete. It is assumed that the partner relationship is dissolved by death only. Death is assumed to occur at advanced ages; namely, during the fifth stage of life. This stage starts at age 65 and is referred to as the elderly period. Table 7.1 summarizes the five stages.

In the remainder of this section, the life courses of individuals and households are estimated. The life courses constituting the household dynamics are viewed as representations of continuous-time stochastic processes. The parameters of the life course processes are instantaneous rates of

TABLE 7.1. The individual life course

Stage	Event-origin	Terminating event	Living arrangement
I	birth	18th birthday	with parents
II	18th birthday	first childbirth	alone or with partner
III	first childbirth	40th birthday	with partner and children
IV	40th birthday	65th birthday	with partner and with or without children
V	65th birthday	death	with partner or alone

TABLE 7.2. Parameters of the life course processes

	Age	Females	Males
1. Survival			
mortality rate	0–64	0.00	0.00
	65+	0.05	0.07
2. Partner relationship			
2.1 Onset of search			
proportion in search at age	18	70%	40%
rate of onset of search	18–39	0.40	0.30
2.2 Arrival of partners			
arrival rate of partners of opposite sex	18–39	0.25	0.27[a]
2.3 Matching			
reservation value	18–39	7.30	10.0
rate of matching	18–39	0.09[a]	0.09[a]
3. Departure from home			
rate of departure	18–29	0.15	0.20
	30+	0.60	0.60
4. Childbearing			
fertility rate at parity 0	18–39	0.25	
fertility rate at parity 1+	18–39	0.10	

[a] Calculated from other life course parameters.

transition (intensities) and are assumed to be given. They are given in Table 7.2. The discussion of the estimation of these parameters from real data is beyond the scope of this chapter. The interested reader is referred to chapter 11 by Courgeau and Lelièvre. The following life course processes are considered:

- survival process for males and females;
- partner relationship process;
- departure-from-home process;
- childbearing process.

For each process and for a combination of processes, the following questions are addressed:

- onset of the process;
- duration of the process, that is, the length of time exposed to the risk of experiencing the life event generated by the process;
- probability of the event occurring in a given interval;
- in case of repeatable events, the number of events occurring during a given interval; and
- time spent in each stage of the life course process.

7.4.1. Survival

It is assumed that deaths occur in stage V of the life course only and that the rate of occurrence is gender-specific but independent of age and household status. The mortality intensity of males is 0.07, implying a life expectancy at age 65 (and hence an average length of stage V) of $1/0.07 = 14.3$ years and a total life expectancy of 79.3 years. The life expectancy of females in considerably higher: 20 years at age 65 and 85 years at birth. The lengths of stages I to IV are independent of mortality, since mortality is absent during these stages.

The probability that the relationship of a woman at any age beyond 65 is dissolved by the death of her partner in a year is 6.4 per cent, assuming that the partner is at least as old as the woman, and independence of mortality between the spouses. It is obtained as the product of her surviving one year and her partner dying in that year:

$$\exp(-0.05) \, [1 - \exp(-0.07)] = 0.064.$$

In general, the probability of widowhood for the woman over a period of t years is

$$\exp(-0.05t) \, [1 - \exp(-0.07t)].$$

Of the women with a partner at age 65, 36.8 per cent are still alive at age 85 and 72.3 per cent of them are living alone as a widow. The probability that the marriage is still intact at age 85 is

$$\exp(-0.05 * 20) \cdot \exp(-0.07 * 20) = 9.1 \text{ per cent.}$$

7.4.2. Partner relationship

On reaching the age of 18, childhood is completed and the young adult enters a new stage of life. She/he enters a period of disengagement from the parental relationship, increasing independence, and, most likely, an engagement in a partner relationship. The disengagement involves leaving the parental home. It is assumed that a young adult engages in a partner relationship and marries or cohabits if she/he finds a suitable partner and is being accepted by the potential partner. In that case, the two persons match. The analysis and modelling of the matching process is treated in this section. If there is no match, either because an acceptable partner does not arrive or if one is rejected, the young adult continues the search and stays with her/his parents, or moves out to live alone. There may be a positive probability of a match never occurring due to the lack of partners (quantity) or too high an aspiration (quality), in which case potential partners are rejected because their characteristics are below given minimum requirements.

The process of relationship initiation or the matching process is viewed as a searching process. The process is analogous to the labour market process matching jobs and people (Flinn and Heckman, 1982). The process has three essential characteristics:

1. the onset of the search process, that is, the age at which one engages in a search for a partner;
2. the arrival rate of potential partners, that is, the rate at which one meets potential partners; and
3. the decision rule governing the acceptance or rejection of potential partners and determining the rate of matching.

1. Onset of search for partner

It is assumed that the onset of the search process coincides with the transition to the second stage of life, which has been fixed at age 18. At that age, 70 per cent of the females and 40 per cent of the males are assumed to engage in a search for a partner. The remaining females and males start the search process at a later age. It is assumed that these females and males engage in a search at a rate of $r_{sf} = 0.40$ and $r_{sm} = 0.30$ respectively. It is further assumed that persons do not initiate a search at an age above 40. Females who are not involved in a search at the age of 18 start a search at age 20.5, on average; at age 25, 98 per cent have at some time initiated a search for a partner. The corresponding figures for the males are 21.3 years and 93 per cent. The probability that a female has at some time engaged in a search before age 22 is:

$$0.7 + 0.3 * (1 - \exp(-0.4 * 4)) = 93.9 \text{ per cent.}$$

The average age at which they engage in a search is 18.38 years and the expected duration of the search at age 22 is 3.62 years if all females ever engaged in a search are considered (Appendix). The expected duration of the search for the females who initiated the search process *after* age 18 is 2.51 years.

2. Arrival of potential partners

The rate at which one meets new potential partners during the search, that is, the rate of arrival of partners, depends on the availability of eligible persons of the opposite sex. A person is eligible if involved in a search process. Formulated more formally, a person is at risk of meeting a potential partner for the duration of the search, which is the average waiting time for a relationship. The arrival rate of potential partners therefore not only depends on the rate at which young adults of the opposite sex enter the search, but also on their success, that is, on their rate of attrition from the search process.

The rate of leaving the process is equal to the rate of success, which is the rate at which two partners match. The probability of a match depends on the attributes of the partners and their perception of the characteristics of a suitable partner (aspirations). The matching process is discussed in the next section. For the moment, we assume that a potential partner is never rejected and that any meeting results in a match.

Assume that the number of males of exactly 18 years is equal to the number of females of that age. The assumption implies a sex ratio of one at ages below 65 since mortality is absent at those ages. Assume further that, once engaged in the search process, a female may expect to wait four years before a relationship occurs. This implies an arrival rate of male partners of 0.25, given that there are enough males participating in the search. If the numbers of males and females involved in a search are unequal, there may not be enough partners to meet at the given rate and the arrival rate of partners may need to be adjusted. The adjustment involves the two-sex problem. To assure that the number of males meeting females is equal to the number of females meeting males, a number of approaches have been suggested in the literature (for a review, see Keilman, 1985). In this chapter, we adopt a simple approach, involving the adjustment of the rate at which males meet females (arrival rate of females). The matching process is discussed for females first, since it is not affected by the availability of males.

(*a*) FEMALES The probabilities that females ever embark upon a search process are discussed above and are shown in the Appendix for selected ages. The Appendix also shows the expected duration of the search given that the search is not interrupted. For instance, a 22-year-old female who has at some time entered the search process has been in the process for 3.62 years on average. At age 22, most of those involved in a search have been in the process for 4 years since 74.5 per cent of females who started the search before age 22 started at exact age 18. The 25.5 per cent who entered the process between age 18 and 22 entered on age 19.5 on average.

Denote the arrival rate of males by $r_{mf}(x)$ and assume it to be constant and equal to 0.25, between ages 18 and 40, that is, $r_{mf}(x) = r_{mf} = 0.25$. The average duration of the search is therefore 4 years. After 1 year of search, 22.1 per cent of the females have found a mate; and after 4 years, 63.2 per cent have been successful, given that males continue to arrive at a rate of 0.25. The probability that a female who started a search at age x before age 22 is still engaged in a search at the age of 22 years is

$$S_{sf}(22) = \exp(-0.25 * (22 - x)).$$

For a female who started the search at the age of 18.38 years, which is the average age at onset of the search for those starting the search before age 22, the probability is 40.4 per cent. The expected age at onset of search for those engaging in a search before age 40 is 18.75 years.

A 22-year-old female who started the search at the average age of onset of a search has been engaged in the process for 3.62 years. The average waiting time for success has been 2.38 years, which is the ratio of the probability of success (0.596) to the rate of success (0.25). If the search has been successful, the average waiting time to the relationship has been:

$$[2.38 - 3.62 * (1 - 0.596)]/0.596 = 1.54 \text{ years.}$$

(b) MALES The probability that an x-year-old male has ever started a search is

$$0.4 + 0.6 * (1 - \exp(-0.3 * (x - 18))).$$

At age 22, 81.9 per cent of all males are engaged in a search (as opposed to 93.9 per cent of the females). The expected age at onset of the search is 18.82 years for males entering a search before age 22 and 19.98 years for all males ever entering a search. Notice that the probability of males participating in a search determines the maximum value of the arrival rate of males. Assume that the onset of the search is at age 18.75 for females and at age 19.98 for males (average ages) and that no one engages in a relationship after age 40. Since the probability that a female is involved in a relationship before that age is 99.5 per cent, the probability that a male is involved in a relationship must be 99.5 per cent too, since the sex ratio at age 18 is one and since there is no mortality before age 40.

A 40-year-old male who at any time embarked upon a search process (99.92 per cent) started the process 20.02 years ago on average. The rate at which males meet females (arrival rate of females) may be obtained from the following equation:

$$99.92 * [1 - \exp(-r_{mf} * 20.02)] = 99.5,$$

where r_{mf} is the arrival rate of females. The rate is 0.2735. Given the dynamics of the search process, eligible males need to meet females at a rate of 0.2735 if females meet males at a rate of 0.25 and consistency is observed. This calculation assumes that the potential partner one meets is selected at random from the pool of eligible persons. In other words, everyone in the search process has the same probability of being met and there is no age-selectivity.

Since almost everyone (99.6 per cent) leaves the search process before age 40, the average duration of the search is about 3.66 years for males (1/0.2735) and 4 years (1/0.25) for females. The mean age at relationship is 23.64 for males (18 + 1.98 + 3.66) and 22.75 for females (18 + 0.75 + 4) given that they entered the search process at the average ages. Females participate in the search process for longer periods of time than males because they start at younger ages at which the eligibility of males is still relatively limited.

3. Matching

Persons engage in a relationship at a rate which is equal to the product of three terms: the arrival rate of potential partners, the probability of accepting the partner, and the probability of being accepted by the partner. In the previous section, it was assumed that everyone met is accepted as a partner. Consequently, any meeting results in a partner relationship. In this section, the possibility of rejecting potential partners is introduced.

Each individual is characterized by a set of attributes. For simplicity's sake, we assume that the attributes may be represented by a single index, which we will refer to as the personality index. It is further assumed that in the population, the personality indices are normally distributed with mean value 10 and standard deviation 5.1 and that both the male and the female population exhibit the same distribution of the personality index. The value of the standard deviation is selected such that the 95 per cent interval is from 0 to 20. The lowest value of the index at which a potential partner is acceptable is called the reservation value, resembling the reservation wage concept in search models of labour economics. The decision rule used is therefore as follows: as soon as a potential partner is met whose qualifications are such that the personality index exceeds the reservation value, he/she is accepted. The reservation value may decrease with age indicating that a person searching for a partner reduces her/his aspirations as time passes and she/he gets older. The variable reservation value may also be used to express that independence and alternative activities such as education are preferred over a partner relationship. Table 7.3 shows the distribution of the personality index in the population. The figures denote the probabilities that the personality index of a person selected at random exceeds a given value.

TABLE 7.3. Probabilities that the personality index W of a potential partner exceeds given value w[a]

w	Probability that W exceeds w
0	0.975
2	0.942
3.5	0.900
5	0.837
6	0.784
7	0.722
8	0.653
9	0.578
10	0.500
11	0.422
12	0.347
13	0.287
14	0.216
15	0.163
16.5	0.100
18	0.058
20	0.025

[a] The personality index is normally distributed with mean 10 and standard deviation 5.1.

For our calculations, the reservation value at age 18 is assumed to be 10 for males and 7.3 for females. The difference expresses the hypothesis that males have higher aspirations than females and are prepared to wait longer to engage in a relationship implying marriage and/or cohabitation than females do. The probabilities that a meeting with a potential partner results in a match is 50 per cent for males and 70 per cent for females. In this chapter, the reservation values are assumed to be independent of age and the duration of the search. The Appendix gives a few indicators of the matching process. The probability that a female who entered the search at the average age of onset of a search finds an acceptable partner and is accepted by the partner by the age of 22 is:

$$[70 + 30 * (1 - \exp(-0.4 * 4))] * [1 - \exp(-0.25 * 0.5 * 0.7 * 3.62)] = 93.943 * 0.2715 = 25.5 \text{ per cent,}$$

with $0.25 * 0.5 * 0.7 = 0.0875$ the rate at which females match.

The probability of a successful match is much lower than the probability of a successful search (55.9 per cent) due to the rejection of potential partners. More than 65 per cent of the meetings do not result in a match because one of the partners is not acceptable to the other. If the reservation values remain constant, 37.3 per cent of the females will not find a suitable partner by the age of 30 and 15.6 per cent by the age of 40, although at age 30 99.7 per cent and at age 40 all have met potential partners.

The average waiting time to a match is 9.6 years for all 18-year-olds and 7.5 years for those who experience a match before age 40. Those who match before age 25 spend 2.9 years in the search process, on average.

The matching process of males is determined by the matching process of females and the consistency condition that an equal number of females and males match. Given that the sex ratio at 18 is one, that no match occurs after age 40, and that age selectivity is absent, the probability that a male finds a suitable partner by age 40 must be 84.4 per cent $(100 - 15.6)$. This condition is satisfied if males match at a rate of 0.0930923, which is higher than the rate for females due to the relatively late entry of males in the search process (average waiting time to onset of search is 1.98 years versus 0.75 years for females). The associated arrival rate of females is $0.266 \ (= 0.093/(0.7 * 0.5))$. Although males engage in the search process later, the process is more intensive.

An 18-year-old male waits, on average, 9.08 years for a match, which is less than an average female. The waiting time is 7.07 years if a match is to occur before age 40, and 2.6 years if the match occurs before age 25.

7.4.3. Departure from the parental home

Young adults not engaged in a relationship stay with their parents or set up their own one-person household. Let us assume that the rate of leaving the parental home to live alone is 0.20 for males and 0.15 for females. Beyond age 30, the rates are 0.6 for both sexes. Assume further that the rates are independent of the duration of search and that the arrival rate of potential partners and the reservation value are independent of the living arrangement. For example, a person aged 25 years who has been searching for a partner for 7 years leaves her/his parental home at the same rate as an 18-year-old.

The rate of leaving home to set up a one-person household depends on the financial resources available. It is assumed that a person who intends to set up a one-person household will do so only if her/his income is adequate. In this chapter, we assume that the income does not constrain the departure from home.

A person may leave home by engaging in a relationship or by setting up a one-person household. The total rate of leaving home is the sum of the rate of leaving to join a partner (0.0875 if one is involved in a search) and the rate of passage to a one-person household (0.15). Since both component rates are assumed to be independent, the classical theory of competing risks applies and the probability that a person leaving home is engaged in a relationship is the ratio of the rate of leaving home to join a partner to the total rate of leaving. The probabilities of particular living arrangements of females at selected ages are shown in Table 7.4. It is assumed that the event-origin which initiates a process leading to a particular living arrangement occurs at the expected age of that particular event. On average, a female participating in the search process leaves home at age 21. By age 30, 94.2 per cent have left the parental home. Of those who have left, 36.8 per cent (= 0.0875/0.2375) left because of a relationship and 63.2 per cent (= 0.15/0.2375) set up a separate household.

TABLE 7.4. Probabilities of a particular living arrangement of females at selected ages[a] (%)

Age	With parents	With partner Previous living arrangement			Alone
		Total	With parents	Alone	
18	100.0	—	—	—	—
19	78.9	8.4	7.8	0.6	12.7
20	62.2	16.0	13.9	2.1	21.8
22	38.7	29.4	22.6	6.8	31.9
25	19.0	45.2	29.8	15.4	35.8
30	5.8	63.9	34.7	29.2	30.3
40	0.5	84.2	36.6	47.6	15.3

[a] For simplicity's sake, it is assumed that all females without a partner participate in the search process.

7.4.4. Childbearing

The engagement in a relationship resulting in marriage and/or cohabitation starts a new process; namely, the fertility process. It is assumed that births outside of a relationship are absent. The fertility rate of couples is assumed to depend on parity only. Three parity categories are distinguished: 0 children, 1 child, and 2 or more children. The fertility rates at parity 1 and at parity 2+ are assumed to be equal. It is finally assumed that women do not have children after age 40.

Let the fertility rates at parity 0 and 1+ be 0.25 and 0.10, respectively. The average waiting time for first birth is 3.87 years given that a birth after age 40 is impossible and that a woman starts a relationship at the expected age at relationship (26.25 years) (Appendix). If a first birth occurs before age 40, the average waiting time is 3.54 years. The waiting time for second birth is 7.1 years for all women with 1 child and 4.9 years for those who have a second child before age 40 (about 71 per cent). The ages of the mother at which the children are born can easily be calculated. An average 40-year-old woman

TABLE 7.5. Age distribution of females experiencing the onset of search (1), match (2), first birth (3), and second birth (4) between ages 18 and 40 (%)

Age	1	2	3	4
18	33.0	3.7	1.1	0.1
19	22.1	5.4	2.3	0.2
20	14.8	6.3	3.5	0.5
21	9.9	6.7	4.7	0.8
22	6.7	6.8	5.6	1.3
23	4.5	6.7	6.4	1.8
24	3.0	6.5	6.8	2.4
25	2.0	6.2	7.0	3.0
26	1.3	5.8	7.0	3.7
27	0.9	5.5	6.9	4.4
28	0.6	5.1	6.6	5.1
29	0.4	4.7	6.2	5.6
30	0.3	4.3	5.7	6.1
31	0.2	4.0	5.2	6.6
32	0.1	3.7	4.7	6.9
33	0.1	3.4	4.2	7.2
34	0.1	3.1	3.7	7.4
35	0.0	2.8	3.2	7.5
36	0.0	2.6	2.8	7.5
37	0.0	2.4	2.4	7.4
38	0.0	2.2	2.1	7.3
39	0.0	2.0	1.8	7.1
TOTAL	100.0	100.0	100.0	100.0

with two children born started to search for a partner at age 18.75 years. She found a partner and matched at age 26.25. The first child was born at age 29.79 and the second child at age 34.04. The children are 10.20 and 5.95 years old. Not all women obeying the life course parameters given in Table 7.2 have two children. Only 52.2 per cent of all women have two children. Of all women 81.7 per cent have at least one child and of all couples 96.8 per cent have at least one child. Childlessness (18.3 per cent) may partly be attributed to the lack of a suitable partner (15.6 percentage points) and to couples remaining childless (2.7 percentage points). About 41 per cent of the women who will ever have a child have the child within 2 years after the relationship. Of those with at least one child, 63.9 per cent have a second child before age 40 (parity progression ratio). Of the women with two children, 45.1 per cent have a third child. The average number of children ever born is 1.91 if all 40-year-old women are considered:

$$1.91 = 0.25 * (29.79 - 26.25) + 0.10 * (40 - 29.79)$$

The average age at which an event (e.g. childbearing) occurs does not give insight into the ages at which the events occur. Table 7.5 shows the ages of women at the time of an event, given that the event occurs before age 40. For instance, 6.8 per cent of the women with a first child before age 40 have the child at age 24 in completed years.

7.5. Conclusion

In this chapter a few ideas are presented to improve household models. It is demonstrated that household dynamics may be viewed as an outcome of several interrelated stochastic processes. Each component process underlies the pattern of occurrence of a single life event. Some of the events are associated with the life course of an individual while other events are part of the life course of relationships between individuals. The life courses of household members and of the relationships between the members need to be understood in order to be able to describe and explain the household dynamics.

The life course perspective leads to a microdemographic model. The household dynamics is described in terms of four life course processes: survival, partner relationship, departure from home, and childbearing. The household structure at each point in time is an outcome of the four processes acting in parallel or in sequence. Much of the complexity of household formation, including the selection processes involved, can be described by a few very simple interacting processes.

The approach presented in this chapter has considerable potential. Much remains to be done, however. Of particular importance is the identification and representation of the interaction or dependence between component processes.

References

BERSCHEID, E. (1985). Compatibility, interdependence and emotion, in: W. Ickles (ed.), *Compatible and Incompatible Relationships* (Springer Verlag, New York), 143–61.

BONGAARTS, J. (1983). The formal demography of families and households: an overview, *IUSSP Newsletter* 17, 27–42.

CLARK, M. S. (1985). Implications of relationship type for understanding compatibility, in: W. Ickles (ed.), *Compatible and Incompatible Relationships* (Springer Verlag, New York), 119–40.

COMBRINK-GRAHAM, L. (1985). A developmental model of family systems, *Family Processes* 24, 139–50.

ELCHARDUS, M. (1984). Life cycle and life course: the scheduling and temporal integration of life, in: S. Feld and R. Lesthaeghe (eds.), *Population and Social Outlook* (Koning Boudewijn–Stichting, Brussels), 251–67.

ELDER, G. H. jun (1978). Family history and the life course, in: T. K. Hareven (ed.), *Transitions: The Family and the Life Course in Historical Perspective* (Academic Press, New York), 17–64.

ERIKSON, E. H. (1980). *Identity and the Life Cycle* (Norton and Co., New York).

—— (1982). *The Life Cycle Completed* (Norton and Co., New York).

FLINN, C. AND J. HECKMAN (1982). New methods for analyzing structural models of labor force dynamics, *Journal of Econometrics* 18, 115–68.

HELD, T. (1986). Institutionalization and deinstitutionalization of the life course, *Human Development* 29, 157–62.

HULTSCH, D. F. AND S. W. CORNELIUS (1981). Kritische Lebensereignisse und lebenslange Entwicklung: methodologische Aspekte, in: S.-H. Filipp (ed.), *Kritische Lebensereignisse* (Urband and Schwarzenberg, Munich), 72–90.

KEILMAN, N. W. (1985). Nuptiality models and the two-sex problem in national population forecasts, *European Journal of Population* 1(2/3), 207–35.

KNUDSON, R. M. (1985). Marital compatibility and mutual identity confirmation, in: W. Ickles (ed.), *Compatible and Incompatible Relationships* (Springer Verlag, New York), 233–51.

LEVINSON, D. J., C. N. DARROW, E. B. KLEIN, M. H. LEVINSON, AND B. MCKEE (1978). *The Seasons of a Man's Life* (Ballantine Books, New York).

MONTGOMERY, H. (1983). Decision rules and the search for a dominance structure: towards a process model of decision making, in: P. Humphreys, O. Svenson, and A. Vari (eds.), *Analyzing and Aiding Decision Processes* (North Holland, Amsterdam), 343–69.

PAYKEL, E. S. (1983). Methodological aspects of life events research, *Journal of Psychosomatic Research* 27, 341–52.

REINKE, B. J., D. S. HOLMES, AND R. L. HARRIS (1985). The timing of psychosocial changes in women's lives: the years 25 to 45, *Journal of Personality and Social Psychology* 48, 1353–64.

Appendix

Life course indicators at selected ages, females

Age x	Probability of event up to and including x (%)	Retrospective indicators			Prospective indicators	
		Expected waiting time to event (years)	Waiting time given event before or at x (years)	Expected duration since event (years)	Expected duration to event given no event up to and including x (years)	Expected duration to event given event between x and 40 (years)
A. Search process. Event: onset of search						
18	70	0.00	0.00	0.00	2.50	2.50
19	80	0.25	0.06	0.94	2.50	2.50
22	94	0.60	0.38	3.62	2.50	2.49
30	100	0.74	0.72	11.28	2.47	2.36
40	100	0.75	0.75	21.25	0.00	0.00
B. Matching process. Event: match, given onset of search						
18	0	0.00	0.00	0.00	9.65	7.51
19	8	0.90	0.46	0.48	9.50	7.29
22	27	3.10	1.71	1.91	8.98	6.63
30	63	7.17	4.73	6.56	6.65	4.29
40	84	9.65	7.51	13.74	0.00	0.00
C. Fertility process. Event: first birth, given presence of a relationship (match)						
18	0	0.00	0.00	0.00	3.87	3.54
19	11	0.45	0.23	0.24	3.85	3.50
22	38	1.52	0.88	1.03	3.79	3.35
30	81	3.22	2.42	4.14	3.34	2.67
40	97	3.87	3.54	10.20	0.00	0.00
D. Fertility process. Event: second birth, given first birth						
18	0	0.00	0.00	0.00	6.39	4.25
19	2	0.02	0.12	0.12	6.31	4.17
22	10	0.10	0.51	0.52	6.00	3.89
30	34	3.39	1.93	2.21	4.55	2.73
40	64	6.39	4.25	5.95	0.00	0.00

8

The headship rate approach in modelling households: The case of the Federal Republic of Germany

W. Linke

ABSTRACT

This chapter presents methods for projecting the number of households, based on the macroanalytical approach. This involves the well-known, and most frequently used, so-called 'headship rate method', as well as a modification of this method, in which the number and age structure of the household members pertaining to the given heads of households are taken into account. Further, a method is presented which is no longer based on headship rates, but on age-specific household membership rates, according to the household size in question. In structure and implementation, this method is somewhat simpler than the above-mentioned methods, and also permits a breakdown of the estimated households by individual household sizes.

8.1. Introduction

THE number and structure of private households are implicitly influenced by demographic and non-demographic factors of population development; for instance, changing attitudes towards marriage, divorce, and birth. In the case of the projection of private households, further non-demographic factors (trend towards consensual unions, and early departure from the parental home) may be at work. The demographic and non-demographic factors which, in a population projection, are considered to be related to individual persons, together influence the entire process of household formation, extension, reduction, and dissolution. Therefore, in the case of household projections, it is both necessary and practicable to proceed, to an even higher degree than in a population projection, from just a few combined trend assumptions. Moreover, the same reservation as in the case of population projections and model computations applies for projections of the number and structure of households: they can only give insight into future household trends if the relevant assumptions come true.

The number of households may be projected by using either the micro-analytical (microsimulation) or the macroanalytical (macrosimulation) approach. In the first case, data for individuals applying to a certain point in time are continuously updated. In practice, this method presumes an adequate basis of individual data, on the one hand, and a relatively large number of assumptions about individual transition probabilities, on the other hand. In the macroanalytical approach, data for groups of individuals are updated, using relatively simple transition assumptions for these groups. One of the best-known applications of the macroanalytical approach is the projection of households, using head of household quotas. The prototype of this projection method was published by the United States National Resources Planning Committee (1938). On the basis of the 1930 census, a projection of the number of households in the USA until the year 1980 was carried out at that time, using the headship rate method. Age-specific and sex-specific rates were kept constant for the entire projection period. The improvement in the basic statistics in the censuses round about 1950 enabled a further series of countries, especially industrial countries, to carry out household projections. In accordance with the methodological development and the data basis existing at the time, the headship rate method proved to be the most plausible and suitable method. The particular advantage of this method, as compared to the simple method of extrapolating the household/population ratio or the life table method (see Brown (1951) and Glass and Davidson (1951)), is the possibility to link up directly with present population projections. Thus changes in the age structure and composition of the population, broken down by sex and marital status, can be taken into consideration. In the 1962 Recommendations of the EEC to its member states, the application of the headship rate method was emphasized as being the most suitable one for household projections (Economic Commission for Europe (1962)). In the following years, in particular directly after the census years, household projections were carried out more and more frequently.

The principle of the headship rate approach is as follows (for details, see United Nations (1973)). The development of households by number and type is described by the development of the proportions of household heads in population categories by age, sex, and possibly by marital status. Analysis and projection thus rely on stock data at specific points in time, mostly census counts. Therefore, the headship rate approach is basically a static method. It describes and projects the results of unobserved dynamic processes of household formation and dissolution.

A recent overview of the historical development of the headship rate method is given by Kono (1986). In addition to this review, he discusses extensions including a multiple decrement headship life table, in which entries to and exits from the headship status can be investigated. Pitkin and Masnick (1986) present an improvement of the headship rate method which includes the relationship between heads and non-heads in the household population. Finally, we mention recent work by Burch *et al.* (1986), who analyse headship indices which indirectly standardize for age, sex, and marital status composition (see also chapter 6 by Schwarz). They compare these standardized measures with more simple ratios, for example crude headship rate (or its inverse: average household size), adults per household, and married persons per household.

This chapter presents the headship rate approach, focusing on the case of the Federal Republic of Germany. It discusses the conventional method, as well as an extension in which the number and the age structure of the household members are taken into account. Also, a method is presented including age- and size-specific household membership rates.

8.2. Projecting households by the headship rate method

8.2.1. Headship rate method I

Methodological explanations

As mentioned above, the headship rate method is frequently used for the projection of private households. The headship rates, that is, proportion of heads of household of a specific age group contained in the total number of persons of the same age group, determined for one or several reference years, as well as the future population in private households[1] by age, provide the basic data for this method. It is possible, in this context, to differentiate between the headship rates according to single-person and multi-person households, as well as by sex of the heads of household. For the projection period, either constant or variable headship rates can be assumed. In the first case, the headship rates determined for the base year or as an average for a certain base period are applied to the projection period. The results of this projection method show how many households, broken down by age of the head of household, would exist in the projection years, if the rates of the base year were also to apply in the future. Methods of estimating variable headship rates will be dealt with in somewhat greater detail later. The projection of private households, in accordance with method I, takes place in six steps.

First, the population in private households, by age group, is estimated from the projection results for the total population:

$$B_{y,t}^P = B_{y,t} \cdot f_y. \tag{8.1}$$

The projected resident population in age group y at time t is defined as $B_{y,t}$. The age group-specific proportions f_y between the two populations are determined by means of data from preceding enumerations or sample surveys:

$$f_y = \left(\sum_{t=1}^{n} B_{y,t}^P / B_{y,t} \right) \bigg/ n,$$

with B^P being the population in private households and B the resident population. For the years $1 - n$, the headship rates, being the proportions of the heads of household among the population of the same age in private households, are determined as:

$$v_{y,t} = H_{y,t}/B^P_{y,t}. \tag{8.2}$$

Here $H_{y,t}$ represents the number of heads of private households in age group y. If variable headship rates are to be assumed, these time series may be extrapolated by means of, for instance, the least squares method. For the same years of observation the proportion of single-person households contained in the total number of private households in the individual age groups is then determined and possibly extrapolated if variable rates are to be assumed.

$$h^1_{y,t} = H^1_{y,t}/H_{y,t}. \tag{8.3}$$

The (constant or variable) age-specific headship rates $v_{y,t}$ according to (8.2) determined for the projection year are then multiplied by the estimated number of persons in private households (8.1). This yields the number of private households and heads of household, respectively, by age group of the heads of household, for each of the projection years:

$$H_{y,t} = v_{y,t} \cdot B^P_{y,t}. \tag{8.4}$$

In order to obtain the single-person households in age group y, the estimated number of heads of household (8.4) is weighted with the extrapolated age group-specific proportions of the single-person households according to (8.3):

$$H^1_{y,t} = H_{y,t} \cdot h^1_{y,t}.$$

The projected number of multi-person households with heads aged y is obtained by subtracting the estimated number of single-person households from the estimated number of households:

$$H^m_{y,t} = H_{y,t} - H^1_{y,t}.$$

Totals may be obtained by addition over ages y. By subtracting the single-person households from the population in private households (8.1) it is possible to estimate the number of persons living in a multi-person household:

$$\sum_y B^{P,m}_{y,t} = \sum_y B^P_{y,t} - \sum_y H^1_{y,t}.$$

Average household size may be calculated as:

$$\sum_y B^P_{y,t} \Big/ \sum_y H_{y,t}.$$

Estimation of variable headship rates

A time series of observed age-specific headship rates may be extrapolated linearly by means of the least-squares method or by using even more advanced curve-fitting methods. In using this method, one intends to show how household figures and structures would change in the future, if the trends observed so far were to continue. Conspicuously progressive or degressive trends would, moreover, have to be checked for their plausibility.

It is also possible to use—as a modified extrapolation—the compound interest formula for estimating future headship rates. As an example, consider the estimation of age-specific headship rates (8.2) for the projection year 1990. They are determined by means of the relevant data from the observation years 1970 and 1975:

$$v_{y,1990} = v_{y,1970} \left(v_{y,1975} / v_{y,1970} \right)^4.$$

The regression method for estimating headship rates presupposes a statistical relationship between headship rates and socio-economic variables, such as income. The headship rate (8.2) is considered here as a dependent variable, and the socio-economic variable, denoted by x, as an independent one. Then one estimates a and b in

$$v_y = a + bx. \tag{8.5}$$

It is assumed that the conditions expressed by (8.5) during the observation period will apply in future, too. When this method is used, the estimation of the change in the headship rates shifts, however, to that of the socio-economic variables. Hence, in the present example, we would be faced with the difficulty of estimating the future level of income.

Another possibility for determining variable headship rates is to set target values to be attained in a specific year. The target values can be estimated by assuming future demographic, social, and economic trends. Alternatively, they may be set using information from other countries (for example, average size of household). The rates for individual projection years are determined by interpolating the values between base year and target year.

8.2.2. Modified headship rate method II

Methodological explanations

In the method described in 8.2.1 the age-specific group of persons from which the heads of household originate is always used as a reference number. The actual number and the age structure of the household members of the relevant heads of household are not taken into account. A method will now be discussed which includes the two latter points in the estimation of the number of households.

The approach used here is similar to the one which Akkerman (1980) employed in his method for projecting households (see also Keilman, chapter 9). Akkerman carried out a projection of the population and households, thereby simultaneously taking into account birth and mortality trends. However, method II, described below, presupposes an independent projection of the population in private households which implicitly contains assumptions about birth and mortality trends, as well as about migration. A further methodological difference to be noted is that according to the term population in private households (see Appendix), one person can be a member of two households (in different places), whereas Akkerman, in his method, assumes that each person is a member of only one household.

The following initial data are required for this method:

1. the projected population in private households, by age groups, $B^P_{y,t}$;
2. the number of heads of household of single- and multi-person households by age groups, $H^1_{z,t}$ and $H^m_{z,t}$;
3. the number of household members (including heads of household), by age groups (y), whose head of household belongs to a specific age group z, $P_{y/z}$.

It is expedient to use Table 8.1 to illustrate the method. Table 8.1 shows the age structure of the heads of household, as well as the age structure and the number of persons in these households. The totals of columns 4–10 show the age structure of the population in private households, in a certain reference year. If possible, this evaluation table should be made for several years, in order to provide a sufficient number of observation years for an extrapolation.

The following preliminary calculations have to be made for each reference year, using the evaluation table.

1. Proportion of heads of household in age group z among the total number of persons in the relevant households:

$$u_z = H_z/P_{./z}.$$

2. Proportion of single-person households among the total number of heads of household in age group z:

$$g^1_z = H^1_z/H_z.$$

3. Proportional breakdown of the total number of household members in age group y by age of the head of household z (relative breakdown of columns 4–10 in the evaluation table):

$$q_{y/z} = P_{y/z}/P_{y/.} = P_{y/z}/B^P_y. \tag{8.6}$$

For the purpose of checking, the following average values can be calculated as well:

TABLE 8.1. Heads of household by age (z), and persons living in the households of these heads of household, by age (y)

Age of head of household	Total number of heads of household	Number of		Age of persons in households y (including heads of household)							
		single-person households	multi-person households	0–20	20–30	30–40	40–50	50–60	60–70	70+	Total
z	H_z	H_z^1	H_z^m				$P_{y/z}$				$P_{./z}$
—	1	2	3	4	5	6	7	8	9	10	11
			(1)–(2)								
0–20											
20–30											
30–40											
40–50											
50–60											
60–70											
70 and over											
Total							$P_{y/.} = B_y^P$				B^P

(a) the average household size, based on all households whose head belongs to age group z

$$D_z = 1/u_z;$$

(b) the average household size, based on multi-person households whose head belongs to age group z

$$D_z^m = (P_{./z} - H_z^1)/H_z^m.$$

In order to project the number of private households, the following five calculation steps are necessary:

1. the projected population in private households by age group is determined using the same procedure as in method I:

$$B_{y,t}^P = B_{y,t} \cdot f_y. \qquad (8.1)$$

The values $B_{y,t}^P$ for the relevant projection year t are entered in columns 4–10 of the total line in the calculation table, which corresponds to the evaluation table mentioned above;

2. assuming that the percentage distribution $q_{y/z}$ calculated in the base year have not substantially changed, the projected results for the population in private households by age group $(B_{y,t}^P)$ are broken down into columns, according to age groups z of the heads of household:

$$P_{y/z,t} = B_{y,t}^P \cdot q_{y,t/z,t}.$$

The changes in age structure which occurred in the projected population in private households, as compared with the base year, are thus considered in the age group of the heads of household, using appropriate weights;

3. the number of relevant household members by age group y, estimated for the individual age groups z of the heads of household, are then added up. The combined sum of these totals (column 11) yields the projected total population in private households for the given projection year:

$$B_t^P = \sum_z P_{./z,t}.$$

The projected number of households of heads of household with age z, is then:

$$H_{z,t} = P_{./z,t} \cdot u_{z,t}.$$

with the necessary condition $H_{z,t} < P_{z/z,t}$. Here, $u_{z,t}$ denotes the constant or extrapolated value of the headship rate of age group z for year t. The sum of these values then yields the projected total number of private households:

$$H_t = \sum_z H_{z,t};$$

4. the estimated number of single-person households in age group z of the heads of household is determined as follows:

$$H_{z,t}^1 = H_{z,t} \cdot g_{z,t}^1,$$

$g_{z,t}^1$ denoting the extrapolated value of the proportion of the single-person households among the total number of households for year t. The sum then yields the projected total number of single-person households:

$$H_t^1 = \sum_z H_{z,t}^1;$$

5. the estimated number of multi-person households whose head belongs to age group z is the difference:

$$H_{z,t}^m = H_{z,t} - H_{z,t}^1.$$

The total number of multi-person households can be calculated analogously:

$$H_t^m = H_t - H_t^1.$$

Estimation of variable rates

An extrapolation of the proportions (8.6) can be made in conformity with method I (see section 8.2.1). However, the difficulty of assessing the plausibility of the changes in the highly detailed groups of persons ($P_{y/z}$) and the necessary adjustments to the estimated values in the relative breakdown among the individual age groups y to 100 per cent should not be underestimated.

8.3. Household membership rate method III

The alternative method described below uses an entirely different approach to the two preceding methods. Instead of the headship rates, age-specific household membership rates, according to the household size in question, are applied. In general, this means that, with this method and the requisite basic data, the criterion head of household is no longer used.

With regard to statistical questions, the head of household question primarily serves the purpose of determining a person after whom the household could be classified and statistically evaluated as a whole, from a demographic, economic, and social point of view. The specific headship rates ascertained through this questionnaire constitute the prerequisite for the application of headship rate projections. In the past ten years, in view of the debate about the emancipation of women and partnership in marriage, the use of the term head of household has been increasingly criticized in some countries, and there have been misgivings about including this question in official censuses. Based on previous experience in connection with the preparation and implementation of censuses in some countries, the question about the head of the household will probably no longer be included in the questionnaires of future censuses, and so the traditional determining of headship rates will no longer be possible.

In structure and implementation, this method is somewhat simpler than the other two estimation methods, and it permits a further breakdown of the multi-person households according to individual household sizes. The possibility certainly also exists, theoretically, in methods I and II. However, in this method, a considerably larger amount of data would be required, and it would also involve greater problems of adjustment.

The following data are required for method III:

1. the projected population by age group, B_y^P, in private households;
2. the population in private households by age y, and the size of the household, i, in which the respective persons live, P_y^i, with $\sum_i P_y^i = B_y^P$.

The decisive value for the calculation using this method is the above-mentioned age-specific household membership rate (HMR), according to the household size. It results, for the individual age groups and household sizes, from the following equation:

$$\text{HMR}_y^i = P_y^i / B_y^P.$$

For each age group y we have $\sum_i \text{HMR}_y^i = 1$. Accordingly, the rate for the single-person households is:

$$\text{HMR}_y^1 = H_y^1 / B_y^P = v_y . h_y^1 \qquad (8.7)$$

It is identical to the product of the values (8.2) and (8.3), used in method I. As the above description shows, method III provides a breakdown by age only in the case of single-person households. Multi-person households are shown classified by household size. The rates can be extrapolated by means of the least-squares method on the condition that $\sum_i \text{HMR}_y^i = 1$ for each projection year and each age group.

The projection of the number of private households, in accordance with method III, is carried out as follows. For the selected projection years, the projected population in private households, broken down by age groups, is first required: B_y^P. These population figures are determined in accordance with the procedure described by methods I and II. As the extrapolated age-specific household membership rates for the single-person households also agree with the product of the extrapolated age group-specific headship rates and the proportions of the single-person households (method I), we may find the number of estimated single-person households using (8.7). Hence, this is identical with the results obtained by method I.

In the further course of the calculations, the projected population in private households is, in each case, separately weighted, according to the household size *i* with the extrapolated values of the age group-specific household membership rates of the persons living in multi-person households:

$$P_y^i = B_y^P . \mathrm{HMR}_y^i.$$

Thus, the projected population in private households is first broken down by household size and age group. The projected number of multi-person households, in the individual household sizes, can then be very easily determined:

$$H^i = \sum_y B_y^{Pi} / i. \tag{8.8}$$

That is to say, the projected population in private households by age group and household size is summed over all age groups and divided by the household size.[2] The total number of multi-person households is then obtained by adding up the estimated values determined in accordance with (8.8).

8.4. Comparing the results of the three methods

For methods I–III, model computations were made, up to the year 1990, on the basis of the results of the 1972–8 microcensuses. Extrapolated values, in accordance with the least-squares method, were used in each case.

Table 8.2 shows that the levels of the total numbers of households projected by method III, as well as the number of multi-person households, fall between the projected household numbers of methods I and II. The total number of private households in 1980, estimated by method III, is 0.8 per cent higher than the result of method I, and 0.8 per cent lower than that of method II. For the projection year 1990, these deviations amount to +2.0 per cent (compared with method I), and −2.5 per cent (compared with method II). Proceeding from the estimated results of method III, there are deviations of approximately the same size for the multi-person households.

The similarity in the trends produced by methods I and II can be ascribed to the fact that the headship rates were applied in both cases. As, in method III, the changes in age structure of the population in private households may be considered to be additional information for the sake of classification by age of the head of household, on the one hand, and the number and age of the

TABLE 8.2. Projections of private households, Federal Republic of Germany (population with Germany nationality only)

Method	1980	1985	1990
	Single-person households (000s)		
I	6,938	7,691	8,473
II	6,999	7,911	8,728
III	6,938	7,691	8,473
	Multi-person households (000s)		
I	15,935	15,610	15,276
II	16,242	16,262	16,340
III	16,119	16,003	15,970
	Total (000s)		
I	22,873	23,301	23,749
II	23,241	24,173	25,068
III	23,057	23,694	24,443
	Average household size		
I	2.48	2.39	2.30
II	2.45	2.30	2.18
III	2.46	2.35	2.24

Source: Linke (1983), p. 44.

household members in the relevant households on the other hand, this results in increases or decreases with respect to method I, depending on the changed structural breakdown of the household members. This, on the other hand, depends on the results of the projected population in private households. At this point it is hard to say which of the two methods can be regarded as the more plausible one.

As methods I and III agree in their methodological approach regarding the estimation of single-person households (8.7), they yield identical results for this type of household. As for the estimation of the number of multi-person households, the approach used to extrapolate the rates heavily influences the results. The use of age-specific headship rates, in combination with the age structure of the members of these households (method II), tends to lead to higher estimates than when the special rates of the other two methods are used.

8.5. Conclusions

The headship rate approach for the projection of households is the best-known method, and can now even be called classical. The prototype of this method was published in 1938 by the United States National Resources Planning Committee. After the 1950 round of censuses, household projections were carried out in other countries, in accordance with this method, which, on account of the existing data basis, proved to be the most appropriate one. In 1962, the use of the headship rate method was emphasized in the EEC recommendations as being the most suitable method for household projections.

The particular advantage of the headship rate method lies in the fact that only simple basic data and a fairly small number of assumptions are used, and that a direct link with existing population projections can be made. In contrast to the microanalytical approach (applying individual transition probabilities), dynamic changes within households are only indirectly expressed via the assumption of a change in headship rates and, possibly, in household size. An examination of the assumptions of variable headship rates, with regard to the plausibility of their future development, can, however, be undertaken with further basic data, for example, the development of marriage, divorce, and widowhood, the trend of adolescents leaving the parental household at an earlier age, and the formation of consensual unions.

A refinement of the headship rate method was, for example, attempted in Sweden in 1965, taking socio-economic variables into account. When headship rates are regarded as dependent variables, however, the problem of estimating changes in headship rates becomes a problem of estimating the change in the socio-economic variables. This may very well be even more difficult for a projection period of ten to fifteen years than a general estimation of changes in headship rates.

A modification of the headship rate method can be carried out in such a way that its rates will not be determined by the headship rate in a specific age group, in relation to the number of persons of the same age in the population. As an alternative, they may be derived from the headship rate in a specific age group, in relation to the total number of persons living in the households in question (method II). This assumes a corresponding classification of the total population in accordance with the above-mentioned combination. A projection of the population in private households can be used as a basis for this method, too.

Compared with the simple, classical headship rate method, the actual number and age structure of the household members, with regard to the head of household in question—these in turn differentiated by age groups—are taken into account here. The particular difficulty with this method, however, lies in the total number of household members in a specific age group, in accordance with the allocation of the heads of household to the individual age groups. Moreover, the difficulty in assessing the plausibility of the above-mentioned percentage breakdown and the necessary adjustments should not be underestimated.

The household membership rate method (III) presents an alternative.

Instead of headship rates, it employs age-specific household membership rates, according to the size of a given household. The term head of household is no longer required for the household membership rate method, which, in structure and implementation, is somewhat simpler than the above-mentioned projection method. According to experience so far, in connection with the preparation and implementation of censuses in some countries, it is highly unlikely that the head of household question will be included in the questionnaires of future censuses, and so the traditional calculation of headship rates will no longer be possible. The household membership rate method can, in this case, be referred to as an alternative solution to the projection of the number of households.

Notes

1. For the definition of the population in private households, see the Appendix.
2. For a household of five persons or more, a corresponding extrapolation has to be made, based on the data of the observation years $t = 1$ to $t = n$.

References

AKKERMAN, A. (1980). On the relationship between household composition and population age distribution, *Population Studies* 34(3), 525–34.

BONGAARTS, J., T. K. BURCH, AND K. W. WACHTER (eds.) (1986). *Family Demography: Methods and their Application* (Oxford, Oxford University Press).

BROWN, S. P. (1951). Analysis of a hypothetical stationary population by family units: a note on some experimental calculations, *Population Studies* 4(4), 380–94.

BURCH T. K., S. S. HALLI, A. MADAN, K. T. THOMAS, AND L. WAI (1986). Measures of household composition and headship based on aggregate, routine census data, in: Bongaarts, Burch, and Wachter (1986).

ECONOMIC COMMISSION FOR EUROPE (1962). Technique of surveying a country's housing situation, including estimating current and future housing requirements, ST/ECE/HOU/6 (Geneva, ECE).

GLASS, D. AND F. G. DAVIDSON (1951). Household structure and housing needs, *Population Studies* 4(4), 395–420.

KONO, S. (1986). The headship rate method for projecting households, in: Bongaarts, Burch, and Wachter (1986).

LINKE, W. (1983). Drei Verfahren zur Vorausschätzung der Privathaushalte, *Zeitschrift für Bevölkerungswissenschaft* 9(1), 27–46.

PITKIN, J. R. AND G. S. MASNICK (1986). The relationship between heads and non-heads in the household population: an extension of the headship rate method, in: Bongaarts, Burch, and Wachter (1986).

UNITED NATIONS (1973). Methods of projecting households and families, Population Studies no. 54 (New York, United Nations).

UNITED STATES NATIONAL RESOURCES PLANNING COMMITTEE (1938). The problems of a changing population (Washington, DC, Government Printing Office).

Appendix: Definitions

- Household: Every group of persons living together and forming an economic unit, as well as persons who live alone and keep house by themselves, counts as a private household. The household may comprise relatives and persons other than family members. Institutions are not considered to be households, but they may include private households (for example, the household of the director of an institution). Households with several dwellings count as more than one (see below).
- Population in private households: The population in private households comprises all persons counted in the community who, either alone or together with relatives, form a residential and economic entity ($= de jure$ population minus institutional population). They include, on the one hand, persons who have their sole residence in the community studied, and also persons with several residences, irrespective of the community in which they live for most of the time. Thus, for instance, the absent head of household who goes to work in another community and has a second domicile, as a subtenant, is a member of two households. On the one hand, he is considered part of the household of his family, and on the other hand, he constitutes, as a subtenant, a single-person household. In this respect, the FRG household statistics are quite untypical as compared to those of most other European countries.

9

Dynamic household models

N. Keilman

ABSTRACT

This chapter reviews dynamic household models that have been constructed recently. The analysis is limited to purely demographic macromodels. We discuss the Canadian model developed by Akkerman, Möller's ISP model for the FRG, the Swedish model constructed by Hårsman, Snickars, Holmberg, and colleagues, the model which resulted from research undertaken by Heida and Gordijn in the Netherlands, and finally the model which is currently being constructed at the NIDI. Our comparison shows that it seems a good strategy to model the behaviour of individuals rather than that of households. Furthermore, it is found that the multidimensional approach holds considerable promise for modelling household behaviour. Difficulties common to most models are the availability of data necessary to run the models, inconsistencies that arise when individuals of different sex are modelled separately, and finally the exponential increase in the number of states when a detailed household breakdown is considered.

9.1. Introduction

M A N Y Western countries have experienced major changes in observed life-styles in the last few decades. The traditional role of the family has weakened: members of married couples often live apart, cohabiting persons are not necessarily legally married, and cohabiting married persons are not always married to each other. This argument shows that an understanding of life-styles cannot be gained by studying marital status and nuptiality processes alone. Rather, the concept of a household should be used as an operationalization of the vague notion of 'life-style'.

Insight into future developments of households—and hence of life-style patterns—is of great value for policy makers in different fields: the housing market, social security, consumer durables, and energy, to name but a few. But the methodology to construct reliable household projection models has greatly lagged behind the increasing need for accurate forecasts. Several factors account for this, the major one being the slow progress that family and household demography has made so far. This in turn was caused by such

123

circumstances as differing concepts of the term household, a great variety of data collection strategies, and the lack of a general framework for the construction of household models.

This chapter tries to contribute to a better understanding of household modelling. In particular, it reviews dynamic household models that have been constructed recently. Four points are due here.

1. The household is here interpreted in quite a strict sense, which means that marital status and nuptiality are not considered as necessary concepts to be contained in the models. This, however, does not mean that they cannot provide useful insights into household modelling. Indeed we shall see that a relatively large number of models contain methodological or substantial issues borrowed from marital status models.

2. The models to be described here are purely demographic, that is, they contain demographic variables and processes only. No models will be dealt with which contain non-demographic variables and which describe interactions between demographic phenomena and economic, social, psychological, and cultural processes. Of course, those other processes cannot be regarded as being of minor importance in describing, explaining, and projecting household processes. However, our strict interpretation is based upon the idea that *structural* issues in household modelling have to be resolved before any *substantive* relationships can be studied adequately. In other words, we first analyse formal relationships between demographic entities, as a prelude to the examination of causal issues. A thorough analysis of patterns, disaggregated by demographic and household characteristics, may itself bring forth explanatory variables which should be considered.

3. Our focus on dynamics leads to a discussion of models that describe household *processes*. Models that treat (possibly changing) headship rates, for instance, thus fall outside the scope of this chapter.

4. Although not explicitly stated in the title of this chapter, it should be understood throughout that we limit ourselves to *macromodelling* efforts. Micromodels are discussed by Galler in chapter 10 of this volume.

In terms of the classification of household models presented in chapter 1 (Kuijsten and Vossen), our discussion concentrates on class 6 models. Five species of such purely demographic and dynamic macromodels were found: the Canadian model developed by Akkerman which was applied to Toronto and to the Haldimand–Norfolk region, Möller's ISP model for the Federal Republic of Germany, the Swedish model which was constructed by Snickars, Hårsman, Holmberg, and colleagues, the model which resulted from research undertaken by Heida and Gordijn at the Netherlands Research Centre for Physical Planning, and finally the dynamic household model which is currently being constructed at the NIDI.

First, in section 9.2, we discuss the five models in turn. Only their main features will be pointed out, details being contained in the references given. Section 9.3 gives a methodological comparison of the models. Topics to be treated include the unit of analysis, the household categories each model contains, the events it describes, and constraints imposed upon model variables. To conclude, section 9.4 gives lessons to be learnt from these modelling exercises.

9.2. Five dynamic household models

9.2.1. The Akkerman model

The household projection model described by Akkerman (1980, 1982) was developed within the framework of regional planning and regional population growth. It was applied to two Canadian regions: the metropolitan area of Toronto and the Haldimand–Norfolk region in Ontario. The model can be viewed as a further extension of the Leslie model. The idea is as follows.

The Akkerman model aims at calculating the number of households as well as their composition by age of the head. It does so by making use of a so-called household composition matrix, which gives the simultaneous distribution of ages of household members and those of heads of household. Define $a(i,j)$ as the average number of household members in age i per household whose head is in age j. The number $(a(i,j) + d(i,j))$ denotes, then, the average number of *all* persons in age i per household whose head is in age j, $d(i,j)$ being one for $i = j$ and zero otherwise. The household composition matrix $\mathbf{A}$ has the following structure

$$\mathbf{A} = \begin{bmatrix} a(1,1)+1 & a(1,2) & a(1,3) & \dots & a(1,n) \\ a(2,1) & a(2,2)+1 & a(2,3) & \dots & a(2,n) \\ a(3,1) & a(3,2) & a(3,3)+1 & \dots & a(3,n) \\ \vdots & \vdots & \vdots & & \vdots \\ a(n,1) & a(n,2) & a(n,3) & \dots & a(n,n)+1 \end{bmatrix}$$

where n is the number of age classes. For any point in time, the relation between the vector K which gives the age distribution of the population and the vector W of households by age of household head can be written as

$$K = \mathbf{A}.W.$$

Since $\mathbf{A}$ is non-singular (Akkerman, 1982, p. 84) it follows that

$$W = \mathbf{A}^{-1}.K, \tag{9.1}$$

or, the distribution of households by age of head can be found after multiplication of the inverse of the household composition matrix and the distribution of the population by age. Now the familiar Leslie projection model

$$K(t + 1) = \mathbf{P}.K(t), \tag{9.2}$$

in which **P** denotes the Leslie matrix, describes the population dynamics in the Akkerman model. The complete model consists of equations (9.1) and (9.2), in which matrices **A** and **P** could possibly be time-dependent.

Several analytical properties of **A** are discussed by Akkerman. For instance, the sum of elements in each column j equals the average number of persons per household whose head is in j. Also, the sum of elements in each row i of **A**, appropriately weighted, equals the average number of persons in age i per household.

9.2.2. The ISP model

Möller (1979, 1982) describes a household projection model which was developed at the 'Institut für angewandte Systemforschung und Prognose' (ISP) in Hanover (Federal Republic of Germany). Constructed within the broader framework of an economic model, the ISP model, too, is based on a usual population projection model in which the population by age and sex is simulated. This gives rise to the events of childbearing, mortality, and external migration.

First, the population is further broken down into dependent children and adults, using age-specific proportions. These proportions are estimated from data on the process of leaving the parental household. Next, another set of proportions, exogenously given, divides the adults further into two groups: married and non-married persons. Using an assumption on headship rates, the number of households is calculated on the basis of the male adults and the non-married female adults. This means that adult males and non-married adult females are always considered as the head of a household.

Given the number of households, the model finally calculates their distri-

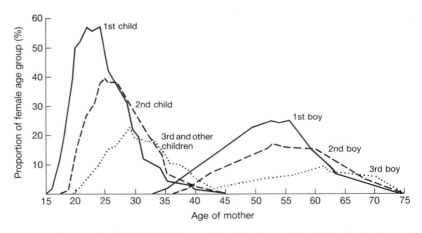

FIG. 9.1. Curves describing fertility and leaving home (boys) by mother's age for parities 1, 2, and 3+, 1974

bution by size. It distinguishes sizes ranging from one (one-married person) to five or more (a married couple with at least three children). Information on the presence of children in the household results from the following algorithm. The age-specific fertility rates, treated by the population projection model for individuals, are broken down according to parity: one, two, and three or more. A convolution of these age- and parity-specific fertility curves and the age-specific curves (age of the *child*!) which describe the process of leaving the parental home results in curves that depict this latter process broken down by age of the *mother* (see Figure 9.1).

Cumulating these curves over the age of the mother and taking the difference between cumulated fertility and cumulated 'home leaving', both by parity, enables one to construct a frequency distribution for the presence of one to three children by the mother's age (see Figure 9.2).

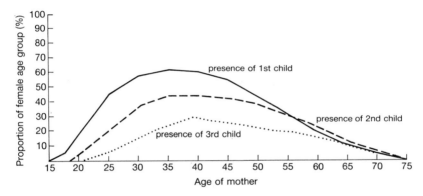

FIG. 9.2. Frequency distribution for 1, 2, and 3 children in mother's household, by age of mother

The same pattern by age of the male is found after a shift of the female curve in the age dimension over a distance equal to the average age difference between the spouses. Adding information on the marital status of the male results in a comprehensive frequency distribution of the household types that the model distinguishes (Figure 9.3). Finally, the model mixes yearly the appropriate numbers of persons with the corresponding frequencies of Figure 9.3. This results in a projection of households by type and size.

9.2.3. The Swedish model

During the late 1970s and early 1980s, a dynamic household model was constructed by Hårsman, Snickars, Holmberg, and others in Sweden. Initially, the project was aimed at projecting regional housing requirements for Stockholm. To date, several versions and applications of the model exist and the

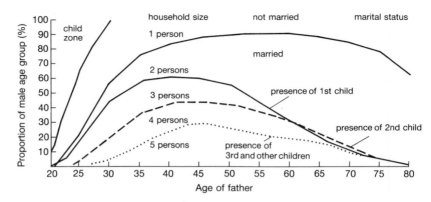

Source: Möller (1979).

FIG. 9.3. Frequency distribution of household types by age of the male

original ideas are updated continually. We shall discuss the model version described in a comprehensive report by Dellgran et al. (1984), as well as in Holmberg (1986). Bugge (1984) applies the method to Norwegian data and Zelle (1982) uses a related approach. Hårsman and Snickars (1983) provide a useful summary of the model.

The Swedish model is based on the observation of the distribution of the population by household category at two consecutive points in time, as well as the change of household status which individuals experience in the particular period. This means that the model follows individuals over a certain time interval, which gives rise to a matrix containing the transitions in household status. The two most important dimensions used to classify individuals by household category are household size (ranging from one to five or over) and whether or not a household contains dependent children. Combining these two dimensions yields nine classes.

The core of the model consists of an optimization algorithm:

min $\sum_{i,j} P(i,j;x) . ln(P(i,j;x)/R(i,j;x))$,

subject to $\sum_{j} P(i,j;x) = P(i,.;x)$

and $\sum_{i,j} P(i,j;x) = P(.,.;x)$,

where $P(i,j;x)$ = projected number of persons aged x having household status i and household status j at the beginning and at the end of the interval, respectively;

           $P(i,.;x)$ = number of persons aged x with initial household status i;

$P(.,.;x)$ = age distribution at the end of the interval, given exogenously;

$R(i,j;x)$ = number of persons aged x making a transition from i to j during an earlier period of time (a priori distribution).

The model makes use of the so-called Minimum Information Principle. It contains an option to constrain the number of projected households of a certain type. This leads to a supplementary condition

$$\sum_{i,x} w(j).P(i,j;x) = H(j),$$

with $w(j)$ = an appropriate weight, being the inverse of the household size of category j;

$H(j)$ = number of households in category j, given exogenously.

The model describes transitions that individuals make. However, a change in household status of an adult in a household of, say, three persons, is accompanied by certain transitions for the remaining members. This poses a consistency problem, which is analogous to the two-sex problem in models of marital status. Therefore, the Swedish model contains a number of additional restrictions. For instance, the number of dependent children in two-person households with children must be equal to the number of adults in that category. Also, the number of children in three-, four-, and five-person households with children should not be less than the number of households of that type. Finally, it should be mentioned that the model may easily be extended to account for births, deaths, and migrants, in order to produce complete projections.

9.2.4. The PRIMOS household model

Heida and Gordijn (1985) of the Netherlands Centre for the Study of Physical Planning constructed a dynamic household model especially suited to applications in the field of housing policy. The development of this so-called PRIMOS household model was commissioned by the Netherlands Ministry of Housing, Physical Planning, and Environment. Brouwer (chapter 15) gives an extensive description of the model. Therefore, we limit ourselves to some methodological issues.

In the PRIMOS household model individuals are distinguished according to age, sex, and household status. The latter dimension contains five basic classes: dependent child, single (never married or cohabited before), married or cohabiting, ever married/cohabited, and living in an institution. This results in a matrix of transitions as shown in Table 15.1 in chapter 15 (Brouwer).

The lack of data on changes in household status created severe difficulties.

Therefore, Heida and Gordijn made rigorous assumptions which were tested later. For instance, they assumed that, in the year 1971, alternative life-styles were scarce in the Netherlands. This enabled them to estimate transition probabilities for events 2, 6, 10, and 14 (see Table 15.1 in chapter 15, Brouwer) using statistics on first marriage, remarriage, divorce, and widowhood of that year. To estimate patterns for event 1 (dependent children starting a one-person household) they took first differences of the 1971 frequency distribution of unmarried persons living in the parental household, analogous to the approach followed in the ISP model. They fitted a curve through the age- and sex-specific patterns of each event for the year 1971: a lognormal curve for events 1, 2, and 6 and a negative exponential curve for events 10 and 14. Normal distributions were used for the entrance into an institution (3, 7, 11, and 15). Next, an assumption was made on the development of the various parameters of these curves in the period 1971–81. The model was tested against information on household structure available from the 1981 Housing Survey. A process of trial and error resulted in correct parameters and satisfying fits. Finally, an extrapolation of these parameters enabled the authors to make projections on households in the Netherlands for the period 1982–2000.

9.2.5. The NIDI household model

The last dynamic household model to be discussed in this section is the one which is currently being constructed at the Netherlands Interuniversity Demographic Institute (NIDI); see also Keilman and Van Dam (1987).

The purpose of the project is to apply techniques and insights of multidimensional demography to the field of household modelling. In particular, attempts are being made to construct a model which accurately describes the dynamics of households. This multidimensional approach facilitates the generation of a series of statistics describing the household-related lives of people. It includes such items as the household history of a cohort, the number of survivors of a given age in each household state, the number of person-years lived beyond a given age by household state, and the life expectancy at a given age by remaining years expected in each household state.

In the NIDI model, several useful concepts of earlier models are synthesized. For instance, it contains elements which bear strong resemblance to the consistency requirements of the Swedish model, whereas events are identified using a table of transitions, as in the PSC model. Also, Akkerman's household composition matrix is used.

The model describes individuals, broken down by age, sex, whether or not they are a dependent child, and household status. The latter contains five categories: single, consensual union (without dependent children), family (married couple with or without children), other family (at most two adults, not married to each other, with children), and non-family household (two or

TABLE 9.1. Table of events of NIDI household model

Household status after transition	Household status before transition						
	1	2	3	4	5	6	7
1. child in two-parent family	—	7	13	x	x	x	x
2. child in other family	1	—	14	x	x	x	x
3. single	2	8	—	19	22	24	27
4. consensual union	3	9	15	—	x	25	28
5. living with marriage partner	4	10	16	20	—	26	29
6. adult in other family	5	11	17	21	23	—	30
7. non-family household	6	12	18	x	x	x	—

— = no event
x = event (direct transition) impossible due to definition of household categories.

more unrelated adults, without children). Dependent children may live in a family, or belong to the group 'other family'. Thus the NIDI model contains seven household classes. This breakdown of individuals by household category was partly inspired by the concept of 'Minimal Household Units' described by Ermisch in chapter 3 (see also Overton and Ermisch, 1984). It is based on considerations with respect to decisions about financial and housing matters, and—no less—about household formation and dissolution.

The seven household categories give rise to the events expressed in Table 9.1.

Altogether, 30 possible events have been identified. Of course, in addition to these transitions between states, events may also be caused by transitions to and from the environment (for instance, death or emigration, or birth or immigration).

The model will be run with parameters that are derived from data describing all relevant events. It will make use of the 1984 ORIN Survey of the Netherlands, in which individuals were asked retrospectively to give their household biography in terms of transitions between the household types mentioned above (see Klijzing, chapter 4). These data permit the calculation of occurrence–exposure (o/e) rates, aggregated over time and over individuals. The observation criterium is of the period-cohort type, that is, events observed for a certain cohort within a certain period. The model transforms the o/e-rates into transition matrices that project the population by age, sex, and household status. The multiregional projection model described by Willekens and Drewe (1984) is used:

$$K(x+1,t+1) = (\mathbf{I} + \tfrac{1}{2}\mathbf{M}(x,t))^{-1} . (\mathbf{I} - \tfrac{1}{2}\mathbf{M}(x,t)) . K(x,t) +$$
$$(\mathbf{I} + \tfrac{1}{2}\mathbf{M}(x,t))^{-1} . O(x,t). \tag{9.3}$$

In equation (9.3), $K(x,t)$ is a vector of persons of a certain sex, aged x at time t, broken down by type of household. $\mathbf{M}(x,t)$ is a matrix of o/e-rates that applies to period $(t,t+1)$, **I** is the identity matrix and $O(x,t)$ is a vector of 'immigrants', that is, the absolute number of persons entering the system in the interval $(t,t+1)$, arranged by household status.

Equation (9.3) describes *individuals* by household category. However, many users of household projections need data on *households*. Therefore, Akkerman's household composition matrix will be used to group individuals in a certain household category. This means that equation (9.3) will be supplemented by the following equation for the households by age of the household head:

$$W(h,t) = \mathbf{A}(h,t)^{-1}.K(h,t)'. \qquad (9.4)$$

In expression (9.4), $\mathbf{A}(h,t)$ denotes the (n by n)-household composition matrix for household type h ($h = 1,2, \ldots ,7$), n being the number of ages. For single persons (household type 3 in Table 9.1), $\mathbf{A}(h,t)$ is equal to the identity matrix **I**. The vector $K(h,t)'$ gives the number of persons in household type h, arranged by age. It can be found after sorting out the appropriate elements of the stacked vector

$$(K(1,t),K(2,t), \ldots ,K(n,t)\,)^T,$$

calculated by (9.3).

As in the Swedish model, the NIDI model is confronted with consistency problems due to the modelling of an individual's behaviour, rather than that of a household. One of the purposes of the NIDI model is to give an accurate description of *events*; therefore, consistency constraints will be imposed upon the model equations of these events, rather than on those for the *stocks*, as was done in the Swedish model. Consistent behaviour of different subgroups will be found by taking a simple harmonic average of the initial numbers of (inconsistent) events and then adjusting the corresponding o/e-rates (see Keilman, 1985, for technical details).

9.3. A comparison of the five models

Table 9.2 compares different aspects of the household models discussed in the previous section. A few comments are due here.

The aspect of *system boundaries* gives an answer to the question as to which persons are covered by the model: those in private households only, as in Akkerman's model, the Swedish model, the NIDI model, and probably in the ISP model (see Möller, 1982, p. 47), or those in institutions as well (the PRIMOS model)? In all models the *unit of analysis* is the individual, although Akkerman (1982, p. 4, p. 82) asserts that his model also treats the household. This, however, is only true in so far as it concerns the clustering of individuals into groups at a certain point in time. The *definition* of the concept of a *household* is often unclear. This does not apply to Möller (1982,

TABLE 9.2. A comparison of five household models

	Akkerman	ISP model	Swedish model	PSC model	NIDI model
1. Purpose	regional planning	income and consumption	housing requirements	housing requirements	general
2. System boundaries	private households only	probably private households only	private households only	private and non-private households	private households only
3. Unit of analysis	individual	individual	individual	individual	individual
4. Household definition	not given	income and consumption unit	not given	not given	housekeeping unit
5. Household categories	1. age head 2. average household size	1. child/adult 2. married/not married 3. head/member	1. whether in household with child 2. household size 3. head/member	1. child/single/married (coh.)/formerly married (coh.)/in institution	1. single/consensual union/married couple/other family/non-family household 2. child/adult 3. (average household size)
6. No. of household events	0	1	72 (transitions)	9	30
7. Household data	household structure from survey	leaving home, age-specific fertility	transitions (linked structures)	vital statistics + household structure to test model	events on changing household type + household structure
8. Controllability	excellent	good	poor	excellent	fair
9. Internal constraints	no	no	yes, on stocks	yes, on flows	yes, on flows
10. External constraints	yes	yes	yes	unclear	no
11. Iterations	no	no	yes?	no?	one-cycle adjustments
12. Analytical properties	excellent	problematic	fair	good	good
13. Other household categories	flexible	difficult	difficult	difficult	difficult

p. 40), who considers the household as an income and consumption (economic) unit. The NIDI model follows the ORIN definition, in which a household is described as a group of persons, sharing a main room and regularly dining together (housekeeping unit).

With respect to the *household categories* that each model contains in its stock variables, an increasing level of detail may be observed when reading from left to right in Table 9.2. Möller does not distinguish cohabiting couples or one-parent families, and the Swedish model disregards possible relationships between household members. The Akkerman model and the NIDI model contain the variable of average household size in their stock variables, measured on a ratio scale rather than on a nominal scale. Of course, the different purposes of the various models are portrayed in the different choices of values for the household variables.

The Akkerman model does not describe any *household events*, that is, events defined by transitions from one household state to another. The ISP model treats just one event, the process of leaving the parental home. The nine household categories of the Swedish model give rise to $9 \times 8 = 72$ different types of transitions, at least in theory. It is unclear how many of these are observed in reality during the 5-year projection interval. Given the experience of the PRIMOS model, in which some of the theoretically identified events are virtually absent in practice, it could be expected that some of the 72 transitions of the Swedish model and some of the 30 events in the NIDI model may be neglected. Note that the Swedish model does not calculate events, but only transitions. Hence, this model does not distinguish between single and multiple events individuals may experience during the unit projection interval. For one-year periods the difference between the numbers of transitions and the numbers of events are only of minor importance. The deviations grow with increasing interval length.[1] The PRIMOS model does not distinguish between events and transitions, or, equivalently, this model may be considered as a first order approximation of the correct (multidimensional) model.[2]

With respect to the *input data* necessary to run the models, Table 9.2 shows a great diversity. Obviously, the Swedish model and the NIDI model need data that are not generally available. The aspect of *parameter controllability* shows the extent to which one can guide the model's behaviour, a necessary requirement when making variant projections, or even forecasts. The Swedish model has the drawback of being less transparent than the others, caused by the a priori transition matrix R and the objective function in which it appears. The NIDI model's behaviour can be controlled adequately (unless the consistency algorithm produces heavy adjustments of the a priori flows). In particular, the NIDI model is able to simulate observed household structures accurately, given observed o/e-rates. For the Swedish model this validity is much less certain. Although Heida and Gordijn (1985) did not report so, the PRIMOS model contains an algorithm to reach consistency between the numbers of males and females that marry or start to cohabit in a particular year. *External constraints* in the form of results of population projections by age and sex are imposed on the Akkerman model, the ISP model, and the Swedish model. However, the question arises as to whether the population covered by these projections corresponds with the population in the household model. Some doubt may be expressed, since these three models treat individuals in private households only. The Swedish model probably uses *iterations* to arrive at a solution, which creates a problem when *analytical properties* of the model are investigated. Indeed, the relative simplicity of his model enabled Akkerman (1982, pp. 106 ff.) to examine the conditions for ergodicity of household populations. His model, given by (9.1) and (9.2) in section 9.2.1, fits entirely within the framework of time-discrete linear systems. Hence, modern systems control theory may also be used to study the properties of the Akkerman model.

Finally, it should be mentioned that Akkerman's model is very flexible, in that it may easily be applied in situations that differ from the one it was constructed for. For example, Akkerman (1985) recently introduced region of residence of the household as one of the model characteristics. The remaining four models need—sometimes considerable—reformulations.

9.4. Conclusion

This chapter reviews dynamic household models, thus seeking to contribute to a better understanding of household modelling methodology. We limited ourselves to macromodels of purely demographic character. Only five models could be traced, all of them constructed after the mid-1970s. This indicates that macromodelling of dynamic household behaviour is a relatively young line of research in demography. But the necessity of having dynamic household models is evident: changes in household structures cannot be adequately understood unless one studies the events that cause these changes. A few general points emerge from this review, admittedly biased by our own point of view.

First, it seems a good strategy to model the behaviour of *individuals*. An alternative could be to follow *households* through time. However, the main difficulty with this approach is that households may dissolve, thus creating two or more different entities. Then the question arises as to which household should be followed as the original one, and which household constitutes a new entity. Individuals do not, of course, suffer from this phenomenon.

Second, the multidimensional approach holds considerable promise for the future of modelling household behaviour. Indeed, three of the five models studied here applied the multidimensional approach—either implicitly (the Swedish model and the PRIMOS model) or explicitly (the NIDI model). The multidimensional approach in household modelling attaches, to every individual, a household state that he or she occupies. The passing from one household state to another introduces household events, and hence the dynamic character of the model. Multidimensional household models are thus not only able to describe household structures at a certain point in time, they can also calculate the household events individuals experience in a given period.

However, and this is our last point, a few difficulties common to almost all models seem to exist. The most important problem is posed by the availability of data necessary to run the models. Statistical bureaus do not routinely collect household information on individuals. Therefore, the models treated in this chapter rely on indirect estimations (the ISP model and the PRIMOS model), on the linkage of successive census registrations and vital registers (the Swedish model), or on a special household survey (the NIDI model). It seems appropriate that, given the often expressed need for better household forecasting methodology, additional means for improved household data collection are provided. Another problem we encountered is that of inconsistencies that are bound to arise when individuals of different sex are modelled separately. The NIDI model solves this two-sex problem in quite a simple manner, but further research is needed to assess the adequacy of this approach. In particular, one may study inconsistencies in household formation and dissolution models in a manner analogous to treatments of the two-sex problem in the context of marital status projection models. Finally, it should be mentioned that, considering the size of the existing models, more detailed household studies can probably not be pursued using the methods described in this chapter. For instance, the NIDI model classifies individuals in seven different household categories, and the Swedish model even uses nine classes. Combining the household dimension with those of sex and age (some 100 age classes are not exceptional) leads to 1,500–2,000 subcategories the modeller has to consider. A higher level of detail is likely to pose various severe problems. Indeed, in the NIDI model, household size was not introduced as a nominal variable (which would have caused an exponential increase in the number of states), but rather as a ratio scale, using Akkerman's household composition matrix.

The problems identified above suggest that the study of alternative modelling strategies could be extremely useful. For example, the microsimulation approach discussed by Galler (chapter 10) avoids problems of consistency and exponentially growing model size. Therefore, it is useful to memorize here the point made by Wachter (1986), who states that micromodelling and macromodelling (as well as analytic treatments) are far better used in tandem on a single problem, than viewed as alternatives.

Notes

1. Assuming a linear distribution of events during the unit projection interval having length h, the relation between the matrix of transition probabilities $\mathbf{P}$ and the matrix of o/e-rates $\mathbf{M}$ is

$$\mathbf{P} = (\mathbf{I} + \tfrac{1}{2}h\mathbf{M})^{-1}.(\mathbf{I} - \tfrac{1}{2}h\mathbf{M}).$$

Expanding $(\mathbf{I} + \tfrac{1}{2}h\mathbf{M})^{-1}$ in a power series gives

$$\mathbf{P} = \mathbf{I} - h\mathbf{M} + (h\mathbf{M})^2/2 - (h\mathbf{M})^3/4 + (h\mathbf{M})^4/8 - \ldots \tag{N1}$$

A model based upon the assumption of constant intensities

$$\mathbf{P} = \exp(-h\mathbf{M})$$

results in

$$\mathbf{P} = \mathbf{I} - h\mathbf{M} + (h\mathbf{M})^2/2 - (h\mathbf{M})^3/6 + (h\mathbf{M})^4/24 - \ldots \tag{N2}$$

Now the matrix $\mathbf{Q}=(\mathbf{I} - \mathbf{P})$ contains on its main diagonal probabilities of experiencing a transition during the interval, while each off-diagonal element contains the value $-p(i,j)$, the opposite of the elements of $\mathbf{P}$. Hence the structures of $\mathbf{Q}$ and $\mathbf{M}$ are identical. Using the expressions given above, one may evaluate the difference between $\mathbf{M}$ and $\mathbf{Q}$ in the case of the linear model as well as for the exponential model.
2. Formulae (N1) and (N2) in note 1 show that for $h=1$, $\mathbf{Q}$ equals $\mathbf{M}$ when terms in $(h\mathbf{M})$ of order two or higher are disregarded.

References

AKKERMAN, A. (1980). On the relationship between household composition and population age distribution, *Population Studies* 34(3), 525–34.
—— (1982). *Demographic Input to Regional Planning: Towards a Household Analysis of Regional Population Growth* (Demosystems, Edmonton).
—— (1985). The household-composition matrix as a notion in multiregional forecasting of population and households, *Environment and Planning A* 17(3), 355–71.
BUGGE, L. S. (1984). Husholdning—struktur og prognose: en metodisk tilnaerming (Household—structure and forecast: a methodological approach), unpublished paper (Institute of Sociology, Oslo University, Oslo).
DELLGRAN, P., I. HOLMBERG, AND P. OLOVSSON (1984). *Hushållsbildning och bostadsefterfrågan* (Household developments and housing requirements), Demographic Research Unit Reports no. 16 (Gothenburg University, Gothenburg).
HÄRSMAN, B. AND F. SNICKARS (1983). A method for disaggregate household forecasts, *Tijdschrift voor economische en sociale geografie TESG* 74(4), 282–90.
HEIDA, H. AND H. GORDIJN (1985). Het PRIMOS-huishoudensmodel: analyse en prognose van de huishoudensontwikkeling in Nederland (The PRIMOS household model: analysis and forecasts of household trends in the Netherlands) (Ministerie van Volkshuisvesting, Ruimtelijke Ordening en Milieubeheer, The Hague).
HOLMBERG, I. (1986). Household and housing forecasting models, in: J. Bongaarts, T. K. Burch, and K. W. Wachter (eds.), *Family Demography: Methods and their Application* (Oxford University Press, Oxford).

KEILMAN, N. W. (1985). Internal and external consistency in multidimensional population projection models, *Environment and Planning A* 17, 1473–98.

—— AND J. VAN DAM (1987). A dynamic household model: an application of multidimensional demography to life styles in the Netherlands (Netherlands Interuniversity Demographic Institute, The Hague).

MÖLLER, K. P. (1979). Die Entwicklung der Haushaltsstrukturen in der Bundesrepublik bis zum Jahre 2000, in: R. Mackensen (ed.), *Empirische Untersuchungen zum generativen Verhalten* (Berlin).

—— (1982). *Die Entwicklung von Bevölkerung und Haushalten in der Bundesrepublik Deutschland bis zum Jahre 2000* (Duncker and Humblot, Berlin).

OVERTON, E. AND J. ERMISCH (1984). Minimal household units, *Population Trends* 35, 18–22.

WACHTER, K. W. (1986). Microsimulation of household cycles, in: J. Bongaarts, T. K. Burch, and K. W. Wachter (eds.), *Family Demography: Methods and their Application* (Oxford University Press, Oxford).

WILLEKENS, F. J. AND P. DREWE (1984). A multiregional model for regional demographic projection, in: H. ter Heide and F. J. Willekens (eds.), *Demographic Research and Spatial Policy* (Academic Press, London), 309–36.

ZELLE, K. (1982). Modelle zur Haushaltsstrukturschätzung, *Mitteilungsblatt Österreichische Gesellschaft für Statistik und Informatik* 12(45), 1–12.

10

Microsimulation of household formation and dissolution

H. Galler[1]

ABSTRACT

Microsimulation provides an approach to simultaneously modelling popula-tion and household structures. Differentiated hypotheses on individual behaviour can be applied to explain changes in household composition. The microsimulation model of the Sonderforschungsbereich 3 is designed to allow projections of population, family, and household structures. Transi-tion probabilities in the model have been estimated from cross-sectional data. In general, simulation results appear to be satisfactory, but for some sub-groups estimates are somewhat biased. It is our intention to improve the structure of the model when longitudinal data is available.

10.1. Problems of modelling household structures

A GENERAL methodological problem of modelling household and family dynamics is to maintain consistency between household and family structures and the corresponding population structure. Since households and families consist of individuals, changes in the structure of the population induce cor-responding changes in households and families. At the same time, population dynamics depend to a large extent on household and family structure. This implies that demographic structures cannot be modelled independently, on the level of individuals, families, and households, but the interdependencies between these structures have to be included to prevent inconsistencies. How-ever, most approaches to modelling households and families start from given population projections.

Some aggregate approaches use headship rates in population subgroups to model changes in the household structure dependent on population forecasts (for example, Herberger and Borries, 1970). However, no assumptions are provided that would link these ratios to individual behaviour and that would allow the deduction of their change if, for instance, mortality or fertility changes. On the other hand, applying constant ratios to varying population structures results in inconsistencies, since the applied ratios imply a popula-tion structure different from the one they are applied to.

Other, more sophisticated approaches (see for instance the work of Möller, 1982, discussed by Keilman in chapter 9) try to obtain the structural information needed for household forecasts from more detailed population projections. By differentiation with regard to marital status and number of children, family structures are derived from population forecasts. Children become members of the mother's family when they are born. 'Splitoffs' of adult children are taken into consideration. But with this approach, difficulties arise if incomplete families or multi-family households are included in the model. Facing the multitude of possible household compositions, further disaggregation of this approach leads to unmanageable models.

Even in very disaggregated models of this type, the problem of finding a causal explanation of demographic change is not solved in a fully satisfactory manner. In such models, survival curves play a major role; they describe, for instance, the probability of children leaving the parental home and forming households of their own. Again, observed data are used, but the causal relationships behind the figures are not introduced explicitly in the model. However, it can be shown empirically that the process of leaving the parental household is closely related to marriage decisions, educational level, and labour force participation (Ott, 1984). If behaviour changes in these areas, household membership curves will also change. However, since these relationships are not included, models are incapable of catching these effects and parameters have to be adapted exogenously.

All these problems demonstrate the need for an approach that allows simultaneous modelling of population and household structures and their dynamics in a unified framework. Only then can the consequences of demographic processes and individual behaviour for the family and household structure be inferred directly and consistently. But this cannot be done feasibly on the group level, since a multitude of explanatory variables must be considered that would lead to an unmanageable number of groups.

We will not present here an extensive discussion of the microsimulation approach and its application to household dynamics. A recent overview was given by Clarke (1986). Our discussion will be fairly general, and we will focus on the model which was developed at the Sonderforschungsbereich 3.

10.2. The concept of microsimulation

In the concept of microsimulation, population structures are represented by microdata of individuals that are grouped into families and households. Data of this type can be obtained, for instance, from the German Mikrozensus or the Current Population Survey in the United States. Both cover members of randomly selected households. In such a data base, each individual is linked to a certain family and household or to an institution. Consequently, aggregate information on population, family, and household structures can be obtained from the same microdata file by simple aggregation.

In a dynamic microsimulation model, the relevant demographic processes are simulated for each individual in the sample by stochastic Monte Carlo techniques. Besides the deterministic process of ageing, other events are simulated stochastically using conditional probabilities. A number drawn from a uniform distribution of the interval $(0,1)$ is compared with the specific conditional probability, and an event is assumed to occur when the drawn number does not exceed that probability. For instance, death is simulated for an individual if the drawn number does not exceed the probability of dying specific for that individual. Similar procedures are used to simulate fertility, marriage, divorce, and transitions between private households and/or institutions.

Such a stochastic simulation process does not provide deterministic forecasts for individual biographies. However, the biographies generated by the model can be interpreted as realizations of the stochastic process described by the model, which is assumed to underlie these biographies, too. Conceptually, both simulated and observed biographies are interpreted as realizations of the same stochastic process. Microdata files generated by the simulation process are therefore interpreted as random samples from the population that would have been observed if the processes modelled would have been effective in the real world.

Due to the stochastic approach, simulated and observed biographies will differ randomly. But according to the law of large numbers, random deviations will tend to cancel each other out when simulation results for different microunits (individuals, families, households) are aggregated. Correspondingly, summarizing statistics can be estimated for the total population or subgroups thereof with little error if a sufficiently large sample is used (Galler, 1983).

Since in the sample each individual is linked to a specific family and household, the consequences of demographic events on the level of individuals for family and household composition are obtained without any problem. If, on the individual level, the birth of a child is simulated, a new data record is created for that child and added to the corresponding family and household in the microdata file. In case the death of a person is simulated, the corresponding record will be deleted from the file. This amounts to changing the composition of the respective family and household correspondingly. Thus, by definition, consistency between population structure and family and household structure is maintained in a microsimulation model.

Besides the 'biological' processes of ageing, fertility, and mortality, family and household structures are changed by transitions of persons between households, or to and from institutions. Here, the formation of new households by children leaving their parents' household is most important. Families and households are split when couples get divorced. Finally, the household composition is changed when persons move into institutions such as sanatoriums or homes for the elderly. In the simulation process, such transitions are modelled by simply changing the links of individuals to households or institutions. If a person moves from one household to another, the corresponding record is deleted from the previous household and added to the new one. The same procedure is applied for transitions between households and institutions.

Transitions are based on individual decisions. At least in principle, the causal relationships behind such decisions can be modelled easily in a microsimulation model, since simulation takes place on the level of individuals. Compared to other approaches, the advantage of microsimulation in this context is that many explanatory variables can be introduced, allowing for rather detailed hypotheses. Since the size of a microsimulation model is not determined by the number of variables included, but by the size of the sample, all necessary information can be stored with each individual, given its availability. This makes it possible to base simulation on theoretically well-developed hypotheses. The modelling approach imposes almost no restrictions. However, modelling efforts are constrained by the limitations of empirical data.

For the microsimulation of household and family composition, additional assumptions are required beyond those used in traditional demographic models. First, conditional probabilities for an individual either to stay with the household in a given situation or to move are needed. For movers, the type of transition must be determined. Additionally, assumptions concerning the structure of families and households are required. If the characteristics of the head of household are dependent variables or are used as explanatory variables, a head must be selected in the simulation process for each household. This information can be observed in the original sample, but an assumption is required for all households created in the simulation process.

This points to a problem of the microsimulation approach. As far as its formal structure is concerned, it is less restrictive and allows for more complex structural relationships than other approaches presently available. Assumptions regarding theoretically important causal factors can be implemented in a differentiated way. This also implies a comparatively high flexibility of the approach with regard to modifying the model structure. The relations used can easily be adapted to changing behaviour or to modified theoretical explanations. This, however, also means that microsimulation requires more modelling efforts and poses higher demands on empirical data.

In other models, for instance in headship rate models, simple ratios which can be obtained from cross-sectional data are used for forecasting. In the microsimulation approach, however, dynamic models of individual behaviour based on longitudinal data become feasible. To exploit fully this advantage, comparatively large efforts are necessary both in theoretical and in empirical work. Due to the relatively complex model structure, computer runs of microsimulation models also tend to be more expensive than those of other, simpler models.

10.3. The micromodel of the Sonderforschungsbereich 3

The demographic microsimulation model developed at the Sonderfors-chungsbereich 3 (University of Frankfurt, Federal Republic of Germany) is part of a more general modelling effort in the field of the analysis of income distribution and social policy. An attempt is made to use quantitative simulation techniques in analysing the dynamics of the personal income distribution and the efficiency of measures of distributional and social policy. In this context, demographic structures and their changes play a major role, since they form the basis of personal income distribution. Thus, the primary purpose of the demographic modelling efforts is to provide differentiated forecasts of demographic structures as a basis for distributional analyses.

The basic structure of the demographic microsimulation model was initially developed by Hecheltjen (1974). It contained a description of demographic processes on the individual level but it was restricted to nuclear families. This means that individuals were grouped into families of parents and dependent children. At the age of 18, children were split off from the parental family, and formed a unit of their own. Thus, no household structures could be simulated with that first version.

Steger (1980) extended the model to families and households by linking persons to families, private households, or institutions and by introducing assumptions for the transitions between these entities. In particular, conditional probabilities were added concerning unmarried children leaving the parental household, the formation of new households at the time of marriage, and transitions between households and institutions. This model was used for projections of the population and of the family and household structure. It still forms the basis of the microsimulation model currently in use. Some efforts are presently being made to improve the modelling of household dynamics.

The microdata file used for the simulation contains a household record for each household and one record for each person in the household. Besides other socio-economic variables, the household record contains the size of the household and a pointer variable indicating the head of household. In the records of the household members, a family number links each person to a family. In addition, personal characteristics are recorded, such as the basic information on gender, age, marital status, duration of present marriage, number of children (both ever-born and still living in the household), and the relation to the head of household. The records of married persons contain pointers to the spouse, those of children point to their parents. This makes it easy to reconstruct family relations.

TABLE 10.1. Transitions between household states in the Sfb 3 Microsimulation Model

Origin	Event	Destination — Private household: Previous household (Previous family)	New family	New household	Household of spouse	Institution (1)	(2)	(3)	(4)	(5)	(6)
Private household	no change	+									
	fertility	+									
	leaving home			+							
	marriage		+	+							
	divorce		+	+	+						
	entering institution					+	+	+	+	+	+
Institution	leaving institution										
1. Education		+				+					
2. Sanatorium		+					+				
3. Old age		+						+			
4. Hostels		+							+		
5. Military		+								+	
6. Other		+									+

Since persons do not stay forever in institutions such as hospitals, schools, or military barracks, but at some point in time return to their original households, individuals leaving a household for an institution are not 'physically' removed from the household but are marked as being absent. Then, the person is not counted in the household but is treated as a separate unit. However, when leaving the institution, that person will be reintegrated into his or her previous household.

An overview of the transitions covered by the model is given in Table 10.1. In the original state, each individual is affiliated to a private household or an institution. Starting from private households, transitions may be induced by demographic events—childbearing, marriage, divorce—or the decision to move on the part of either children leaving the parental home or persons entering an institution. Individuals linked to an institution either remain in the institution or move back to their previous household. Thus, formation of new families and households always starts from an existing private household.

The general structure of the demographic simulation process is presented in Figure 10.1. After a household has been read from the input file, the demographic processes on the individual level that might result in a person leaving the household are simulated first. Here, the first step is ageing and the simulation of mortality. Age is increased for each person. Using mortality probabilities broken down by gender, age, and marital status, a decision is taken whether the person survives or will be marked as deceased. In a similar procedure, divorces are simulated using probabilities specified by duration of marriage. Transitions into and out of institutions are simulated depending on sex, age, and marital status and, in the case of military service, school attendance.

In the next step, using marriage probabilities disaggregated by gender, age, marital status, and school attendance, unmarried men and women are selected randomly as marriage candidates. While the empirically observed frequencies are applied for women, those for men are increased by some exogenously set factor to guarantee an oversupply of males on the marriage market. This procedure was chosen to ensure that all women to be married can be matched to a proper spouse. In a final step, for all children still living in their parents' household and not participating in the marriage market, splitting off and formation of new households is simulated. Here, probabilities conditional on gender, age, and marital status are applied.

In the first block, individuals are only marked to split off from a household. Actual transitions are performed in the second block by deleting the corresponding records from the household and linking them to a new household. Household variables of both households are updated accordingly and family links are reorganized. However, transitions into already existing households are not simulated since these are negligible in the Federal

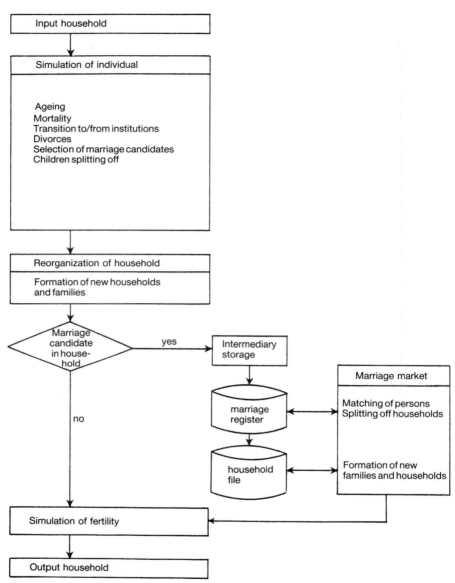

FIG. 10.1. The basic structure of the micromodel

Republic of Germany. But in principle, such transitions could be included in the model using a matching process similar to that implemented for the marriage market.

If a person has been marked to be a marriage candidate, the corresponding household is stored in an intermediary file. The relevant characteristics of the individual, together with a pointer to the household, are entered into a register file and simulation is continued with the next household.

If there are no marriage candidates in the household, fertility is simulated in a final block for all female household members in the corresponding age bracket. Birth is simulated stochastically, depending on marital status, parity, and completed duration of marriage for married women, or age for unmarried women. In the event of a birth, a record for a child is created and added to the household. If necessary, the family structure is reorganized. Finally, the household is transferred either to other simulation modules or directly to the output data file.

After all households from the input data file have been processed, the marriage register contains information on every individual participating in the marriage market. Starting from women, men are selected using matching probabilities conditional on age, occupational status, and marital status. Nationality is not used for matching due to deficiencies of the available data. For each woman the 'desired' characteristics of the spouse are determined randomly, using a joint probability distribution for the two partners, and a male meeting these requirements is selected from the register. If no full match is reached, a second-best solution is chosen based on a distance function.

Since marriage candidates are matched to form a new couple, consistency between the number of males and females marrying is automatically guaranteed. However, in the present version of the model, no feedback is incorporated that would link individual marriage behaviour to the market conditions. The propensity to marry as well as the matching probabilities governing the allocation process are set exogenously in the simulation. Therefore, these parameters are independent of the number of individuals available for marriage as well as their characteristics. Only some adaption to the market conditions takes place in the matching process, when, due to a short supply of males, some matches cannot be formed according to the exogenous matching probabilities. In such a case, 'second-best' matches are formed using a distance function. In addition, adjustments of the parameters to changes in the population structure have to be provided exogenously.

When a couple has been matched, it is randomly decided whether it will form a new household or stay with one of the two original households. Depending on the outcome of the random drawing, individuals are moved between households and household variables are updated accordingly. Children of both spouses belonging to their families are moved together with their parents. Households containing no other marriage candidates are then passed to the simulation of fertility and output from the demographic simulation module. In case there is still another marriage candidate in the household, it is written back to intermediary storage, and address pointers are updated accordingly.

After every woman on the marriage market has been married, males who have not been selected for marriage are 'left over', since men are over-sampled. For them, splitting off the parental household is simulated by the same procedure as the one used for those not having entered the marriage market. This procedure had to be adopted since the probabilities of splitting off have been calculated, conditional on the fact that persons involved do marry in the course of the given year. Therefore, marriages must be simulated first and then splitting off of unmarried children can take place. Again, new households are formed for those leaving the parental household. All households are passed through the simulation of fertility and are also transferred from the demographic simulation module.

10.4. Parameters of the model

In the microsimulation model, probability tables are now used for the simulation of demographic processes containing the probabilities of specific events conditional on explanatory variables. This is quite similar to the approach of more traditional demographic models. However, as can be seen from Table 10.2, more detailed tables than the usual ones are employed. Probabilities for mortality, nuptiality, fertility, and divorce have been taken from official statistics or have been calculated from official data. In some cases

TABLE 10.2. Probability tables used in the micromodel

Simulation step	Observation period
Mortality	by sex and age, 1969 and 1970[b] by marital status, age and sex, 1971–1978[a]
Marriage	never-married: by sex and age, 1969–1978[a] others: by sex and age, 1969–1978[a] matching probabilities by sex, age, and marital status, 1969–1975[a]
Divorce	by marriage duration, 1969–1978[b]
Fertility	married women: by marriage duration and parity, 1969–1978[b] unmarried women: by age, 1969–1978[a]
Splitting off	from household: by sex, calculated from cross-sectional data of the Mikrozensus 1969[a] from/to institution: by sex, calculated from cross-sectional data of the Mikrozensus 1969 and Census 1970[a]

[a] Own calculation.
[b] Material of the Federal Statistical Office.
Source: Steger (1980).

unpublished material had to be used.

More complications arose with regard to the transition probabilities between households and for those between households and institutions. They have been calculated by Steger (1980) using cross-sectional information from the German Mikrozensus of 1969 and the National Census of 1970. Longitudinal data that would have been more appropriate for the model were not available at that time. Since the situation has not improved substantially, simulations are still run with these parameter values. However, attempts have been made in the meantime to check the validity of the model using longitudinal data from surveys.

In principle, the calculations by Steger were based on a comparison of the percentage of individuals of different age cohorts living in different types of households or institutions in 1969 (a similar approach was followed by Möller, and by Heida and Gordijn—compare chapter 9 by Keilman). After accounting for marriages and deaths as well as controlling gender and marital status, the change in the proportion of persons living in a given type of household was used to estimate net transition probabilities. Additional explanatory variables, such as school attendance or labour force participation, could not be included since the necessary information was not available and the approach on the group level did not allow further differentiation.

From such calculations, only unidirectional net flows can be estimated. In addition, age-specific effects cannot be separated from cohort-specific effects. However, these are probably similar for neighbouring age cohorts and are therefore differenced out when changes between cohorts are analysed. Another deficiency is that net transitions had to be modelled, not the bi-directional gross flows of individuals. After all, doubts still remain with regard to the validity of some such calculations based on cross-sections for the simulation of household dynamics.

To validate the approach, in addition to information on household composition, further data on all persons having left or entered the household since 1975 were collected in 1980 for a sample of about 4,000 private households by retrospective interviews. With these data it is possible to estimate the transition rates to and from private households (compare Ott, 1984). However, households which were dissolved during that period are not covered by the survey. Also, due to limited funds, no exact dating of events was possible. Thus, the survey data have some deficiencies of their own.

In Table 10.3, the proportion of sample households is given in which, during the 1975–80 period, at least one person entered or left the household, not counting births or deaths. There are only few transitions into existing households. A substantial part of them are spouses entering a household. Excluding these cases, only very few transitions into households are observed. These figures may be biased somewhat downward if persons who temporarily left a household were not reported as exits or re-entrants. But even accounting for that, it can be concluded that primarily transitions out of

TABLE 10.3. Households with persons entering or leaving the household, 1975–1980, except for birth and death

Age of head	Cases	Transiton (%)	
		into household	out of household
Under 20	24	8.3	4.2
20–30	488	2.7	5.9
30–40	601	1.0	7.3
40–50	822	1.6	16.8
50–60	697	1.0	24.0
60+	1,450	0.3	7.2
Total	4,082	1.1	11.9

Source: Survey data (see text).

existing households occur. A modelling approach based on net outflows, like that of Steger, will then not produce severe errors.

In the survey, not all information necessary to compute transition rates had been collected. However, some estimates can be produced with a few auxiliary assumptions concerning the distribution of exits over time. Figure 10.2 shows such estimates together with the corresponding values calculated by Steger. Exit rates of unmarried children for 1975–80 tend to exceed those computed from the cross-section of 1969. Presumably, these differences are not primarily caused by biases in the calculations by Steger, but to a large extent reflect an increasing propensity to leave the parental household in the 1970s. Simulations based on the rates calculated by Steger will therefore probably be biased toward underestimating the number of small households of younger persons. However, due to the small sample size and the assumptions needed, the survey estimates are not very dependable either. Therefore, the cross-sectional estimates are still used in the micro-simulation model.

However, improved longitudinal data will be available in the near future. Information on the process of household formation and dissolution is gathered in panel studies which are now being conducted at the Sonder-forschungsbereich 3 (Hanefeld, 1984) and by other institutions (Pohl, 1982; Kaufmann *et al.* 1982). Longitudinal data on the biographies of selected cohorts including data on household and family affiliation are available from a retrospective life history survey conducted at the Sonderforschungsbereich 3 (Mayer, 1984). Finally, the Mikrozensus of the Federal Statistical Office has a partial panel design, which could be exploited for such analyses if the data were made available to science.

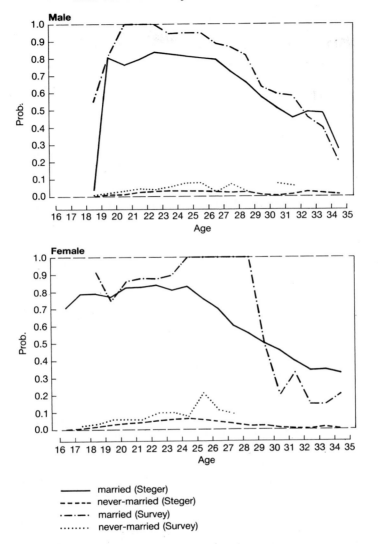

FIG. 10.2. Age-specific transition probabilities for leaving the parental household

10.5. Some simulation results

Attempts to evaluate demographic models have to deal with two major problems: definitional inconsistencies and differing assumptions with regard to exogenous parameters. First of all, different models use divergent definitions of the population covered, ranging, for instance, from the 'German population in private households' to the 'German population including institutionalized persons' or the 'Total population including foreigners'. At the same time, different definitions of households are used based on either economic criteria or the residence of individuals. Depending on which definitions are used, different structures will be found that are not directly comparable.

A second problem consists of differing assumption concerning the values of exogenous parameters. Since parameters like those for mortality, nuptiality, and fertility are defined exogenously in all demographic models, but at the same time are of crucial importance for the results, different assumptions will lead to different results that cannot be compared directly.

Similar difficulties arise when ex-post simulations are compared with actual data. Here, differing definitions in the model and in the statistical data pose similar problems. Since the results achieved by a model depend on both the model structure and on the exogenous parameter values, we can, by comparing simulation results with actual data, only infer the combined effect of both the model structure and the parameter values. The modelling approach can be validated on its own by performing ex-post simulation using the observed values for the parameters of the model. Remaining differences between model results and actual values can then be ascribed to the modelling approach.

The following tables give simulation results for 1978, together with the actual values for a simulation that started from the 1969 microdata file of the Sonderforschungsbereich 3. This is a sample of about 120,000 persons or 0.2 per thousand of the population. Starting in 1969, simulations were run through 1978 using the observed values for the model parameters as far as they were available. In particular, the observed probabilities for fertility, nuptiality, and mortality have been used. However, for the transitions between households, constant probabilities as calculated by Steger have been applied.

The start file of the simulation is representative of the residential population in 1969 with households defined according to the concept of family residence which is basically an economic concept. During the course of simulation, no provisions were made for migration. Thus population gains by net immigration are not covered by the model. Additionally, the total number of children born is underestimated since children born to foreign women who immigrated during that period are not taken into account. This results in an underestimate of the overall population in 1978 by 2.3 million as compared with the population statistics for that year, as shown in Table 10.4 (compare Helm and Lempert, 1982).

Due to the differences in population size, comparisons of absolute numbers are not very instructive. Therefore, the relative shares of subgroups are compared. The age distribution in Table 10.4 clearly shows underestimates in the

TABLE 10.4. Population in 1978 by gender, age, and marital status

	Total		Never-married		Married		Other	
	Wb78[b]	Sim[a]	Wb78[b]	Sim[a]	Wb78[b]	Sim[a]	Wb78[b]	Sim[a]
Males	(000s) 29,210.4	28,075.0	(%) 43.6	42.3	51.7	52.9	4.7	4.8
Age	(%)							
0–5	5.2	4.2	100.0	100.0	—	—	—	—
5–10	6.9	6.4	100.0	100.0	—	—	—	—
10–15	9.0	9.1	100.0	100.0	—	—	—	—
15–20	8.6	8.7	99.6	100.0	0.4	0.0	—	—
20–25	7.6	7.5	81.3	89.6	18.3	10.4	0.4	0.1
25–30	7.5	7.2	41.3	50.2	56.0	48.4	2.7	1.4
30–35	6.7	6.2	20.4	19.0	75.0	78.4	4.7	2.6
35–40	8.6	8.6	12.7	10.0	82.4	85.8	4.9	4.2
40–45	7.9	8.2	9.0	7.1	86.4	87.5	4.7	5.4
45–50	6.5	6.8	6.4	3.2	89.0	90.8	4.7	6.0
50–55	5.7	6.3	4.7	3.3	90.5	91.1	4.8	5.6
55–60	4.7	5.1	3.9	1.6	90.6	91.8	5.6	6.6
60–65	3.4	3.5	3.9	1.9	88.8	92.8	7.4	5.3
65–70	4.4	4.4	4.0	3.3	85.3	86.6	10.7	10.1
70+	7.3	7.9	4.3	2.6	70.6	72.1	25.1	25.3
Females	(000s) 32,116.1	30,902.5	(%) 35.4	35.1	47.2	47.5	17.4	17.4
Age	(%)							
0–5	4.5	3.6	100.0	100.0	—	—	—	—
5–10	6.0	5.6	100.0	100.0	—	—	—	—
10–15	7.8	7.7	100.0	100.0	—	—	—	—
15–20	7.5	7.7	95.4	98.7	4.6	1.3	0.0	0.0
20–25	6.7	6.5	53.4	63.0	45.2	36.2	1.4	0.8
25–30	6.5	6.0	19.1	21.3	76.6	75.3	4.3	3.2
30–35	5.7	5.6	8.7	10.3	85.2	84.9	6.1	4.8
35–40	7.3	7.3	6.6	6.1	86.7	88.1	6.8	5.8
40–45	6.8	7.1	6.3	6.2	86.2	87.2	7.5	6.8
45–50	5.7	5.8	7.3	7.1	83.1	84.7	9.7	8.2
50–55	6.2	6.3	9.0	7.6	76.9	79.6	14.2	12.8
55–60	6.2	6.7	9.2	7.9	67.3	69.5	23.6	22.6
60–65	4.7	4.6	8.5	8.0	54.1	54.6	37.3	37.4
65–70	6.2	6.3	8.6	7.2	44.3	46.9	47.1	45.8
70+	12.3	13.0	11.1	11.3	23.4	22.7	65.5	66.0

[a] Sim = simulation results.
[b] Wb78 = residential population 1978.
Source: Helm and Lempert (1982).

lower and middle age brackets since immigration is not included. For males, immigration of foreigners is concentrated in the age bracket 25 to 35 years. For women, deficits occur in the age bracket 25 to 30 years. The number of children is significantly underestimated since children born to female immigrants are missing.

The breakdown of age groups by marital status also shows substantial differences in the percentages of never-married and married persons, respectively. For men aged between 20 and 30 years and for women between 20 and 25 years of age the simulation results in a substantially higher percentage of never-married persons. Correspondingly, the share of married persons is underestimated. This points to a problem not yet satisfactorily solved: it can be shown empirically (Galler, 1979) that the propensity to marry is significantly lower for persons attending school. However, it has not yet been possible to calculate marriage probabilities disaggregated by school attendance in addition to age and marital status.

As an approximation, persons attending school are excluded from marriage. But marriage probabilities for other individuals have not been increased accordingly. Consequently, the number of marriages is underestimated in that age bracket. However, marriages are made up for by applying higher marriage probabilities when persons have left school. Thus, the total number of marriages is estimated correctly but the age at marriage is somewhat overestimated, and marriage duration of married persons is underestimated.

Differences in population size result in 1.2 million fewer households in the simulation as compared with official statistics. Therefore, Table 10.5 also gives percentages of household types. The breakdown by household size shows that the percentage of two-person households is slightly underestimated whereas single-person households as well as households with five or more persons are somewhat overestimated. A slight underestimate of the proportion of households with two children appears in the breakdown by number of dependent children in the household.

The share of single parents with dependent children is underestimated significantly in the breakdown by household size and number of dependent children. One reason for this could be that the model only accounts for divorces but not for separations without formal divorce. No adequate data are available to extend the model in that direction. The share of households consisting of a married couple with one or two children is also underestimated wheras the share of large households is overestimated. Obviously, there is a bias toward multi-generation and multi-family households.

This result is due, at least in part, to differing definitions. In the model, persons are counted as being part of a household if they belong to it economically, regardless of whether they have another residence. Official statistics, however, are based on residence as the only criteria. Moreover, splitting off by children has been modelled but transitions by other relatives

TABLE 10.5. Private households 1978, by size and number of dependent children

| | Total | | With dependent children under 18 years | | | | | |
| | | | 1 child | | 2 children | | 3+ children | |
	StBA[a]	Sim[b]	StBA[a]	Sim[b]	StBA[a]	Sim[b]	StBA[a]	Sim[b]
	(000s)		(%)					
Cases	24,212	23,017	16.8	16.7	12.4	11.3	5.9	5.8
Size of household	(%)							
1	29.3	30.2	—	—	—	—	—	—
2	28.5	26.9	10.6	6.2	—	—	—	—
3	18.0	18.2	65.0	63.4	4.7	4.7	—	—
4	14.8	14.1	17.1	19.5	78.6	73.9	3.6	3.0
5+	9.5	10.6	7.3	10.9	16.7	21.3	96.4	97.0

[a] StBA = Statistical yearbook 1980.
[b] Sim = Simulation results.
Source: Helm and Lempert (1982, p. 27).

or non-related persons in the household have not. Here, additional assumptions are needed. However, due to the size of the corresponding groups, these errors are not substantial.

A comparison of the observed and the simulated family structures in Table 10.6 shows an underestimate of about one million families due to the smaller actual population size. The percentage of families with one or two children is too low in the simulation because of the smaller number of children actually born. The breakdown by family type reveals that the share of single adults, especially that of single women with dependent children, has been under-

TABLE 10.6. Families in 1978 by family type and number of children

| | Total | | Headed by married couple | | Headed by unmarried person | | Headed by unmarried female | |
	StBA[a]	Sim[b]	StBA[a]	Sim[b]	StBA[a]	Sim[b]	StBA[a]	Sim[b]
	(000s)		(%)					
Cases	22,431	21,400	67.5	69.1	32.5	30.9	25.5	24.7
	(%)							
no child	51.5	52.1	38.1	38.4	79.2	82.6	77.3	80.2
1 child	22.3	21.7	26.3	27.0	13.9	10.0	15.2	12.3
2 children	16.9	15.9	22.8	21.1	4.6	4.2	5.0	4.7
3 children	6.2	6.4	8.5	8.6	1.5	1.4	2.5	2.7
4 children	3.1	4.0	4.2	4.9	0.8	1.8	0.0	0.0

[a] StBA = Statistical yearbook 1980.
[b] Sim = Simulation results taken from Helm and Lempert (1982), p. 28.

TABLE 10.7. Simulation results for the household structure 1970–2000

Year	1970	1975	1980	1985	1990	1995	2000
Persons (000s)	57,132	56,396	54,734	53,078	51,908	50,710	48,970
Households (000s)	21,623	22,118	22,394	22,704	22,941	22,804	22,344
Persons living alone (%)							
male	7.1	8.5	9.6	10.3	11.0	12.1	13.4
female	20.4	21.7	22.7	23.0	22.8	22.3	22.0
Marriages (%)							
no child	22.4	22.9	23.0	23.9	24.6	24.9	25.0
1 child	16.1	15.6	16.0	17.2	18.4	18.3	17.2
2 children	12.9	12.5	12.0	11.1	10.3	10.0	9.9
3+ children	8.5	8.0	6.5	4.5	3.1	2.6	2.6
Other households (%)							
2 persons	5.1	4.4	4.4	4.5	4.8	5.2	5.6
3 persons	2.5	2.3	2.3	2.1	2.0	1.9	1.9
4 persons	1.8	1.6	1.5	1.4	1.3	1.3	1.2
5+ persons	3.2	2.6	2.2	1.9	1.7	1.5	1.3
Average household size	2.70	2.61	2.51	2.40	2.32	2.28	2.24

Source: Steger (1980, p. 300).

estimated. This is probably linked to the problem of separation of spouses.

An example of long-term simulations with the micromodel is the projection of household structures conducted by Steger (1980). Based on the microdata of the 1969 Mikrozensus by the Federal Statistical Office, the population of West Germany has been simulated up to the year 2000. Fertility was assumed to drop until 1980 and subsequently to rise to the level observed in 1972. Migration was not included. With these rather restrictive assumptions, the simulation represents a conditional projection that cannot claim general validity.

In this simulation, the population decreases in the thirty-year period after 1970 by more than eight million persons. However, as can be seen from Table 10.7, during the same period the number of households increases by more than half a million. As the breakdown by types of households shows, the share of single male households increases steadily while the share of single female households remains constant following a rise until 1980. As for the assumptions concerning fertility, the number of childless marriages will increase, as will those with one child, whereas the percentage of marriages with two or more children will decrease. For the other households, consisting mainly of incomplete families and multi-generation households, the structure will not change substantially. Average household size will decline from 2.7 in 1970 to 2.2 in 2000.

As the example demonstrates, the model proves to be stable in long-term projections. The results are plausible, but differ from other forecasts since they are based on other assumptions. This makes direct comparison difficult. In addition, comparisons are complicated by differing definitions.

10.6. Conclusions

In general, both the ex-post and ex-ante results appear to be satisfactory. But it is also obvious that further improvements are necessary. First of all, external migration is a problem to be tackled. At present, migration is accounted for by weighting the microdata. However, a preferable solution would be to include immigration and emigration explicitly in the model by generating or deleting individuals in the data file. But for such an approach more information is needed on the structure of migration.

As far as migration of family members of foreigners living in the country is concerned, rather detailed data will become available from the panel study conducted by the Sfb 3. There, for a sub-sample of foreigners living in the Federal Republic of Germany, information on spouses and children living abroad is gathered and migration of individuals and households will be observed. This will provide a basis for the simulation of the most important part of external migration. However, other migration processes remain, such as immigration of persons applying for political asylum, which probably cannot be endogenized in the near future.

Another drawback of the present model specification is that it does not allow for consensual unions; only formal marriages are covered. However, integrating informal unions into the model in principle poses no problems. In the simulated marriage market both formal and consensual unions can be formed, depending on specific propensities. In the same way, the simulation of divorces can be extended to the separation of informal partnerships. As yet, however, few quantitative data are available on the formation and stability of consensual unions. Again, some information will become available from the panel studies now being conducted.

In addition, an attempt should be made to improve the substantive hypotheses. This is most obvious with regard to the dependence of the propensity to marry on the supply conditions on the marriage market. As far as ex-post simulations are performed and observed frequencies are used, the present solution is appropriate. However, especially in long-term ex-ante simulations, the present approach may give rise to errors if rapid changes in demographic structures occur. For such cases, it might be useful to apply behavioural relations that link nuptiality to supply indicators in addition to individual characteristics (compare Pollard, 1977). If such relations are specified in a time-recursive way—linking marriage behaviour in one period to market conditions in preceding periods—they can be easily integrated into the present model structure.

H. Galler

Similar arguments can be put forward for other parts of the model. The hypotheses used to simulate demographic processes are still rather crude. At present, the model depends heavily on exogenous parameters like those for nuptiality and fertility specified by demographic characteristics. Moreover, socio-economic variables such as occupation or income are probably also important. More detailed behavioural relations may seem appropriate. But attempts to improve the model in this direction are restricted by deficiencies of both the theoretical concepts and of the availability of empirical data.

However, these problems also point to an advantage of microsimulation models as compared with other approaches. If improved behavioural hypotheses become available, they can easily be incorporated into the model. Since simulation is performed on the microlevel of individuals, all information available on each individual in the sample can be used to explain the demographic event under consideration. This allows for rather complex causal structures without influencing the size and complexity of the total model. This may be the most important advantage of the microsimulation approach, since it provides a very flexible tool for the development of behavioural hypotheses and their application to simulation and forecasting.

Notes

1. The demographic micromodel is part of the microsimulation model of the Sonder-forschungsbereich 3 developed by the author and his research team. The present form of the demographic model has been designed and implemented by Almut Steger. Successive updates, simulations, and evaluations have been provided by Iris Lempert. I am indebted to them and to all the other colleagues who collaborated in the development of the model.

References

CLARKE, M. (1986). Demographic processes and household dynamics: a micro-simulation approach, in: R. Woods and Ph. Rees (eds.), *Population Structures and Models: Developments in Spatial Demography* (Allen and Unwin, London), 245–72.

GALLER, P. (1979). Schulische Bildung und Heiratsverhalten, *Zeitschrift für Bevölkerungswissenschaft* 5(2), 199–213.

—— (1983). Mikrosimulationsmodelle als demographische Planungsgrundlage, in: H. Birg (ed.), *Demographische Entwicklung und gesellschaftliche Planung* (Frankfurt), 143–78.

HANEFELD, U. (1984). The German Socio-Economic Panel, in: American Statistical Association, 1984 Proceedings of the Social Statistics Section (Washington).

HECHELTJEN, P. (1974). *Bevölkerungsentwicklung und Erwerbstätigkeit* (Opladen).

HELM, R. AND I. LEMPERT (1982). Ausgewählte Ergebnisse des Mikrosimulationssystems (Querschnittsversion 81.6), Sfb 3 Working Paper no. 69, Frankfurt.

HERBERGER, L. AND H. BORRIES (1970). Vorausschätzung der Zahl der Privathaushalte bis 1980, *Wirtschaft und Statistik*, 504-9.

KAUFMANN, F. -X., A. HERLTH, J. QUITMANN, R. SIMM, AND K. -P. STROHMEIER (1982). Familienentwicklung: generatives Verhalten im familialen Kontext, *Zeitschrift für Bevölkerungswissenschaft* 8(4), 523-45.

MAYER, K. U. (1984). The process of leaving home: a three cohort comparison for West Germany, paper presented at the seminar on 'Demography of the later phases of the family life cycle', International Union for Scientific Study of Population, 3-7 Sept. 1984, Berlin.

MÖLLER, K. P. (1982). *Die Entwicklung von Bevölkerung und Haushalten in der BRD bis zum Jahre 2000* (Duncker and Humblot, Berlin).

OTT, N. (1984). Analyse der Haushaltsmobilität 1975-1980, Sfb 3 Working Paper no. 157, Frankfurt.

POHL, K. (1982). Konzeption und derzeitiger Stand der Paneluntersuchung des Bundesinstituts für Bevölkerungsforschung zu Fragen des Familienbildungsprozesses, *Zeitschrift für Bevölkerungswissenschaft* 8, 499-525.

POLLARD, J. H. (1977). The continuing attempt to incorporate both sexes into marriage analyses, in: International Population Conference, Mexico 1977, vol. 1 (IUSSP, Liège), 291-309.

STEGER, A. (1980). *Haushalte und Familien bis zum Jahr 2000* (Campus Verlag, Frankfurt).

11

Estimation of transition rates in dynamic household models

D. Courgeau and E. Lelièvre

ABSTRACT

This chapter deals with the estimation of instantaneous transition rates in nonparametric, semiparametric, and parametric models. The bivariate and multivariate problems are introduced and discussed using data from a retrospective life history survey, undertaken in France, 1981.

11.1. Introduction

THE construction of dynamic household models requires comprehensive knowledge of the demographic events which lead to household formation and dissolution. The interplay between these events in individual cases may be observed by using prospective or retrospective data sets. We will here show how such data sets allow the estimation of transition rates between states of the family cycle. Such transition rates can be applied in macromodels (as discussed by Keilman in chapter 9) as well as in micromodels (examples of which are given by Willekens in chapter 7 and by Galler in chapter 10).

There are three types of interactions between demographic phenomena: interactions in which one phenomenon prevents the occurrence of another phenomenon, those that create the preconditions for new phenomena, and those that neither impede nor bring about a phenomenon (Courgeau, 1979).

An example of the first type of interaction is the selection which occurs by virtue of survival when studying marriage. In order correctly to estimate probabilities for each event in the pure (undisturbed) state, one usually makes the hypothesis of 'non-dependence', namely, that an individual who died single would have had the same behaviour, had he lived, as individuals who did not die at the same age (Henry, 1972).

The second type of interaction concerns events that enable the occurrence of other events which would not have been possible without the occurrence of the initial event. For instance, marriage allows legitimate reproduction.

The third type is intermediate: the disturbing phenomenon neither impedes nor brings about another phenomenon. The concept of local dependence may be introduced (Schweder, 1970) to study these interactions. This concept formalizes the intuitive notion that a stochastic process may influence the development of another process. Hence, local dependence is a dynamic property developing with time. It always has a certain direction since the first process may be locally dependent on the second one, while this second process is locally independent of the first one (Aalen *et al.*, 1980). Such a situation may be extended to more than one type of event for each interacting phenomenon.

Different types of observational plans may be available to collect the information, and since the measurement of the interactions is dependent on these plans, we must introduce the two principal ones: prospective and retrospective observational plans.[1]

In a prospective observational plan the individuals are sampled randomly before the events of interest take place. Such a sample may be a cohort of individuals born in a given year followed prospectively by a follow-up survey. Some of the individuals may die before the events take place, others may experience these events. Such a follow-up design is rarely used in demographic studies because it is expensive and often not cost-effective, given the often considerable amount of drop-out. Moreover, the time needed to get sufficient information on household formation and dissolution prevents prompt reporting. However, the accuracy of such reports may be excellent.

In a retrospective observational plan, data are collected only from survivors, which induces a selection by virtue of survival; reliability and validity of retrospectively reported information is not assessed here (Hoem, 1983); nor are register and survey data compared (Lyberg, 1983). However, such an observational plan, which needs only one interview, is an appealing alternative. It is mainly used for demographic studies in countries where register data either do not exist or are unable to provide an answer to specific research questions.

These two kinds of observational plans create problems of censoring which are important for this paper. Right censoring, which occurs in both prospective and retrospective observations, is not too problematic. We will see later how we can obtain unbiased estimates of transition rates. Left censoring, which may occur when the observation starts at an arbitrary point in time, presents more complicated problems.[2] In such cases we are unable to estimate the effects of past history, occurring before this arbitrary time, without making far-reaching assumptions. We may assume either that the process studied begins at the first date of observation, or that the history of the process prior to this date does not affect the future of the process. Such an assumption is not always realistic. Yet it is necessary because of the extremely complicated analytical problems that would arise if it had not been made.

This paper deals with the estimation of instantaneous transition rates, which generalize hazard functions for multivariate event histories of individuals. We will restrict our discussion to right-censored event histories since, as we have seen, left censoring is very problematic.

The survey data used here record to the nearest month the dates of status changes. Such detailed event histories will allow us to work with continuous time models (Tuma and Hannan, 1984, pp. 82–8). However, it seems important to go beyond this concept. It appears that, even if the exact timing of each event is correctly registered, such a precise time may be far removed from the time generated by the relational systems within which an individual lives. These events do not occur in a linear and continuous time but in a more 'fuzzy time'. It thus seems important to introduce this 'fuzzy time' concept. Let us see how this can be done.

We will consider here the interaction between leaving the agricultural sector and marrying. In a number of cases these two events may take place almost simultaneously for the same individual, some marrying shortly before leaving the agricultural sector, others leaving the agricultural sector shortly before marrying. Under these conditions it is not significant which event takes place first. The two events can therefore be considered to occur simultaneously, even if there is a certain time-lag between them. The introduction of a 'fuzzy time' allows us to analyse these almost simultaneous events. We will see later how this concept of fuzzy time may be defined.

We will present here different methods of analysing these interactions. The first approach (section 11.2) is a nonparametric one, which generalizes the usual demographic methods of longitudinal analysis to the case of complex interactions. A new impetus was recently given to the development of the mathematical apparatus needed to estimate hazard rates and to construct confidence intervals for such nonparametric models (Aalen, 1978; Johansen, 1983). The second approach is semiparametric or even fully parametric (section 11.3). The introduction of (semi)parametric models in demography took place only recently, but their use is rapidly becoming more widespread. Here, we will consider the instantaneous transition rate as a dependent variable, and introduce a relationship between this rate and a variety of observed variables.

The purpose of this paper is to develop methods for estimating transition rates, using a detailed data set. Rather than presenting general techniques, we prefer to discuss a few concrete examples, since they illustrate appropriately the problems that arise when estimating these rates. However, the methods presented here are quite general and they may, with slight modifications, be used in very diverse situations.

The data used here consist of the retrospective life histories of a random sample of individuals aged 45–69, living in France in 1981. These data were collected from a nationwide sample and for this survey we obtained 4,602 questionnaires, with a response rate of approximatively 89 per cent. Its purpose was to study the migration, family, and work histories of the French population (compare Courgeau, 1985).

11.2. Nonparametric methods of analysis

The first type of method is a classical longitudinal analysis, generalized to deal with more complex dependencies between life history events. Let us first consider the very simple case of an independent sample from a homogeneous population with a single event.

Let T be a non-negative random variable indicating the time at which a particular event occurs. The survivor function is the probability that T is at least as great as a value t:

$$F(t) = Pr(T \geqslant t).$$

The key nonparametric approach to estimating the survivor function is derived from Kaplan and Meier's (1958) paper giving a product-limit estimator for the survivor function where no assumption is made about its functional form.

Another concept closely related to the survivor function is the hazard function. It specifies the instantaneous failure rate at $T = t$, conditional upon survival to time t, and is defined as:

$$h(t) = \lim_{\Delta t \to 0} \frac{Pr(T < t + \Delta t \mid T \geqslant t)}{\Delta t} = - \frac{d \log F(t)}{dt}.$$

Thus the logarithm of the Kaplan–Meier estimator can be used to estimate the hazard function. This will give good asymptotic estimates of the hazard function for large samples. However, for small samples the Kaplan–Meier approach is biased and therefore Aalen (1978) used martingale theory to derive a better estimator. These functions may arise in the same way for continuous and discrete cases where the Dirac delta functions handle the discrete distributions.[3]

When some individuals are censored at time t they are usually included in the number of individuals under consideration until, and at, time t. After this time they will no longer appear in this population.

Let us now first consider the bivariate case, before trying to handle the multivariate case.

11.2.1. The bivariate problem

We will here consider the relationship between getting married and leaving the agricultural sector. But as we said earlier, such a model is applicable to any bivariate situation.

Here, we work in terms of the state space diagram, given in Figure 11.1. We now have two types of failure time represented by random variables T_1 and T_2: T_1 is the age at leaving the agricultural sector; T_2, the age at marriage. In our sample everybody starts in state 0. However, an individual in state 1 may

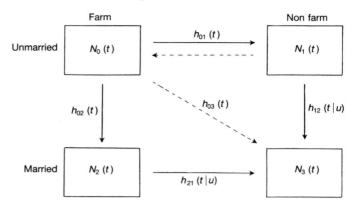

FIG. 11.1. State space diagram for the bivariate case

return to state 0 if he is not married. On the other hand, we consider only first marriage.

The previous hazard function defined in the univariate case can be generalized into four hazard functions:

$$h_{01}(t) = \lim_{\Delta t \to 0} \frac{Pr(T_1 < t + \Delta t \mid T_1 \geqslant t, T_2 \geqslant t)}{\Delta t}$$

with a similar one for $h_{02}(t)$, while

$$h_{12}(t \mid u) = \lim_{\Delta t \to 0} \frac{Pr(T_2 < t + \Delta t \mid T_1 = u, T_2 \geqslant t)}{\Delta t}, \, t \geqslant u$$

with a similar one for $h_{21}(t \mid u)$.

It is also possible to introduce simultaneous occurrence of the two types of failure $h_{03}(t)$.

Though a fully satisfactory nonparametric procedure of estimation has not yet been found (Cox and Oakes, 1984, p. 163), we will present some approximated estimates. To do this, we have to gain insight into the studied phenomena.

As mentioned above, these events do not occur in a linear and continuou· time but in a 'fuzzy time'. It therefore seems more important to introduce this fuzziness than to give a nonparametric procedure of estimation.

Let us first consider, for example, the marriage behaviour of men who are on the verge of leaving the agricultural sector. Such behaviour may be closer to that of men who have already left this sector, than to that of men who remain in it. It therefore seems better to consider such individuals as having left the agricultural sector.

On the other hand, let us consider the attitude towards the labour market of men who are on the verge of marrying. Again, such behaviour may be closer to that of men who are already married than to that of bachelors. It thus seems better to consider such individuals as being married. The problem is now how to introduce such a 'fuzzy time'.

Different possibilities are open to us. We may focus on the decision-making process. Let us assume a time-lag t_1 between actually leaving the agricultural sector and the decision to leave it, and another time-lag t_2 between marriage and the decision to marry. Although we realize that taking such decisions is a gradual process, we may introduce different time-lags, from one month to one year, for example, and observe how the results differ.[4]

We used a similar procedure for our French survey, taking a one-year time-lag. This procedure, less accurate than the previous one, is easier to implement, as it introduces a time-discrete version of the nonparametric model. Let us have a closer look at the estimates to which it leads. Censored individuals will not be taken into account.

Let $N_i(t)$ ($i = 0,1,2$) be the population in state i at the beginning of year t. Let $n_{ij}(t)$ be the number of occurrences of type j in the population in state i. Let $r_{10}(t)$ and $r_{32}(t)$ be the number of people returning to the agricultural sector.

We assume that the simultaneous events occurring to the same individual during the same year (this occurs only for 5 per cent of the observed population) are related to the corresponding population at risk.[5] As we have a limited number of observations (668 men and 519 women) we assume that the behaviour of the observed individuals will depend only on their age and not on the time the previous event occurred. With this assumption we can estimate the following hazard rates by observed occurrence/exposure rates using the total time at risk during year t and assuming that both types of events occur uniformly throughout the interval:

$$\hat{h}_{01}(t) = \frac{n_{01}(t)}{N_0(t) - \frac{1}{2}(n_{01}(t) + n_{02}(t) - r_{10}(t))},$$

$$\hat{h}_{21}(t|u) = \frac{n_{21}(t)}{N_2(t) - \frac{1}{2}(n_{21}(t) - n_{02}(t) - r_{32}(t))},$$

$$\hat{h}_{02}(t) = \frac{n_{02}(t)}{N_0(t) - \frac{1}{2}(n_{02}(t) + n_{01}(t) - r_{10}(t))},$$

$$\hat{h}_{12}(t|u) = \frac{n_{12}(t)}{N_1(t) - \frac{1}{2}(n_{12}(t) + r_{10}(t) - n_{01}(t))}.$$

We are then able to compare $h_{01}(t)$ with $h_{21}(t)$ (respectively, $h_{02}(t)$ with $h_{12}(t)$) to see whether or not the behaviour of unmarried individuals (of individuals working in the farming or nonfarming sector, respectively) is different. To do this, we may use test statistics given in Hoem and Funck Jensen (1982).

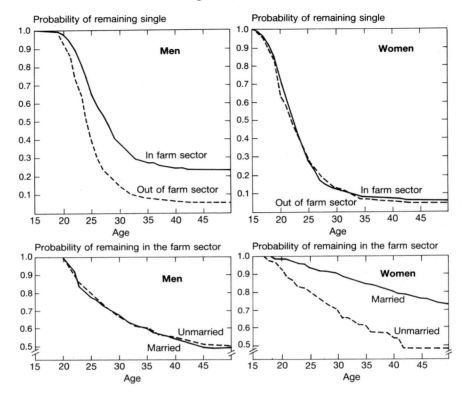

FIG. 11.2. Probabilities of remaining single inside or outside the farm sector, and probabilities of remaining in the farm sector, by marital status

Figure 11.2 shows the results for the estimated survivor functions in each of the four defined states. The behaviour of men and women is very different. For men, the probability of remaining single is significantly higher for those in the agricultural sector than for others, while for women it is the same in both categories. On the other hand, for men there is no significant difference in the probability of leaving the agricultural sector between those who are unmarried and those who are married, while married women remain in the farming sector significantly more often than unmarried women. Hence, in terms of local dependence, we find the following: for men, being in the farming sector diminishes their probability of marriage, while being married or not does not influence the probability of them leaving the farming sector. For women the reverse is true.

11.2.2. The multivariate problem

We will consider here, as an example of the multivariate problem, the interaction between migration occurring after marriage and marital fertility. The state space is presented in Figure 11.3. We can also introduce failure times represented in each of the two dimensions by random variables T_1, $T_2 \ldots T_k \ldots$ for migration and T^1, $T^2, \ldots T^n \ldots$ for childbirths.

A state is specified as an ordered pair (k,n) where k is the number of moves previously experienced and n the number of children previously born. We have hazard functions between all these states of the following kind (for migration):

$$h^n_{k,k+1}(t\,|\,u_1, \ldots, u_k, v_n, \ldots, v_1) =$$

$$\lim_{\Delta t \to 0} \frac{Pr(T_{k+1} < t + \Delta t \,|\, T_{k+1} \geq t, T_1 = u_1, \ldots, T_k = u_k, T^n = v_n, \ldots, T^1 = v_1)}{\Delta t}.$$

Evidently, such a model cannot be estimated with a small number of individuals, as in our survey, and we have to make some further assumptions. Let us assume that a migration hazard function is dependent on its rank, on the time since the last move (u) and on the time since the last childbirth (v). With these assumptions, we can write for the hazard function

$$h^n_{k,k+1}(t\,|\,u,v) = \lim_{\Delta t \to 0} \frac{Pr(T_{k+1} < t + \Delta t \,|\, T_{k+1} \geq t, T_k = u, T^n = v)}{\Delta t}.$$

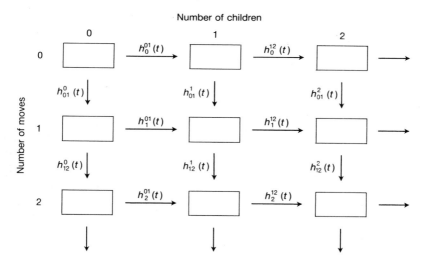

FIG. 11.3. State space diagram for the multivariate case

For the childbearing hazard function we have similar hypotheses:

$$h_k^{n,n+1}(t\,|\,u,v) = \lim_{\Delta t \to 0} \frac{Pr(T^{n+1} < t + \Delta t\,|\,T^{n+1} \geqslant t,\, T_k = u,\, T^n = v)}{\Delta t}.$$

We assume further, that both of the two previous functions are independent of u and v, and that $h_{k,k+1}^{n}(t)$ depends only on n, whereas $h_k^{n,n+1}(t)$ depends only on k.

Under these assumptions it is possible to estimate the hazard rates. They will allow us to answer the following two questions:

- What will be the effects of n births after marriage on the migration process?
- What will be the effects of having undertaken k moves after marriage on the childbearing intensity?

We can obtain a cumulative spatial mobility index until time t for the hypothetical population of women of parity n (or the cumulative fertility of women with k moves). However, as the risk set may be small for short durations and values of n or k greater than zero, we assume that if the risk set contains less than 50 individuals, the cumulative mobility index (or the cumulative marital fertility) of couples with n children (k moves) is the same as that of couples with $(n-1)$ children ($(k-1)$ moves).

Figure 11.4 gives the results for women born in 1911–25, married to men born in 1911–35.[6] We classify these women according to their age at marriage (15–22, 23–30). For women who married young, there is a clear effect of family size on the cumulative number of moves: the greater the size, the more mobile the subpopulation will be. However, such an effect, although striking for the lower birth ranks, is less perceptible for the higher ones. For the same women we can also see that some moves are undertaken to provide for forthcoming births.

For women married after the age of 22 years, the effect of family size on the number of moves undertaken has entirely disappeared. These women, compared with the younger ones, appear to have a dwelling sufficiently large to anticipate their ultimate family size. But, on the other hand, the cumulative fertility of these women according to their number of previous moves indicates that some of those moves are undertaken to provide for forthcoming births. Thus, in this case, we have a local dependence of fertility on spatial mobility: if no more moves are undertaken after or during the year of a birth in the household, it appears that some moves may be undertaken in expectation of future births.

The assumptions applied here seem very restrictive, because they take into account only the longer term effects on the level of each of the two status dimensions considered (childbearing parity and number of moves experienced). It will then be important to take into account the short-term after-effects of the occurrence of one event on the other. In this case, if the birth of a child modifies the migratory behaviour of his parents, then

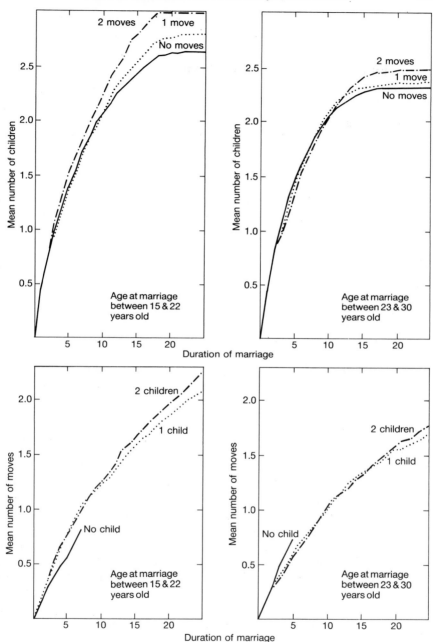

FIG. 11.4. Mean number of moves for women having 0, 1, or 2 children, and mean number of children for women having undertaken 0, 1, or 2 moves, according to age at marriage and marriage duration (women born in 1911–1925)

$h_{k,k+1}^n(t|u,v)$ should depend on v, at least for small v, and this effect will come in addition to its possible dependence on t and we shall have to estimate $h^n(t|v)$. In the same way, if a new spatial move modifies the couple's reproductive behaviour, then $h_k^{n,n+1}(t|u,v)$ should depend on u, at least for small u, in addition to its possible dependence on k. We will have to estimate $h_k(t|u)$. However, the limited number of surveyed persons does not allow us to go further. In order to extend such an analysis, we need parametric methods.

11.3. Semiparametric and parametric methods of analysis

When trying to introduce some exogenous variables into the previous analysis, it seems easier to discard the interaction point of view we took in section 11.2 and to introduce a more causal analysis on the studied phenomena. However, such an analysis is, as yet, not wholly causal. It is only a one-sided point of view of two or more interacting phenomena.

11.3.1. The bivariate problem revisited

We will now attempt to introduce exogenous variables into the previous bivariate analysis. We shall consider a semiparametric model for the hazard function of leaving the farming sector. Suppose, the hazard is affected by marriage but that it is independent of the waiting time u. We use a model considered by Crowley and Hu (1977). It uses proportional hazards for the two rates. Then we have

$$h_{01}(t|z) = h(t)\exp(z\,\beta_1),$$

$$h_{21}(t|u,z) = h(t)\exp(z\,\beta_1 + \beta_0 + z\,\beta_2).$$

The parameters β_0, β_1, β_2 can be estimated by partial likelihood methods (Kalbfleisch and Prentice, 1980). Table 11.1 gives estimates of the regression coefficients for models introducing different kinds of variables.

Recall that for men, leaving the farming sector is independent of marital status, whereas married women remain in the farming sector to a far greater degree than unmaried women. This is consistent with the results given by model 1, where only marital status is considered: this variable appears to be associated significantly with an important decrease in the exit risk for the female population only.

Then the number of siblings (model 2) appears to have an impact on unmarried women only: they leave the farming sector at a rate which increases concomitantly with the number of siblings. On the other hand (model 3), elder women, when unmarried, leave this sector to a lesser extent. Once married, there is no interaction between these two variables, so that their effect will remain at the previous level.

TABLE 11.1. Regression coefficients for a semiparametric model of exit from the farming sector

Model	Variables	Indicator		Main effect (β_1)		Marital status (β_0)		Interactions (β_2)	
				Males	Females	Males	Females	Males	Females
				$\times 10^{-3}$					
1	Marital status	0 unmarried 1 married		—	—	-171	-835^a	—	—
2	Number of sibs	number		3	16^a	-170	-835^a	-0	-3
3	Elder	0 if not 1 if elder		-67	-412	-161	-930^a	-46	258
4	Father farmer	0 if not 1 if farmer		-563	-950	-483^a	-1255^a	490	608^a
5	Father-in-law	0 if not 1 if farmer		—	—	189	-563^a	-580^a	-452^a

[a] One-sided test significant at the 5 per cent level.

When introducing the father's occupation, a number of interesting results appear (model 4). Unmarried men and women exhibit the same behaviour when their father is a farmer: they leave the farming sector to a lesser extent than married men and women. This may be because they are to inherit their father's farm. Once married, the interaction is significant but in the opposite direction. There is no longer any difference in behaviour between them, irrespective of whether or not their father is a farmer.

Model 5 includes a covariate in the time-dependent part of the model and not in the constant part. It measures whether or not the father-in-law is a farmer. Again, such a variable has a very clear effect: it lowers the degree to which both sexes leave the agricultural sector, once married. However, these rates remain very close to previous ones.

This example shows how such an approach will be important for future demographic research, especially when improving it by introducing interaction effects. We will not consider them here.

11.3.2. A split of the multivariate problem into parametric models

We shall now introduce exogenous variables into the previous analysis of migration related to childbearing. To do this we will split up this complex problem into parametric or semiparametric models. Let us take the migration process as being the main one, and introduce the other variables as explanatory variables.

As before, let T_i^0 be the duration of residence of an individual. We can write his survival probability as a function of a vector x_i of characteristics of the individual at the beginning of the observation period. Hence

$$F(t; x_i, \theta) = Pr(T_i^0 \geqslant t; x_i, \theta)$$

where θ is a parameter vector which we have to estimate.

We can also define a probability density function for migration as:

$$f(t; x_i, \theta) = \lim_{\Delta t \to 0} \frac{Pr(t \leqslant T_i^0 < t + \Delta t; x_i, \theta)}{\Delta t}$$

$$= -\frac{\partial F(t; x_i, \theta)}{\partial t}.$$

However, as we are working on retrospective survey data we have for some duration of residence a censored observation, so that $T_i < T_i^0$. As censoring times are in this case stochastically independent of each other and of the failure time, we can write

$$Pr(T_i < t + \Delta t; \delta_i = 1, x_i, \theta) = O_i(t) f(t; x_i, \theta) \Delta t,$$

$$Pr(T_i < t + \Delta t; \delta_i = 0, x_i, \theta) = q_i(t) F(t; x_i, \theta) \Delta t,$$

where δ_i is a dummy variable that is equal to zero if the ith item is censored, and equal to one if it is not censored; $O_i(t)$ and $q_i(t)$ are the survivor and density functions for censoring.

As neither O_i nor q_i are informative about θ, the likelihood of the data is proportional to

$$\prod_{i=1}^{n} f(t_i; x_i, \theta)^{\delta_i} F(t_i; x_i, \theta)^{1-\delta_i}$$

where n is the number of observed durations of residence.

It is then possible to estimate the parameter vector θ with maximum likelihood methods. It has been shown that the asymptotic distribution of θ is multivariate normal with mean $\hat{\theta}$. When using the Newton–Raphson technique to find the maximum of the likelihood function, we also have an estimate of the covariance matrix of these parameters.

We suppose here that the instantaneous migration rate is related to the observable variables in a generalized Gompertz model:

$$h(t; x_i, \theta) = \exp(\theta x_i + \theta_0 t).$$

Previous migration analyses show a very good fit of regression models to Gompertz's duration of residence effect (Ginsberg, 1979). We suppose that the other variables act multiplicatively on the migration rate.

We will not present here the detailed analysis we undertook in another paper (Courgeau, 1985), using 37 variables, introducing first age group variables with duration of residence, then family life cycle variables, tenure status variables, career variables, and finally some more general variables introducing war periods or periods of economic crisis. We will only give as an example the reduction of age effects when introducing different kinds of variables. Figure 11.5 shows the multiplicative effect of age on mobility

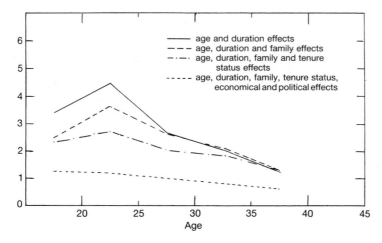

FIG. 11.5. Age-specific multiplicative effect on mobility according to the set of considered variables: males born in 1931–1935

according to the set of considered variables, for the male cohort born in 1931–35.[7]

When introducing only age and duration effects, we have a curve that is very close to the curve we obtain with period data: a maximum migration rate for the age group 20–4 years, and an important reduction for the older age groups. When introducing family variables, this age effect is reduced for the age group 15–24. Introducing tenure status variables yields a new reduction of this age effect for all age groups. Later, the introduction of the whole set of variables cancels out any age effect. Hence, for this cohort we are able to explain all age effects usually noted in the different stages of the individual's family, economic, and political life.

11.4. Conclusion

We have here covered the entire spectrum of analyses, from nonparametric models to fully parametric ones, via semiparametric models. We have also introduced univariate analyses, bivariate ones, and finally more complex multivariate analyses. Through this exploration, some important issues for future research have appeared. We will pin-point them and give some suggestions for future research.

An important problem was that we were not able to estimate complete models because this would require a huge sample with many observations in each cell. Such detailed information was not available. Therefore, we introduced some assumptions on the main effects. In order to do so we mainly used earlier experiences with demographic data. For example, this applies to the prominent effect of the duration since the last event rather than to the duration since earlier ones. Such hypotheses need to be explored in more detail. With more surveys containing event history data, we will be able to give a more solid basis to these hypotheses. However, to do this we will need larger samples than usual.

Another problem will be to introduce more time-dependent explanatory variables into these analyses. When revisiting the bivariate problem we introduced such a time-dependent variable, namely, being married or not at time t. Such an approach needs to be generalized. In the parametric approach we only allow for the value of the parallel process at the beginning of each event interval. Obviously, these life cycle variables, tenure status variables, and career variables may change in between moves or births. It will be important, in future work, to try to incorporate such time-dependent explanatory processes as well.

A third problem did not appear clearly from the previous analyses but seems very important for further research. We introduced previously different explanatory variables to control their effect. However, other characteristics of the studied individuals interfere with them, while we do not have any possibility of measuring these characteristics. We can incorporate this unobserved heterogeneity (Tuma and Hannan, 1984, pp. 155–86) into the models. However, research on this problem has only just begun, and its possible solutions will most likely appear in future research.

Last but not least, we have introduced a 'fuzzy time' that leads to very important problems which are difficult to deal with. The estimation of transition rates needs a very precise time scale on which events can be placed. However, when studying demographic events, we do not observe such a time scale, but rather a more 'fuzzy time'. It does not seem important, when working with a time interval of six months or even a year, to know which event occurred first (for example a birth or a migration). The analysis on a very precise time scale may lead to inconsistent results with a sociological analysis. One way to avoid such inconsistencies may be to introduce a time which is not ordered linearly. For example, this may occur in a two-dimensional time-space: the first dimension may be our common time; the other, a hazardous time that will be added to or subtracted from the continuous time. This possibility is open to further research.

Acknowledgements

The authors are indebted to Richard Gill for valuable comments and discussions on a preliminary version of this paper and to Stephen Clarke for correcting the English.

Notes

1. We will not consider here another commonly used observational plan, namely panel data. Such data are usually so scarce that it is difficult to know the exact timing of every demographic event.
2. In demographic surveys, such as the O R I N Survey in the Netherlands, left censoring, rather than left truncation, arises (Klijzing, chapter 4). Left truncation arises when individuals come under observation only some known time after the natural time origin of the phenomenon under study. That is, had the individual failed before the truncation time in question, that individual would not have been recorded (Cox and Oakes, 1984). Such a truncation leads to a maximum likelihood fitting of any parametric or nonparametric model.
3. Such a function $\delta(t)$ is defined so that $\delta(t)\, dt = 1$ if $t = 0$, otherwise $\delta(t)\, dt = 0$.
4. Nico Keilman is trying to use this approach to study interrelations between migration and birth events.
5. It is also possible to exclude them and to compute rates as $h_{03}(t)$ in Figure 11.1.
6. For reasons of clarity, we consider only moderate family size and moderate numbers of migration.
7. Such an effect is measured by the antilog of the parameters ($\exp \theta$). When it is equal to one, the behaviour of the considered age group will be the same as the behaviour of the comparison group (40 years and over). To undertake this analysis we use the Fortran computer programme 'R A T E', written by N. Tuma and D. Pasta.

References

AALEN, O. (1978). Nonparametric inference for a family of counting processes, *The Annals of Statistics* 6, 701–26.

—— Ø. BORGAN, N. KEIDING, AND J. THORMANN (1980). Interaction between life history events: nonparametric analysis for prospective and retrospective data in the presence of censoring, *Scandinavian Journal of Statistics* 7, 161–71.

COURGEAU, D. (1979). Migration and demographic phenomena in France, in: J. White (ed.), *The Urban Impact of Internal Migration* (Chapel Hill, University of North Carolina Press), 1–32.

—— (1985). Interaction between spatial mobility, family and career life cycle: a French survey, *European Sociological Review* 1, 139–62.

COX, R. AND D. OAKES (1984). *Analysis of Survival Data* (Chapman and Hall, London).

CROWLEY, J. AND M. HU (1977). Covariance analysis of heart transplant data, *Journal of the American Statistical Association* 72, 27–36.

GINSBERG, R. (1979). Timing and duration effects in residence histories and other longitudinal data, II: studies of duration effects in Norway, 1965–1971, *Regional Science and Urban Economics*, 369–92.

HENRY, L. (1972). *Démographie: analyse et modèles* (Larousse, Paris).

HOEM, J. M. (1983). Weighting, misclassification and other issues in the analysis of survey samples of life histories, Stockholm Research Reports in Demography, 11.

—— AND U. FUNCK JENSEN (1982). Multistate life table methodology: a probabilist critique, in: K. C. Land and A. Rogers (eds.), *Multidimensional Mathematical Demography* (Academic Press, New York), 155–264.

JOHANSEN, S. (1983). An extension of Cox's regression model, *International Statistical Review* 51, 165–74.

KALBFLEISCH, G. D. AND PRENTICE, R. L. (1980). *The Statistical Analysis of Failure Time Data* (John Wiley, New York).

KAPLAN, E. L. AND P. MEIER (1958). Nonparametric estimation from incomplete observations, *Journal of the American Statistical Association* 53, 457–81.

LYBERG, I. (1983). The effects of sampling and non-response on estimates of transition intensities: some empirical results from the 1981 Swedish fertility survey, Stockholm Research Reports in Demography, 14.

SCHWEDER, T. (1970). Composable Markov processes, *Journal of Applied Probability* 7, 400–10.

TUMA, N. B. AND M. HANNAN (1984). *Social Dynamics: Models and Methods* (Academic Press, Orlando).

PART IV

Applications

12

Application of household models in studying the family life cycle

A. Kuijsten

ABSTRACT

After discussing some shortcomings of the family life cycle concept, it is suggested that one way to overcome these shortcomings is by constructing family life cycle tables. The author has constructed such family life cycle tables from input and output of a macrodemographic projection research project. Next, the modelling strategy for this project is discussed. In the final sections, the user's influence on the research project, the use of its results in policy, and future research opportunities in the field of family life cycle modelling are discussed.

12.1. Introduction

IN 1975, the Netherlands Ministry of Social Affairs initiated a research project dealing with the projection of the Dutch female population, disaggregated by age, marital status, and number of dependent children. The Ministry aimed at using the project results as a point of departure for estimating future labour force participation of ever-married women. Age, marital status, and number and age of dependent children were considered important determinants of future female labour force participation.

This project initiated a 10-year period of research on the demography of households and families. At this moment, a decade later, the original projection results have partly become obsolete. Nevertheless, new directions in research have been explored on the basis of the original projection model, leaving its main principles intact.

The original projection model, notwithstanding the restrictions necessitated by the funding agency's application intentions, proved to be a practical tool for modelling the family life cycle development of female first-marriage cohorts. The result was a set of family life cycle tables.

My contribution to this volume serves a dual purpose. Its main part (section 12.4) discusses the impact of data availability on the modelling strategy and on the specification of assumptions on behalf of the original projection research. The outcome of my modelling efforts at the time had a direct bearing on the way I later calculated the above-mentioned family life cycle tables. The second purpose is, then, to describe in a nutshell the main features of and analytic possibilities offered by these tables.

This description, given in section 12.3, is preceded by a paragraph dealing with the family life cycle concept, its main points of criticism, and the way I think these may be overcome by the demographically inspired life table method. The family life cycle table is regarded as a possible means of modelling the family life cycle, that is, a means of modelling a very important facet of the process of household formation and dissolution. This part of the household formation and dissolution process can be wholly described by demographic factors. The modelling efforts discussed in this chapter basically focus on the very same entities which Ermisch calls 'Minimal Household Units' (see chapter 3). They differ only from Ermisch's concept in that it is the ever-married woman who is systematically taken as the 'reference person' or 'marker' (Brass, 1983; and chapter 17, Keilman and Keyfitz) and in that they are restricted to the age range 15–49 years (in the projection research) and to the first 25 years after the year of marriage (in the family life cycle table).

The chapter concludes with some remarks on the funding agency's influence on the research project, on the use of the model in policy (section 12.5), and on future research opportunities (section 12.6).

12.2. Theoretical background

The 'family life cycle approach' or 'developmental approach', which has its roots in the 1930s and 1940s, has acquired a firmly established position in family sociology. In this approach the family is regarded as a configuration of individuals experiencing, in the course of time, significant processes of formation, growth, consolidation, and contraction (Hill and Rodgers, 1964; Cuisenier, 1977; Young, 1977; Glick, 1947, 1977). Therefore, typical stages in the life course of a family may be distinguished. Each stage is characterized by its typical 'developmental tasks' of the family members involved (the qualitative aspect) as well as by typical compositional attributes (the quantitative aspect). Both aspects are assumed to be closely related to one another. Compositional attributes, therefore, may serve as indicators for the family development in terms of its qualitative aspects.

Efforts to model the dynamics of these compositional attributes, identifying major 'transition points' marking the family life cycle stages, have to deal with many kinds of events at the microlevel of the family as a configuration of individuals that demographers are used to deal with when modelling macrolevel population dynamics: marriage, childbearing, survival. The same events have relevance for household modelling too. Both household modelling and family life cycle modelling differ from macrodemographic population modelling, in that the latter is based on the individual as the modelling unit, whereas household and family life cycle modelling deal with configurations of individuals as modelling units. Household modelling may differ from family life cycle modelling in as far as the former has to account for a larger variety of relevant events of change, the (nuclear) family concept being more narrowly defined than the household concept. Family life cycle modelling, then, may be regarded as a subcategory of household modelling.

The family life cycle concept has met with severe criticism. The main stream of criticism has focused on the so-called 'normative underpinnings' of the developmental approach, and its quantitative aspects in particular. A fine collection of quotations with respect to the interrelated 'partial' and 'normative' characteristics of the family life cycle concept may be found in Höhn (1982, pp. 84–8). With respect to the concept's partial character, Elder (1977, p. 295) wrote:

The most common stage models of the family cycle are all best described as delineating **stages of parenthood**—before children, the active phase of parenting, the departure of children, and the 'empty nest'. Moreover, these stages follow a preferred script of a marriage which bears children and survives to old age; deviant patterns are excluded—childless marriages, children before marriage, the widowed and divorced with or without children, serial marriages, or an extended phase of living together which is eventually formalized by marriage. There is no limit to the models that could be developed for life patterns that deviate from the preferred or conventional type.

Its normative character has been criticized by Nock (1979, p. 16) in the following way:

. . . families are without exception in abiding by normative constraints. All couples will have children or at least desire them. In addition, it must be assumed that families abide by normative constraints in that they do not terminate as a result of divorce or separation. The normative underpinnings of developmental approaches are obvious and essential. Any other assumption makes the approach impractical as an orienting strategy for studying the family.

These criticisms of the family life cycle concept, although fully justified in themselves, have also, of course, received much impetus from empirical developments. When increasing numbers of families in reality deviate from the prescribed family life cycle script (by voluntary childlessness, unmarried cohabitation, divorce, or serial marriage) the concept's shortcomings become clear.

Another point of criticism regards the quantification of the family life cycle stages and their transition points. From a demographer's point of view, these quantifications often suffer from a lack of precision. Many studies of the family life cycle (in majority based on cross-sectional census data) abound in presenting relatively precise values of median transition points for comparatively crude and/or imprecisely defined categories of individuals (women or mothers, born at 10-year intervals, and/or 'approximately' married in a 10-year time interval), as, for example, Glick (1977) has done. The series of transition points presented for these categories of women too easily negate the fact that these categories of women are, without exception, sequentially non-homogeneous with respect to the sequence of events measured in terms of some average point in time at which these events occur. This heterogeneity is not restricted to the kind of events, pointed to by the critics of the concept's partial character. It essentially extends to all events of interest. Calculations of differences between average points in time at which transition points A and B occur are meaningful only in those cases in which all individuals who have experienced event A also experience event B. The usual transition points in family life cycle measurement seldom meet this condition. Moreover, if they did do so, such a difference between average points in time is a meaningful measure only when arithmetic means, not medians, are taken as average points in time, as is sometimes done. Despite the points of criticism mentioned above, there is no need to conclude that the family life cycle concept should be discarded. There are several ways of overcoming the concept's shortcomings of normativity, partiality, and inexactitude. It can retain its usefulness as a tool for measuring and analysing what may be called 'household and family dynamics' in situations where the traditional family life cycle sequence of marriage–parenthood–child departure–'empty nest'–death has lost ground.

A first possibility is what has been called the 'expanded family life cycle analysis' (for example, Spanier and Glick, 1980). In this kind of analysis, the concept's partial character, and implicitly its normative character as well, are corrected by incorporating those events that have tranditionally been neglected: divorce, remarriage, childlessness. Moreover, by decomposition into subcategories having experienced similar critical life histories, the criticism of sequential heterogeneity is automatically obviated to a considerable extent. A case in point is the research by Norton (1983), who distinguished birth cohort subcategories according to significant differences in life histories, such as 'once-married, never-divorced', 'married twice, currently married, whose first marriage ended in divorce', etc. Family life cycle measures are then calculated for each subcategory separately.

A second possibility is to incorporate the family life cycle analysis into the much broader concept of life course analysis. The life course refers to pathways which individuals follow through age-differentiated roles and events (Elder, 1977). This life course is multidimensional, being 'a product of multiple histories, each defined by a particular timetable and event sequence—histories of education and work life, marriage and parenthood, residence and civil involvement' (ibid., 282–3).

In this way, the criticisms of partiality and normativity may be overcome as well. An additional advantage is that linkages can be established between the family life history and the other histories, yielding more insight into some of the social and economic determinants of the family life history.

A third possibility is to incorporate family life cycle variables into dynamic household modelling. Depending on its specification, typical family life cycle variables such as mean transition points and numbers and ages of children present in the home may result from adequate household modelling. Macro- and microsimulation models (Bongaarts, 1983, p. 33) seem to be most appropriate to the task.

The research reported in this chapter may be viewed as a stepping-stone to a macrosimulation approach to this modelling challenge. The application of life table techniques, within the framework of this macrosimulation approach, not only adds to a greater precision of the family life cycle measures calculated, but it also adds a completely new category of family life cycle measures to those already existing: mean sojourn times or mean number of person-years to be lived in family life cycle stages, specified by marital status of the parent(s) and by number (and, eventually, by age) of the children present in the home. For many policy usages, such person-year measures are more significant than the traditional family life cycle measures.

12.3. A general presentation of the research

The original projection research aimed at forecasting the Dutch 15 to 49-year-old female population over the period 1975–90. The projected number had to be disaggregated by:

- age in 5-year age groups (15–19 up to 45–49);
- marital status (currently married, divorced, and widowed); and
- parity status, in the sense of the number of 0 to 14-year-old children living in the woman's household (parity status running from 0 to 5).

It was agreed upon that the projection results should fit in with the results of the 1975 national forecast (CBS, 1976). These national forecast results consisted of future age–sex structures for the population as a whole, supplemented by age–marital status structures for the female population only.

I did not expect to achieve this goal of optimal fit by way of adequate modelling itself. The aims of my projection were such that a model characterized by a high degree of analogy with the national forecast model would not meet the requirements of the funding agency. In order to achieve a nice fit on the output level, the sole remaining possibility was, therefore, to conform as best I could to the national forecast hypotheses. Some of the modelling problems engendered by this approach predominate in the discussion in section 12.4.

The projection model constructed operated along the following lines:

Step 1: The initial size of a first-marriage cohort is determined.

Step 2: A family life cycle history of the first-marriage cohort is simulated according to: (i) its future marital status distribution, yielding the numbers in the currently married, the divorced, and the widowed states; (ii) its future distribution by number of children ever born; and (iii) its future distribution by marital and parity status combined, integrating the results of (i) and (ii).

Step 3: Rearrangement of the cohort-wise arranged output of step 2 (iii) into cross-sectionally classified output, implying: (i) disaggregation of step 2 (iii) output, proportional to the cohort's initial composition by exact age; and (ii) regrouping according to exact ages of the women on 31 December of each projection year, and aggregating over 5-year age groups.

The first-marriage cohorts involved were those for the years 1950–89, subdivided into five age-at-marriage groups (15–19, 20–24, 25–29, 30–34, and 35–49).

For an English-language formal description of the model, I refer to an earlier publication (Kuijsten, 1977). Many of the projection results have been published in Dutch-language publications (Kuijsten, 1979; 1978/1980); an extensive English-language publication on the model, its input, and its results appeared recently (Kuijsten, 1986). In the latter publication a comparison is made between this model and multidimensional models (see, for instance, Schoen, 1975; Willekens and Rogers, 1978).

The projection model may be characterized as:

- demographic: the model population is represented as a set of individuals who conform to a given definition (Ryder, 1964), disaggregated by attributes that may or may not change over time in ways that depend on purely demographic parameters of change only;
- dynamic: the model describes the changes over time within the set of individuals constituting the model population;
- deterministic: no parameters have been used for which a probability distribution has been specified; and
- time-discrete: the model population's attribute composition is measured at specific moments only, namely 31 December of each projection year from 1975 to 1989.

Moreover, because it was not possible to project the model population from a known situation, the model reconstructs its own baseline population from observation-based input for first-marriage cohorts 1950–74. This is clarified in Figure 12.1.

After the projection research had been finished, it seemed that the strict longitudinal approach of this model would be a perfect precondition for another approach to the problem of modelling family life cycle dynamics. In order to give a description of the projection results for just one marriage cohort, the projection model could be applied as a life table model. In this way, family life cycle tables could be constructed for all cohorts involved in the original projection research.

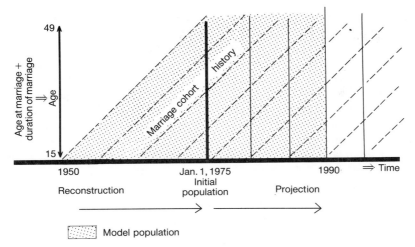

Source: Kuijsten (1986), p. 51.

FIG. 12.1. A schematic representation of the projection model's basic framework

Such a family life cycle table describes the cohort's life course in terms of one absorbing state of death and a number of inter-communicating states according to a state space defined by the two attributes 'marital status' and 'parity status'.

Three marital states are considered: (1) currently married (remarrying divorced or widowed women return to this stage); (2) divorced; and (3) widowed. Six parity states are considered, referring to the number of 0 to 14-year-old children living in the woman's home; this number runs from 0 to 5. Combination of marital states 1–3 with parity states 0–5 gives a state space of 18 states, which is extended to 19 by addition of the absorbing state of death.

The life history of women from first marriage to the end of duration score $n = 25$ is described in the table by the variable $S(n)$, representing the numbers of individual women occupying state S at the end of the seniority variable 'duration n', that is, at the end of the nth calendar year after the calendar year that forms the interval origin. Variable $S(n)$ can take 19 values, 18 of them being combinations of marital status values m ($m = 1,2,3$) with parity status values p ($p = 0,1,2,3,4,5$), written as $S(m,p,n)$, the nineteenth being the cumulating absorbing state of death written as $S(4,-,n)$. The table radix of 100,000 women starts, by definition, in state $S(1,0,-\frac{1}{2})$: currently married ($m = 1$) and no children present ($p = 0$) at the exact date of first marriage, so at the average halfway duration score $n = 0$ (the interval-origin) or at an average exact duration score of $n = -\frac{1}{2}$.

Changes in the numbers in states $S(m,p,n)$ as compared with those in states $S(m,p,n + 1)$ are generated by events which take place in the course of duration interval $n + 1$. With respect to the marital status dimension of the state space, events of interest are divorce, transition to widowhood, remarriage, and death. With respect to the parity status dimension of the state space, events of interest are childbearing, death of a child before it reaches age 15, or the child's survival to age 15. The event of childbearing generates an advance on the parity state score; this can occur when the individual woman occupies marital state 1 only. The two other events generate retreats on the parity state score; these can occur in all three marital states.

From the numbers $S(m,p,n)$ in the family life cycle table, and/or from relevant input data, several unconditional or population-based table measures can be calculated. These table measures are:

- mean numbers of person-years spent in a state, or mean sojourn time in a state, within the frame of duration intervals 0 to 25, and mean number of person-years not lived because of death before attaining the end of duration score 25;
- mean duration scores at which major events of state change take place;
- mean intervals between events of state change, where applicable in case the demand of homogeneity could be fulfilled.

The first category of table measures, of course, adds up to 25.5 years for each first-marriage cohort. The truncation of the family life cycle table influences the interpretation of the second and third category of table measures. Both mean duration scores and mean interval length always pertain to those events of the table only that occur before the end of duration score 25. In order to give an example of the results, Table 12.1 summarizes the mean sojourn times in states $S(m,p)$ for selected first-marriage cohorts aged 20-4 at the time of first marriage.

12.4. The impact of data availability on the modelling strategy and the specification of assumptions

The process of model-building is a process of decision-making. A modelling strategy emerges from a mentally interactive process.

The researcher attempts to combine the more or less clearly articulated demands of the funding agency (in this case, the Netherlands Ministry of Social Affairs), his experience in model-building, his demographic expertise, his acquaintance with the available statistical data (in this case, historical observations as well as input and output of the 1975 national forecast), and his awareness of the missing data (most important in this case, the lack of an observation-based base-line population decomposed by the required attribute categories).

A first and very fundamental decision involved the choice between a so-called 'headship rate approach' and 'vital statistics approach' (United Nations, 1973) as a starting-point for the modelling efforts. I decided to

TABLE 12.1. Mean sojourn time or mean number of person-years lived in marital/parity states over the period extending from first marriage date to the end of the 25th calendar year after the calendar year of first marriage, for selected first-marriage cohorts with age at first marriage 20–24

Marriage cohort	Currently married					Divorced					Widowed				
	Total	of which in parity state				Total	of which in parity state				Total	of which in parity state			
		0	1	2	3–5		0	1	2	3–5		0	1	2	3–5
1954	24.45	5.52	6.69	6.07	6.16	0.47	0.16	0.14	0.10	0.08	0.35	0.14	0.10	0.06	0.05
1959	24.22	5.65	6.88	6.76	4.93	0.71	0.26	0.21	0.15	0.09	0.35	0.15	0.10	0.06	0.03
1964	23.91	6.24	7.29	7.22	3.15	1.02	0.40	0.31	0.22	0.09	0.35	0.18	0.10	0.06	0.02
1969	23.63	7.94	7.23	6.75	1.71	1.31	0.56	0.39	0.28	0.07	0.34	0.19	0.09	0.05	0.01
1974	23.39	10.18	5.85	5.89	1.48	1.55	0.78	0.40	0.30	0.07	0.34	0.21	0.08	0.04	0.01
1979	23.27	10.63	5.62	5.69	1.34	1.67	0.88	0.43	0.31	0.06	0.33	0.21	0.07	0.04	0.01
1984	23.25	10.49	5.60	5.79	1.37	1.70	0.89	0.43	0.31	0.06	0.33	0.21	0.08	0.04	0.01
1989	23.25	10.29	5.69	5.85	1.41	1.70	0.88	0.44	0.32	0.06	0.33	0.20	0.08	0.04	0.01

Note: Mean sojourn times in parity states 0 to 5 have been calculated on the basis of cohort-specific fertility hypotheses that fit in the low-fertility variant used in the 1975 national forecast. For each cohort, fertility after the duration interval corresponding with calendar year 1974 is derived from these hypotheses. Fertility up to and including 1974 is based on observations.

reject the possibility of pursuing a headship rate approach, for the following reasons (see also Linke, chapter 8):

- such an approach would require at least the availability of an observation-based base-line population, disaggregated by age, marital status, and parity status. If possible, a longer time series of such figures would be preferable. Such data did not exist, which was one of the reasons for the funding agency to have them generated through my research;
- such an approach would imply that I would have been capable of 'translating' a priori the combined effect of the 1975 national forecast assumptions on the future course of nuptiality, divorce, mortality, and fertility into a plausible and consistent set of assumed age- and-marital-status specific future parity status distributions. It would have meant that I could 'predict' a priori the outcome of a projection according to a vital statistics approach, especially as far as the effects of the hypothesized profound changes in levels of fertility and divorce on the demanded parity status distributions are concerned.

The modelling strategy, therefore, started with the decision to investigate the possibilities of building a model based on a vital statistics approach. As a consequence, the chosen vital statistics approach would also have to be employed in order to reconstruct the projection's base-line population on 1 January 1975, from observations over a period long enough to make the reconstruction results cover the model population on this starting date (see Figure 12.1).

A vital statistics approach to the modelling problem is based on a system of accounting numbers of events (by balancing equations) which are generated by applying event probabilities to stock numbers at risk (by flow equations). From a formal point of view, the projection model may also serve as a model to reconstruct the past. The main difference lies at the input level: in the reconstruction mode, the event probabilities are based on observations, whereas in the projection mode they are based on assumptions. In the discussion below, both observation-based and assumption-based event probabilities are called 'data'.

These data typically pertain to the experiences of people as *individuals*: if specified according to additional attributes, these attributes are measured at the level of the individual also. It is the 'atomistic' individual who is the unit of observation as well as the unit of projection, in traditional demographic analysis, in official observation-based data collection, and in traditional population projection. Household modelling, in contrast, should ideally take some 'molecular' aggregate of individuals (households or families) as the unit of observation and projection. The emerging sub-discipline of household and family demography has to cope with the problem of defining event probabilities dependent on a set of individual and/or collective attributes of members of the molecular aggregate.

This task still lies ahead, as it did in the mid-1970s, when I carried out this research.

Perforce, then, in the modelling strategy I had to try to generate 'molecular' output (family composition variables as 'attributes' of individual women) from a model that would, as artfully as possible, combine the effects of all relevant 'atomistic' input variables, in full awareness of the fact that this strategy was merely 'second best' to a mature family-demographic model.

Such a strategy of combining 'atomistic' input variables in order to generate 'molecular' output can succeed only when the populations at risk of the event probabilities are defined such that they may be regarded as optimally homogeneous with respect to the event probabilities employed. This recognition automatically leads to a longitudinal or cohort approach. The Ministry was interested in the ever-married female population only. Moreover, as far as projection of future numbers of live births is concerned, the 1975 national forecast model leaned heavily on the projection of legitimate births within marriage cohorts, extra-marital births being assessed as remaining on the 2 per cent level of the projected annual numbers of legitimate live births only.

Therefore, the modelling strategy focused on the longitudinal approach of the model body, provisionally regarding the female marriage cohort as the most homogeneous kind of subpopulation from the point of view of the necessity of combining 'atomistic' input variables. The major consequences of this decision were:

- extra-marital fertility was excluded from the data, and so its possible effects were excluded from the resulting parity status distributions. Because of the very low levels of extra-marital fertility in the Netherlands up to 1975 and the 2 per cent assumption in the 1975 national forecast, I accepted this omission of pre-marital births; that is to say, I preferred the certainties connected with their exclusion over the uncertainties connected with the use of assumptions about their distribution over the brides at the starting-point of their marital careers. Had I known then that present levels of extra-marital fertility would be much higher than envisaged in the mid-1970s, my decision would surely have been different;
- all members of any marriage cohort would start their family life cycle history, to be projected by the model, in the parity zero status. In this way, for all children to be born to the cohort members, the difference between their birth year and the cohort's interval-origin could serve as a perfect and unambiguous 'marker' of their age, at all stages of their mother's family life cycle. This makes it possible to operationalize the child-presence dimension of the family life cycle in any conceivable way, in terms of numbers of children below some age and/or more refined age specifications of the children present in the home.

Marriage cohorts with a very wide age-at-marriage range are much too crude with regard to the assumptions of constant proportionality to the cohort's initial composition by separate age, on which step 3 of the model should be based. Last but not least, available observations on duration-specific fertility and divorce for marriage cohorts, decomposed by age at marriage, do show significant differences in patterns of fertility and divorce by age at marriage. Marriage cohorts in which all women married at ages 15 to 49 are taken together are clearly not homogeneous enough with respect to the major events of interest for the cohort's family life cycle history.

Therefore, in the model, marriage cohorts were distinguished by age at marriage. The problem as to which classification should be chosen could be solved easily by conforming to the age-at-marriage classification in use for observations on cohort marital fertility by the bride's age at marriage (15–19, 20–24, 25–29, 30–34, and 35–49) for a time series starting with marriage cohort 1950. Moreover, the available cohort observations on divorce, dis-aggregated by the bride's age-at-marriage groups, could be dovetailed easily into the above-mentioned classifications of age at marriage. The major con-sequences of this decision were at the level of specification of a number of input variables:

- as far as marital fertility input is concerned, the 1975 national forecast input on marital fertility of marriage cohorts that had not been disaggre-gated by age at marriage was used as a constraint. Although the method did not yield implausible or even suspect results, the series of extrapolated cohort input values showed small irregularities which would not have occurred if I had applied unconstrained extrapolation methods indepen-dently for each marriage cohort.
- in the 1975 national forecast age-specific divorce probabilities had been extrapolated on the basis of an assumption about a further increase in the annual total frequency of divorce per 1,000 married women. Therefore, I had to make my own extrapolation of marriage cohort-specific annual divorce probabilities, starting with the cohort-specific observations up to and including 1974. In this case, the total annual numbers of divorcing women under age 50 according to the 1975 national forecast had to be used as a constraint. Again, extrapolated series of cohort-specific divorce prob-abilities showed greater irregularities than other, unconstrained methods would have yielded.

The data on marital fertility by marriage cohort, observed until 1975 as well as those hypothesized for 1975 and beyond, were fertility data expressed per 1,000 of the initial cohort size, the marriage cohorts consisting of first and non-first marriages of the women concerned. Non-first marriages do link these cohorts: in the course of their lives, women may belong to two or even more of such marriage cohorts, and so does their contribution to cohort marital fertility. But, in the birth order classification of these cohort fertility data, birth order is defined with respect to the current marriage, and not with respect to the life course of the mother. Such fertility data, therefore, are contrary to the aim of optimal homogeneity of cohorts with respect to the most relevant life course events. Moreover, the output demands were clearly in terms of numbers of children with respect to the mothers, and not with respect to the mother's current marriage only. As a matter of fact, remarrying women usually bring their children from a previous marriage into the new marital union.

The modelling strategy, therefore, was aimed at removing the non-first marriages from the marriage cohorts discussed so far. This was done by defining the marriage cohort as a first-marriage cohort, and by placing remarrying women back into the currently married state of their original first-marriage cohort stock, instead of allocating them to a new marriage cohort according to their year of remarriage and age at remarriage. One of the modelling consequences was that:

- the complete cohort-specific fertility input, originally expressed per 1,000 women of cohorts containing first and non-first married cohort members, was assumed to pertain to cohorts consisting of first-married women only. In spite of the distortions that would occur in this way in each separate marriage cohort history, I assumed that these distortions would to a large extent be cancelled at the level of the model population as a whole. Although plausibility tests of the results gave me confidence as to the 'correctness' of the last-mentioned assumption, the procedure as such remains unsatisfactory.

The last major modelling decision had to do with the way in which, within the framework of step 2 (iii), in each duration interval, parity status attributes should be attached to the women who in that duration interval made a marital status change according to step 2 (i). Generally speaking, the observation data could not give sufficiently precise answers to questions about the degree to which the parity status distributions of women who change marital status would differ from the parity status distributions of the marital status category to which they had belonged immediately prior to the marital status change. As a working hypothesis, then, I assumed that the parity status distribution of women undergoing whatever marital status change in whatever interval of a cohort's family life cycle history would be equal to the parity status distribution of the marital status category to which they had belonged at the beginning of the duration interval concerned.

- With respect to divorcing women, this meant the implicit assumption that all 0 to 14-year-old children of a divorcing couple would remain in their mother's care.
- With respect to remarrying women, this meant the implicit assumption that their new husbands would not themselves bring 0 to 14-year-old children into the newly founded family.

12.5. User's influence on the project, and the use of the model in policy

The original projection research has been funded by the Netherlands Ministry of Social Affairs. As the prime potential user, therefore, this Ministry might be expected to have exerted a significant influence on the project. It has done so indeed, be it in the first stages of the project only. Its influence has been most manifest in the way in which I have tried, in the modelling strategy and otherwise, to stick as closely as possible to the Ministry's output demands, as laid down in its first project documents. These demands, in their turn, have been closely related to the Ministry's intended use of the projection results, namely, as a point of departure for estimating the future labour force participation of ever-married women. Marital status, number of dependent children, and age of these children were regarded as important determinants of the future labour force participation of Dutch women.

It must be stressed once again that the modelling strategy was aimed at constructing a purely demographic model. The model is not explanatory, in so far as it does not incorporate behaviouristic parameters alongside the demographic events of status change (such as, for instance, entry into or exit from the labour force). Within this rather narrow framework, however, the modelling strategy aimed at constructing a model which would be as appropriate as possible a point of departure for several kinds of applications, without failing to miss the originally demanded answers: decomposition of the female population relevant to labour force participation estimates.

In view of all the efforts to reach this aim, it is a pity that the Ministry has never, as far as I know, carried into effect its original intentions of making an estimate of future female labour force participation on the basis of my projection results. It did use the results, however, for calculating the budgetary reservations to be made for some social security payments.

Further, the projection results have been used in the report 'Beleidsgerichte Toekomstverkenning' (A policy-orientated exploration of the future) by the Netherlands Scientific Council for Government Policy, in its paragraph on future population prospects for the Netherlands (WRR, 1980, pp. 81–2).

12.6. Future research opportunities

The research reported on may be viewed as a stepping-stone to a macro-simulation model of the family life cycle. The family life cycle table in particular may serve as a useful tool for the sake of policy making, because this life table approach yields mean sojourn times which are not produced by conventional family life cycle analysis. For policy applications, insight into the mean points in time at which transitions between states take place is less relevant than insight into the mean lengths of time individuals occupy these states. From the point of view of making the necessary reservations for future social security payments to divorced women or female-headed one-parent families, for instance, expected mean sojourn times in these states are much more directly related to estimated annual social security expenses than are statistics such as mean age at divorce or the percentage of marriages ending in a divorce. From the point of view of housing policy, for example, expected mean sojourn times in distinct parity states are more directly related to problems of housing differentiation—in terms of square meters of floor space and/or numbers of rooms—than are statistics such as the expected mean number of children born into families, or mean ages of the mother-at which first or last children are born or leave the parental home. The main strength of the table approach to family life cycle modelling, in my opinion, is that it can directly convert assumptions on the future course of relevant events of status change (marriage, divorce, transition to widowhood, child-bearing, children leaving home) into expected sojourn times in policy-relevant states.

There will be two major types of future research. First, studies aimed at overcoming the 'atomistic', individual-based nature of the current model by trying to model on the basis of either households or minimal household units, being configurations of individuals serving as 'molecular' units of analysis and projection. Second, studies aimed at incorporating extra-demographic variables, in search of an explanation of inter-cohort differences in family life cycle courses and, by consequence, in mean sojourn times in policy-relevant marital/parity states.

References

BONGAARTS, J. (1983). The formal demography of families and households: an overview, *IUSSP Newsletter* 17, 27–42.

BRASS, W. (1983). The formal demography of the family: an overview of the proximate determinants, in: The family, Proceedings of the British Society for Population Studies Conference, 1983, Office of Population Censuses and Surveys Occasional Paper no. 31 (OPCS, London), 37–49.

CBS (NETHERLANDS CENTRAL BUREAU OF STATISTICS) (1976). *De toekomstige demografische ontwikkeling in Nederland na 1975* (The future demographic development in the Netherlands after 1975) (Staatsuitgeverij, The Hague).

CUISENIER, J. (ed.) (1977). *The Family Life Cycle in European Societies* (Mouton, The Hague, Paris).

ELDER, G. H. JUN. (1977). Family history and the life course, *Journal of Family History* 2(4), 279–304.

GLICK, P. V. (1947). The family life cycle, *American Sociological Review* 12, 164–74.

—— (1977). Updating the life cycle of the family, *Journal of Marriage and the Family* 39(1), 5–13.

HILL, R. AND R. H. RODGERS (1964). The developmental approach, in: Harold T.

Christensen (ed.), *Handbook of Marriage and the Family* (Rand McNally, Chicago), 171–211.

HÖHN, C. (1982). *Der Familienzyklus: zur Notwendigkeit einer Konzepterweiterung* (The family life cycle: on the necessity of an extension of the concept), Publication Series of the Federal Institute of Population Research, vol. 12 (Boldt-Verlag, Boppard am Rhein).

KUIJSTEN, A. C. (1977). A projection model of families according to family phase, Working Paper no. 7, Netherlands Interuniversity Demographic Institute, Voorburg.

—— (1979). De toekomstige gezinsfase-ontwikkeling van de aantallen gehuwde en gehuwd geweest zijnde vrouwen in Nederland (The future family life cycle distribution of ever-married women in the Netherlands), Internal Report no. 14, Netherlands Interuniversity Demographic Institute, Voorburg (in Dutch).

—— (1978/1980). De toekomstige gezinsfase-ontwikkeling van gehuwde en gehuwd geweest zijnde vrouwen in Nederland (The future family life cycle distribution of ever-married women in the Netherlands), 1: het vooruitberekeningsmodel (the projection model), *Bevolking en Gezin* 1978(3), 413–32; II: hypothesen en uitkomsten (hypotheses and results), *Bevolking en Gezin* 1980(2), 235–57.

—— (1986). *Advances in Family Demography*, Publications of the Netherlands Interuniversity Demographic Institute (NIDI) and the Population and Family Study Centre (CBGS), vol. 14, NIDI, The Hague.

NOCK, L. (1979). The family life cycle: empirical or conceptual tool?, *Journal of Marriage and the Family* 41(1), 15–26.

NORTON, A. J. (1983). Family life cycle: 1980, *Journal of Marriage and the Family* 45(2), 267–75.

RYDER, N. B. (1964). Notes on the concept of a population, *The American Journal of Sociology* 69 (1964) 5, 447–63.

SCHOEN, R. (1975). Constructing increment–decrement life tables, *Demography* 12, 313–24.

SPANIER, B. AND C. GLICK (1980). The life cycle of American families: an expanded analysis, *Journal of Family History* 5(1), 97–111.

UNITED NATIONS (1973). *Methods of Projecting Households and Families*, Population Studies no. 54 (United Nations, New York).

WILLEKENS, F. J. AND A. ROGERS (1978). Spatial population analysis: methods and computer programs, Research Report RR-78-18, IIASA, Laxenburg, Austria.

WRR (NETHERLANDS SCIENTIFIC COUNCIL FOR GOVERNMENT POLICY) (1980). Beleidsgerichte toekomstverkenning (A policy-orientated exploration of the future) (Staatsuitgeverij, The Hague).

YOUNG, C. (1977). The family life cycle, Literature review and studies of families in Melbourne, Australia, Australian Family Formation Project Monograph no. 6, The Australian National University Press, Canberra.

13

Some issues in modelling household behaviour of the aged in Hungary

F. Kamarás

ABSTRACT

This chapter analyses the household situation of an increasingly important population category: the aged. Household data from the Hungarian 1970 and 1980 Population Censuses serve as the basis for analysis, as do the results of projections until the turn of the century. The analysis is carried out by the headship rate method; projections were made on the basis of constant 1980 headship rates. This chapter tries to reveal the factors influencing changes in the headship rates and discusses the flaws connected with projections made on the basis of constant rates. Special attention is paid to the development of one-person households and to possibilities for modelling the demographic factors affecting the evolution in numbers of these households.

13.1. The demographic development of the aged in Hungary

POPULATION ageing is one of the remarkable demographic trends of our time. The process has a long tradition, starting with the decrease in mortality and followed by falling fertility. These two basic demographic processes affect the age structure. Mainly as a result of the decrease in infant and child mortality, ever growing proportions of birth cohorts have attained old age, which in this contribution will be set at the age of 60. This process can be illustrated nicely with Hungarian data, according to which life expectancy at birth increased by 30 to 35 years since the beginning of the century, and life expectancy at age 60 increased by 2 to 6 years in the same period (Klinger, 1983).

In economically developed countries the ageing process may be expected to continue at a more rapid pace. This has two major reasons. First 'inner reserves' for a further mortality decrease are most manifest in the older population groups. Second, the continuing low level of fertility. The latter reason may play an important role in future, especially if its level remains below that ensuring population replacement. This is exactly the situation in Hungary, where the number of births has not reached the replacement level for almost 25 years now. Therefore, the ageing process occurs hand in hand with a decrease in population size. If the hypotheses with regard to mortality

F. Kamarás

and fertility currently in use do indeed materialize, then—by the turn of the century—the population number will drop by about 4 per cent, whereas the number of people over age 60 will grow by about 5 per cent. In the early 1990s the number of persons over 60 as well as their ratio to the total population will equal the number and proportion of the 0 to 14-year-old population.

The age structure of the elderly is unbalanced. The generations born during World War I reached old age in the past decade and will age through the top of the age pyramid during the decades to come. The size of these generations is about 40 per cent smaller than that of the generations following and preceding them. That is why in the 1970s the ageing process of the total population seemed to come to a halt: the proportion over 60 years no longer increased. But in the same period the number of persons over age 70 grew dramatically: within the aged part of the population the ageing process continued. Parallel to this, the proportion of women within the aged population increased.

The absolute number of males over 60 did not change significantly during the 1970s and it is expected to decrease by 3 per cent by the turn of the

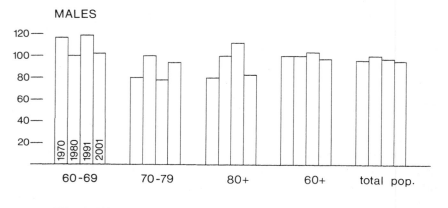

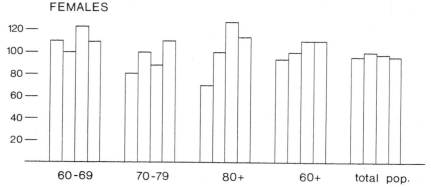

FIG. 13.1 Indexed numbers of aged population, by sex and age, Hungary, 1970–2001 (1980 = 100)

century. The absolute number of aged females, on the other hand, increased between 1970 and 1980, and by the turn of the century their number will presumably have increased even further, by about 10 per cent (see Figure 13.1). All this will cause a further shift in the sex ratio of the aged. Therefore, the social problems of the aged will become increasingly similar to the problems of elderly females.

Besides, there are large regional differences in amount and in tempo of the ageing process. In the last decade, the ageing process was most profound in the capital of Budapest and in the rural areas. Nowadays, two-thirds of the total population live in these two regions, whereas nearly three out of four persons over 60 live there. In the next two decades ageing will be most manifest in the rural areas, because the total rural population will fall by nearly 20 per cent (mainly due to outmigration), whereas the number of aged in the rural areas is expected to change only slightly.

13.1.1. Some household characteristics of the aged

The demographic processes mentioned will thus not only affect the number and age structure of the population, but its sex and marital status composition and its regional distribution too. Through them, they will also influence the population's family and household situation. The decrease in average household size found in the Western world as a whole also applies to Hungary. This is not caused by demographic factors alone; there are also socio-economic reasons. Examining the Hungarian data, one sees that the decline in average household size is clearly characterized by the fact that, whereas in 1970–80 the total population grew by 4 per cent, the total number of households increased by 10 per cent and the number of one-person households even by 24 per cent in the same period. When looking at the period 1960–80, these differences are even more dramatic: the total number of households grew by 21 per cent, the number of one-person households by 63 per cent, whereas the total population increased by 9 per cent only.

These figures reflect the decrease in average family size caused by the drop in fertility, changes in the family life cycle, the increase in the divorce rate, and changes in customs and opportunities with regard to intergenerational cohabitation. No doubt, however, ageing also played an essential role in these changes, since among heads of household the proportion aged is much higher than among the total population. For example, in 1980, 18 per cent of the population living in households were over 60; among heads of household this proportion was 27, whereas 50 per cent of the people living in one-person households were 60 years or older.

When studying the household and family situation of the elderly more thoroughly, it seems expedient to make a distinction between three categories, each with their own repercussions for family and social care. The first category consists of elderly people living in family households, either as

198   *F. Kamarás*

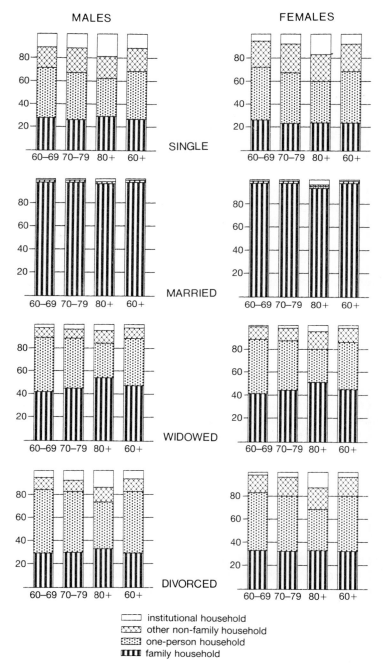

F<small>IG</small>. 13.2. Distribution of the aged population over household types, by age, sex, and marital status, Hungary, 1980 (Census data)

spouses or as parents living with married children or as widowed, divorced, or single people living in the household of a child, grandchild, other relatives, or non-related persons. The second category covers those who do not live in family households: they may be subdivided into those living alone and those living with other people (a relative such as a brother or sister, or a non-relative) without forming a family. The inhabitants of institutions form the third category; they are usually treated separately in household statistics.

When we differentiate between three categories according to their household situation and according to demographic criteria, it is remarkable to discover that neither age nor sex nor residence figure as prominently as marital status does. This is shown very clearly in Figure 13.2, made on the basis of data from the 1980 Census. Among the non-married elderly, widows show the greatest proportion living in family households, whereas the proportion of people living alone is highest among the divorced of all age groups and of both sexes. The proportion living in institutions is highest among aged singles—males and females—who also show the highest proportion of those living together in non-family households. Though it cannot be concluded from the graphs, it is worth mentioning that 9 per cent of single elderly men and 14 per cent of the divorced live in consensual unions: the actual proportion of people really living alone is thus somewhat lower.

Changes over time in the household situation of the aged can be illustrated with the aid of changes in their headship rates. The headship rate method, as recommended by the United Nations, is one of the basic methods in use for making projections of households, their numbers as well as their composition.

Projections of families and households for Hungary on the basis of the headship rate method have been made before (Tamásy, 1965), but their results have not been published. Recently, new projections of this type have been made on the basis of the latest population forecast. Their results have first been published for the total numbers of families and households only and for the major family types (Szabó, 1984). Later on, projection results have been published that are disaggregated by age and marital status also, on the basis of constant headship rates but using hypotheses about future changes in marital status distributions of the elderly (Csernák and Szabó, 1985).

Table 13.1 presents the headship rates of the elderly, split up by age group, sex, and marital status. I calculated these rates on the basis of the number of families and households according to the 1970 and 1980 Censuses. The 1970 Census contained a direct question with respect to the person regarded as being the head of household. In contrast, the 1980 Census only asked about the family status; in case of households consisting of more than one family, the census instructions provided rules to decide which family head should be considered the head of household.

Table 13.1 shows that the headship rates of aged males increased modestly

TABLE 13.1. Headship rates of the elderly and proportion of aged heads of household living in one-person households, by age, sex, and marital status, Hungary, 1970 and 1980

Age groups	Single		Married		Widowed		Divorced		Total	
	1970	1980	1970	1980	1970	1980	1970	1980	1970	1980
Headship rates (%)										
Males										
60–64	67.4	69.9	92.1	90.4	68.1	72.2	86.6	84.2	89.7	88.6
65–69	68.7	70.4	88.3	89.7	58.9	69.8	83.0	84.3	84.7	87.1
70–74	68.5	69.6	85.7	89.2	50.8	63.3	79.7	80.6	79.1	84.3
75+	64.3	63.8	81.1	87.4	39.2	51.0	70.2	74.9	66.2	74.7
total 60+	67.2	68.9	88.3	89.4	49.7	59.0	82.7	82.2	82.1	84.2
Females										
60–64	52.5	62.0	2.3	2.4	55.5	65.4	60.7	68.7	23.5	28.2
65–69	54.5	64.0	1.9	2.2	52.1	62.9	58.4	67.4	28.4	34.0
70–74	54.7	63.7	1.8	2.1	47.2	59.2	56.6	65.0	32.2	39.7
75+	52.2	60.9	2.0	2.6	38.3	49.3	49.3	58.7	33.8	42.6
total 60+	53.5	62.7	2.1	2.3	46.8	56.7	58.0	65.8	28.8	36.8
Proportion in one-person households (%)										
Males										
60–64	63.2	68.1	1.6	1.1	52.6	64.1	60.2	67.6	7.0	8.2
65–69	62.2	69.2	1.6	1.9	63.3	69.5	63.5	70.6	9.1	10.6
70–74	63.0	68.7	1.6	1.8	66.9	73.6	63.1	71.1	11.3	13.6
75+	64.2	66.8	1.5	1.7	65.6	72.7	61.7	69.7	16.8	20.2
total 60+	63.4	68.2	1.5	1.8	63.0	70.7	61.8	69.8	9.7	12.7
Females										
60–64	82.3	77.3	73.9	70.8	68.5	70.3	75.1	72.1	71.1	71.6
65–69	83.1	77.2	78.9	77.3	77.0	76.3	81.5	77.9	78.2	76.8
70–74	81.2	76.4	77.8	76.2	79.2	78.2	84.3	79.1	79.5	78.1
75+	80.1	74.7	75.0	73.1	72.3	72.8	82.2	77.0	73.0	73.0
total 60+	81.7	76.2	73.9	74.4	74.4	74.8	79.3	76.3	75.3	74.7

between 1970 and 1980, whereas those of elderly females increased more strongly. This increase in headship rates has been most conspicuous for widowed males and for single women. At first sight the explanation seems simple: we know from other calculations, not shown in the table, that the proportion of household heads living alone has increased considerably. Such an increase automatically boosts their headship rates. After examination of the lower panel of Table 13.1, however, one may wonder if this explanation is correct. It may be concluded that the moderate increase in the headship rates of males might indeed be explained by the growth of the proportion living alone. In the case of females, however, the proportion living alone decreased slightly. It must be borne in mind that part of the explanation may also be found in the between-census differences in the definition of head of household mentioned above.

Such problems of definition do not arise, however, when comparing the categories of one-person households, which constitute the majority of the households headed by the aged. In spite of this it is still difficult to give an explanation for the increase in the proportion of people living alone in most of the categories of non-married of both sexes. On the one hand there is the growing proportion of elderly people living in non-married cohabitation, but on the other hand the proportion divorced has grown as well. It seems that—parallel to the increase in headship rates—the proportion of persons living alone and of elderly people living in other non-family household types has grown. For the widows at least, who constitute the greater part of elderly people living alone, an acceptable explanation may be found. Because of the decrease in average family size mentioned above, and due to changes in the habits of intergenerational cohabitation (among other reasons because of improved housing conditions), the proportion of married couples living in households of their own, without children or other relatives, has grown. In such cases, when one of the spouses becomes widowed, this will automatically increase the proportion of people living alone. This is most relevant for the female subpopulation, taking into account the worsening mortality conditions for males that have been observed in the past fifteen years.

13.1.2. Expected developments in the household situation of the aged

At the moment it is difficult—though not impossible—to imagine that the headship rates among the elderly will increase further, as they did in the past decade. Instead, it seems more likely that the more important future changes will be related to the composition of aged household heads by type of household; for example legislation now discouraging remarriage of widows below age 55—because of the cessation of the widow's pension rights—may lose its importance in the future. This problem can be solved by cohabitation outside of marriage, but changed legislation in answer to changed norms may be important too. Considering the demands and needs of institutional care for the aged, the proportion of the elderly living in institutional households will probably grow, which is another factor that may depress further growth of headship rates.

It is not my intention to prove or disprove the reliability of the projection made with constant 1980 headship rates. The projection is meant in the first place as a methodically sound experimental calculation to demonstrate the effects that will take place because of changes in the sex and age structure of the population only. This is of particular interest in countries such as Hungary, where there are great differences in size between adjacent age

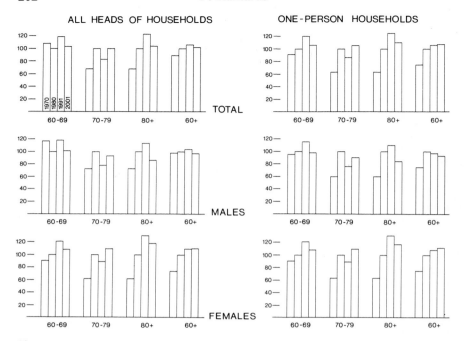

Notes:
    1. The numbers for 1991 and 2001 have been calculated on the basis of constant 1980 age- and sex-specific headship rates.
    2. Since in the age classification for 1970 the age groups 70–79 and 80+ have been taken together, in each category in the graph the two left bars for these age groups are of equal length, representing the indexed numbers of the age group 70+.

FIG. 13.3. Indexed numbers of aged heads of households, by sex and age, Hungary, 1970–2001 (1980 = 100)

groups, especially, but not exclusively, among the aged. Figure 13.3 illustrates the developments that can be expected in the absolute numbers of elderly heads of household until the year 2001. As can be seen from the graphs, the trends observed in the 1970s will continue even when assuming constant 1980 age-, sex-, and marital status-specific headship rates. The total absolute number of households, however, will not change significantly over the projection period, whereas the total population will presumably decrease by 4 per cent. Among heads of household, the proportion of aged heads will continue to grow. From 1990 onwards, the proportion of aged heads of households living alone will increase dramatically. Care for old people will, I believe, have to concentrate more and more on aged females living alone. At present, as many as 79 per cent of the elderly living alone are females: by the turn of the century this proportion will probably have reached 81 per cent.

    In Figure 13.4, these findings have been differentiated by marital status, as far as the elderly living alone are concerned. Because of their large propor-

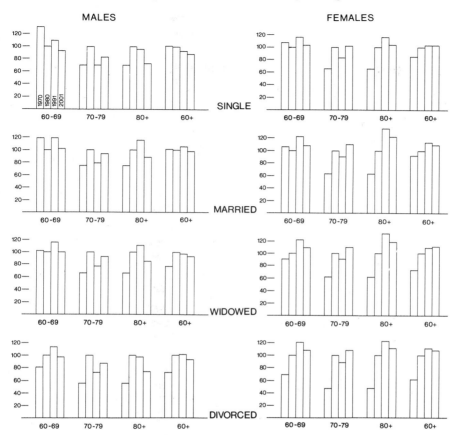

Notes: See notes 1 and 2 in Figure 13.3.

FIG. 13.4. Indexed numbers of aged heads of one-person households, by sex, age, and marital status, Hungary, 1970–2001 (1980 = 100)

tion, the situation of widowed women again deserves most attention. Both among heads of household and among persons living alone, the numbers of widows will grow constantly. Among women of other marital states and among males, the numbers of heads of household and of persons living alone show fluctuations; they are mainly determined by the expected dynamics of the age structure of the elderly.

What is the possible error of a forecast carried out on the basis of these constant headship rates? This question cannot be answered easily, since many factors must be taken into account. From past experience, however, one can gain some information on this matter with the aid of the so-called *ex-post* evaluation method. If we had projected, for instance, in 1970, the 1980 number and composition of aged household heads, assuming that the 1970

TABLE 13.2. Projected indexed numbers of aged heads of household, 1980, on the basis of constant 1970 headship rates (1970 = 100), by age, sex, and marital status, Hungary

Age groups	Single	Married	Widowed	Divorced	Total
	All households				
Males					
60–64	96	102	94	103	101
65–69	98	98	84	98	97
70–74	98	96	80	99	94
75+	101	93	77	94	89
total 60+	98	98	81	99	96
Females					
60–64	85	94	85	88	86
65–69	85	86	83	87	84
70–74	86	85	80	87	81
75+	86	78	78	84	79
total 60+	85	87	80	87	82
	One-person households only				
Males					
60–64	89	94	77	92	87
65–69	88	82	77	89	82
70–74	90	89	73	87	79
75+	97	82	69	83	73
total 60+	91	86	73	89	79
Females					
60–64	90	97	83	92	86
65–69	92	90	83	91	85
70–74	91	87	81	93	83
75+	92	78	77	90	79
total 60+	91	90	80	91	83

headship rates would remain constant, we would have obtained numbers of household heads that would be 4 per cent lower than those observed for the males, and 19 per cent lower than those observed for the females (Table 13.2). When decomposed by marital status, great differences appear between the projected and the observed numbers of aged heads of household; among males, mainly in the case of widowers, among females in all marital states. This difference would have been even greater in the numbers of elderly people living alone, particularly those widowed.

How should these proportional errors be evaluated? Projections of total numbers of aged people can be done quite reliably, since they depend basically on mortality hypotheses. Projections of sex and marital status distributions of the aged are rather less reliable; in the case of the aged, mortality has a significant indirect effect on the distribution by marital status, in addition to the effects of other marital status changes. Notwithstanding these uncertainties, some trends can be observed. The proportion divorced started increasing long ago, but it is still comparatively low among the elderly. Since 1970, the proportion widowed decreased slightly and the proportion married increased to a small extent for both sexes in the age group over 70. But in age group 60–69 the situation is the reverse. These changes in marital status proportions, however, played an insignificant role in the changes in headship rates as compared with the simultaneous changes in the household situation. This can be illustrated with an alternative projection on the basis of the 1980 headship rates instead of the 1970 ones: in this case, the 1980 number of female widowed heads of household is overestimated by about 2 per cent.

In conclusion it may be stated that in a household projection for the elderly population uncertainties about the demographic factors do play a role, but the major uncertainties are non-demographic. Many socio-economic and cultural factors determine the future household situation of the aged, among which are the development of the housing situation, preferences for, and possibilities of, intergenerational cohabitation, and legal provisions facilitating or impeding remarriage or unmarried cohabitation.

13.2. Possibilities for modelling household dynamics of the aged

The analysis and modelling of household dynamics is a relatively new field in demography. With respect to the aged, special demographic modelling approaches have to be developed because of their particular socio-economic situation, demographic characteristics, and therefore their particular family and household situation (see, for instance, the different distributions of the marital status categories by household situation in Figure 13.2). When developing specific modelling approaches for these later phases of the life cycle, one must reveal those household particularities characteristic of the elderly and use these as a basis for modelling. Besides, it is important to ask to what extent society is willing to take up responsibility for the care for the elderly in the long run, or to what extent it wants to place this responsibility on the shoulders of the family itself, by way of a policy of incentives. In other words, the evolution of the household situation of the aged is not a demographic and/or socio-economic problem alone, but a socio-political problem as well. The situation of the aged is a complex problem that will emerge sooner or later in all economically and demographically developed countries.

13.2.1. Data sources

With respect to information on characteristics of the household situation of the aged, difficulties arise for lack of sufficiently detailed data. On the basis of Hungarian Census data, the household situation of the aged can be analysed in two ways. The first way is to take the household as the unit of observation and analysis and describe it with the aid of demographic characteristics of the household head. However, there are few tabulations by age of the household head, and these do not indicate the sex and marital status distributions of the heads. From these tables it can be stated that the overwhelming majority (80 to 90 per cent) of households with an aged head consist of one- and two-person households. As a rule, if the household head is married, this means elderly married couples living together, and if the household head is not married he or she lives alone. Aged non-heads as a rule are members of households of other people. The proportion of the elderly living in institutional households is low in Hungary.

This information leads us to the second type of analysis. It characterizes individuals living in households, by household and by family status. Such data are available by age, sex, marital status, and even by region.

13.2.2. The selection of methods of analysis

The headship rate method was chosen for two reasons. First, headship rates can be calculated easily from the second type of census tabulations, as mentioned earlier. The projection of headship rates of elderly people living in non-family households, however, causes problems. Second, such future headship rates can easily be applied to the results of standard population projections. Yet it still remains problematic how to estimate the extent and direction of change in the headship rates. The change in the headship rates for one-person households, constituting the majority of aged heads of household, can be modelled with the aid of demographic table methods; for example, life tables by sex and marital status. Divorce is rare among the aged, divorced elderly people as a rule enter old age in that marital status. The population projection did not include marital status distributions, hence household projections with unchanged marital status structure presuppose, for example, that mortality among the aged does not depend on their marital status. This supposition is not true, however, as is well-known (Mádai, 1982). Cohort studies of marital status changes may also contribute to the formulation of hypotheses about marital status changes (Csernák, 1983; Csernák and Szabó, 1985). Data on cohabitation, however, are available only for census dates, that is, every ten years.

Changes in headship rates are influenced not only by the demographic processes just mentioned, but by other processes as well, the modelling of which is difficult. The spread of non-married cohabitation is influenced by changing norms and attitudes, as well as by changes in opportunities and laws. The proportion of elderly people living alone may be affected by government policies to increase the number of institutions for the aged and by policies aimed at increasing the role and responsibilities for taking care of one's aged relatives. In forecasting, the proportion of the aged living in non-family households and aspects of housing policy must be taken into account. Such factors seem to have a greater bearing on the future household situation of the aged than 'pure' demographic factors may have.

13.3. Conclusions

Application of the headship rate method to modelling the household situation of the aged has many advantages. The method is relatively simple and the required data are available. The method provides information on heads of household as well as on some characteristics of their households, by age, sex, and marital status of the head. Thus the distribution of the entire population living in households can be established, by household and family status. However, the method does not give the distribution of the population by household size, nor by household composition. For the aged, this is not very problematic, since the majority of households with elderly heads consists of one- or two-person households. We know little, however, about the household composition of the aged living with other families or in non-family households, that is, about the household situation of about 20 per cent of the aged. Methods of combining individual data from other sources seem to be the best solution to that problem. This would greatly enlarge the possibilities for modelling household formation and dissolution.

References

CSERNÁK J. AND K. SZABÓ (1985). A családok és háztartások elöreszámitása, 1981–2001 (Family- and household projections, 1981–2001), Publications of the Demographic Research Institute no. 59, Budapest 1985/1.

CSERNÁK, M. (1983). Development of first marriages in Hungary after World War II, marriage tables of birth cohorts, Publications of the Demographic Research Institute no. 54. As elsö házasságkötések alakulása Magyarországon a II. világháboru után születési kohorszok házassági táblái, A Népességtudományi Kutató Intézet Közleményei 54, Budapest.

KLINGER, A. (1983). Demographic aspects of aging: the demographic situation and problems of the old population. Az öregedés demográfiai vonatkozásai: az idöskoru népesség demográfiai helyzete és problémái, *Statisztikai Kiadó Vállalat*, 19–51.

MÁDAI, L. (1982). Relations between marital status and mortality and their recent tendencies. A családi állapot és a halandóság összefüggései és ujabb tendenciái, *Demográfia* 25, 257–80.

SZABÓ, K. (1984). The development of some characteristics of families and households, 1981–2001, Preliminary variant, Research Reports of the Demographic
Research Institute no. 16. Családok és háztartások néhány jellemzöjének
alakulása, 1981–2001, Elözetes változat, A Népességtudományi Kutató Intézet
Kutatási Jelentései 16, Budapest.

TAMÁSY, J. (1965). Projections of families in Hungary, United Nations World
Population Conference, Belgrade.

UNITED NATIONS (1973). *Methods of Projecting Households and Families*,
Population Studies no. 54 (United Nations, New York).

14

Application of household models in regional planning

H. ter Heide and H. Scholten

ABSTRACT

Regional planning aims at improving the balance between population, resources, and amenities, both within regions and with respect to the distribu tion across regions. To be able to prepare forecasts and assess policy impacts regional planners require recursive models showing the interdependency of population redistribution (migration) and household formation and dissolution. This is illustrated in this paper by a discussion of the models developed in the Netherlands. When confronted with actual trends in migration patterns, regional population structures, and household formation, these models prove insufficient for the task in hand. To solve this problem, techniques for linking existing models should be developed, while further research, especially with respect to unstable components of household formation and migration processes, is desirable.

14.1. Regional planning

14.1.1. Objectives of regional planning

THE concept of regional planning is not unambiguous. Economists, demographers, geographers, physical planners, and ecologists all interpret it somewhat differently. When these interpretations are compared and combined, however, they turn out to refer to different aspects of the same phenomenon: the preparation of policy relating to the development of regions and/or to the distribution of population and activities over regions. This phenomenon is very widespread.

Economists tend to speak of regional policy when referring to policies aimed at redistributing economic activity. Such policies are pursued to combat the problems of unemployment and industrial decline in peripheral regions or regions with outdated industrial structures, or to make better use of regional potentials and thus enhance the contribution of the various regions to national economic development. Regional economic policy is a common feature in most European countries (see, for example, Yuill *et al.*, 1980).

209

Demographers and geographers take great interest in population redistribution policies (for example, Webb *et al.*, 1981). United Nations surveys show that a large majority of countries are dissatisfied with their spatial population distribution and either consider, or actually implement policies to influence this distribution (compare Fuchs and Demko, 1983). In most cases such policies aim at decelerating or reversing rural–urban migration. However, declining population growth and widespread (sub)urbanization may stimulate governments to modify these policies (Ter Heide and Eichperger, 1978; Ter Heide, 1979).

Physical planners and environmentalists are more inclined to look at only one region when speaking of regional planning. In their view, the concept refers to the preparation of a land use plan for a region. It should not be thought, however, that they disregard relations with other regions when preparing such a plan. The economic, social, and environmental functions which the region fulfils for the country as a whole or for other regions are taken into account, as well as the resulting in- and outflow of migration and traffic and the regional–economic input and output (for example, Paelinck, 1971).

The common element in regional economic policies, population redistribution policies, and spatial policies is that they aim at improving the balance between population, resources, and amenities, both within regions and with respect to the distribution across regions. The interpretation of this aim, however, differs from one country to the next and may change with time. In analysing these differences and changes, several authors have pointed to efficiency and equity considerations as the dominant factors in goal interpretation (for example, Richardson, 1969; Folmer, 1983). Which balance between efficiency and equity considerations is striven after depends on the specific situations and values found in each country. Instances of concrete objectives which may be chosen are: bringing into line supply and demand in the labour market or in the housing market; making better use of natural resources; combating long-distance commuting; counteracting pollution and other threats to the natural environment; and improving the accessibility of social and cultural facilities. In developed countries, such as in Europe, equity and environmental considerations predominated during the 1950s and 1960s, but after the oil crises of the 1970s, efficiency considerations, such as the desire to make better use of resources and the promotion of national economic development, were once again emphasized.

14.1.2. Population-responsive and population-influencing measures

Willekens (1984a, pp. 21–2) has pointed out that the realization of a balanced spatial distribution of population and activities calls for two types of policy measures: population-responsive and population-influencing measures. He defines this distinction by saying that the provision of infrastructure, employment, and educational, cultural, and health facilities falls under the first type of policy measure, whereas the second type is designed to influence the size, composition, and distribution of the population.

The two types of policy measures are easily recognizable in the description of regional planning given in section 14.1.1. Regional economic policy is population-responsive, population redistribution policy is population-influencing, whereas regional physical planning may involve both elements. The reasons for the twofold approach to regional planning are also evident: some amenities can easily be provided in regions where they are not in sufficient supply for the present—or future—population numbers (for example, schools, medical facilities), while others can hardly be moved (for example, employment in port industries). Moreover, the preservation of certain natural and scenic amenities may require that population growth in the neighbourhood be restricted.

In his discussion of the two types of policy measures, Willekens (1984a, p. 22) goes on to say that they entail different research requirements. This, however, is only part of the story, as can be seen from an analysis of policy-orientated demographic research in the Netherlands (Ter Heide, 1984; Willekens, 1984b). The interdependency between the two types of policy measures has to be taken into account. Population-responsive measures may affect migration propensities and thus have population-influencing effects. On the other hand, in preparing projections for population-responsive policies one has to take into account the effects of population-influencing measures, which raises the difficult question as to how to predict the future success of such measures. We will encounter examples of this interdependency in section 14.3.2.

The interdependency between population-responsive and population-influencing measures gives rise to a demand for recursive or iterative models. By this, we mean models which can be used in various ways, namely:

- to forecast future population trends on the basis of assumptions regarding, in particular, migration factors;
- to simulate the effects of specific policy measures;
- to assess the conditions which would have to be met to achieve certain policy targets;
- to estimate the limits within which developments can be influenced by policy.

Moreover, as will be shown in the next section, the models will have to allow for disaggregation.

14.1.3. The significance of population structure and households

The demand for employment, housing, social and cultural facilities, and infrastructure depends not only on the size of a population but also on its composition. In addition to age, sex, and socio-economic status, household composition is particularly relevant. The number of households of various types determines the demand for dwellings, and influences labour supply (through differences in participation rates) and the demand for certain facilities (for example, schools, homes for the elderly). For population-responsive policies, information concerning population structure and households is thus required.

The same applies for population-influencing regional policies, since migration is distinctly selective as to age, socio-economic status, and type of household. This selectivity of migration is well documented. As far as the type of household is concerned we refer to, among others, Stapleton (1980), Clark and Onaka (1983), and Op 't Veld *et al.* (1984).

Of particular interest is that not only is migration selective as to type of household, but there is also a direct connection between migration and household formation and dissolution. Except when a single person dies, household formation and dissolution always involves one or more persons moving house: young adults leaving the parental home, couples marrying or starting to cohabit, divorce, elderly people entering a nursing home. If such a move involves crossing regional boundaries, migration takes place.

This means that regional planners have to consider not only the household composition of the population concerned and the possible influence of this household composition (and other aspects of population structure) on migration, but also, when proposing population-influencing measures, the possible impact of such measures on household formation and dissolution. For example, providing more dwellings in a region in an attempt to influence migration might also lead to an increased rate of household formation, for example, by young people who take advantage of the increased housing supply and who leave the parental home sooner than they would otherwise have done.

The models we are looking for in regional planning may thus be described as recursive models showing the interdependency between migration and household formation. It should be possible to use them to prepare forecasts as well as to assess policy impacts, policy conditions, and policy constraints. They should yield results disaggregated in such a way as to make it possible to calculate the demand for housing and social/cultural facilities. Moreover, they should be relatively simple so that policy makers will feel confident in using them.

Needless to say, we do not yet actually have such models. The best we can do in this paper is to describe what partial models we do have, mainly with respect to migration, and to discuss possible directions for further study.

14.1.4. The regional planning system

To clarify our approach further, in Figure 14.1 we give a schematic representation of the aspects of the regional planning system discussed above. A

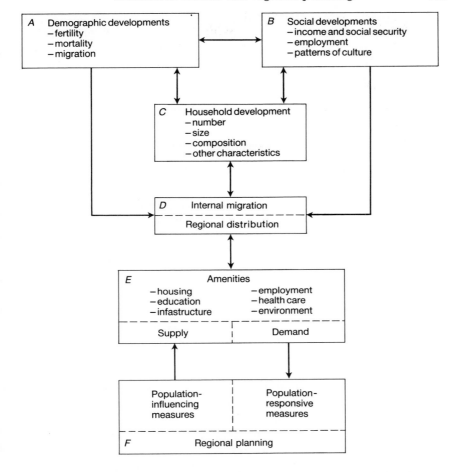

FIG. 14.1. Variables and interrelationships relevant to regional planning

distinguishing element in this diagram is box D: internal migration/regional distribution. The central position of this element in the system indicates the special complications involved in the use of household models in regional planning.

To deal with these complications, we will introduce two restrictions to the analyses presented in this paper. Firstly, we will only pay attention to boxes A, C, and D of the diagram, apart from the occasional passing reference to the link with social developments (box B). Secondly, we will base our arguments on a discussion of problems in only one country: the Netherlands. We feel justified in doing so in view of the fact that, as illuminated in section 14.1.1, regional planning is everywhere based on the same principle: promoting balanced development both within and between regions.

In order to be able to use the Dutch example for our exposition, we will first have to describe population and household developments in the Netherlands. This will be done in section 14.2, thus providing an empirical basis for the presentation of some Dutch models in section 14.3.

14.2. Population and household development

14.2.1. Regional demographic developments in the Netherlands

In the past hundred years, the population of the Netherlands has increased considerably. The number of inhabitants rose from 4 million in 1879 to 14.4 million in 1984. Until 1965 this growth was mainly the result of a high excess of births over deaths. After 1965 natural increase declined, but this decline was offset by a high migration surplus which resulted from a heavy influx of guest workers in the early 1970s, followed by their families in the second half of the same decade. In addition to this, large numbers of people from Surinam, which gained independence in 1975, took up residence in the Netherlands. At the moment, partly as a consequence of the economic recession, these flows have come to a virtual standstill. As a result of differences in natural increase and in the location of immigrants, and especially as a result of internal migration, population growth was distributed across the various regions and settlements in the country. The distribution pattern was, however, not stable, as regards the direction of migration flows. Until 1960 the structure can be characterized very simply: outward migration to foreign countries, especially Canada and Australia, mainly from the large urban settlements, but also—to a surprising degree—from the northern Dutch provinces. The North was also the source of large migration flows to the big cities or to places with developing industries.

In the period 1960–5 immigration set in, and there was a sharp decrease in internal migration to the large cities. After 1965 we were confronted with the phenomenon of suburbanization, initially mainly around the large cities in he West (the Randstad Holland), later also elsewhere.

In the 1970s, suburbanization was at its height and, moreover, there was a new outward migration flow from the West to the adjacent provinces of Gelderland and North Brabant. Government attempted to concentrate this deconcentration by designating a number of growth centres, where construction was to take place at a rapid rate. The northern provinces were less involved in the suburbanization process. The outward flow of young people from these provinces did, however, decrease, and there was a certain influx of elderly people (Vergoossen, 1983). A further phenomenon of the 1970s was a marked decrease in total mobility (from 5.3 persons per 100 in 1973 to 3.8 per 100 in 1979).

From the processes described above, it will be clear that significant differences in population structure have emerged between and within the provinces. For instance, in the northern provinces the percentage of elderly people exceeds 13.5, as against an average of 11.5 for the country as a whole.

If we analyse migration by distance, we find that in 1980 62 per cent of the migrants moved within their municipality, 22 per cent within their province, and 16 per cent between provinces. The percentage of moves over longer distances, often motivated by job opportunities (Clark, 1982), has remained constant. Distances of moves, mainly for the purpose of improving the residential situation, have become shorter. Young families often look for a residence in the city. Consequently, in suburban commuting municipalities very young children are now much less common than children of school-going age. In the large cities there is a sharp decline in the number of departures, even though net outmigration continues. Government is attempting to further the process of decreasing departures by making the urban residential environment more attractive through large-scale urban renewal projects.

14.2.2. Development of households

Having discussed the demographic component, we have dealt with the most important factor in the development of the number of households. However, Figure 14.1 shows that several social factors also play an important role in the development of households. In summary, we arrive at the following major changes in the last fifteen years:

- the number of children per family has decreased;
- there has been a relative decrease in the number of marriages;
- there has been a sharp increase in unmarried cohabitation;
- the number of divorces has increased;
- young people leave the parental home at an earlier age, while old people retain their independence for a longer period of time.

The result of these factors has been that the number of households in the Netherlands has increased sharply, and that the average size of the households has decreased (see Table 14.1).

The distribution of these households across the provinces corresponds only to a limited degree with the distribution of the population. There are particularly large differences in the distribution of households according to size. For instance, in 1977 the percentage of one- and two-person households was 55 in Groningen and 41 in North Brabant. Within the provinces, there are large differences between the big cities and the rural and suburban municipalities.

The causes of these differences are to a large extent demographic, that is to say, age-related. To some degree the differences result from migration processes. It is found that one- and two-person households in particular move to the city, while families with children leave the city (see Hoekveld, 1981). But there are also geographic differences in the formation of households. For

TABLE 14.1. Number of households, average size of households, and percentage distribution of households according to size, the Netherlands

	Number of households (000s)	Average size of household	Size of households (%)		
			1 + 2	3 + 4	5 or more
1960	3204	3.50	36	37	27
1971	4056	3.15	43	37	20
1977	4719	2.89	48	38	14
1980	4907	2.81	50	38	12

Source: Bureau for Strategic Marketing Research, 1983.

instance, the formation of one-person households, resulting from the dissolution of larger households, is a process which is encountered much more often in large cities than in smaller cities (see Hårsman and Snickars, 1983).

The regional planning questions emerging from the developments described above will be clear. As a consequence of migration in particular, large differences in population composition and household structure have arisen between urban and rural areas, and to a lesser degree between different parts of the country. The question arises as to the extent to which these differences will influence future developments. In this context, one should not lose sight of the decreased population growth and reduced mobility. Does this mean that the present population structure in the various regions will exert a strong influence on the further demographic development of these regions, or should it be assumed that selective migration will continue to influence population distribution? In either case, accomplishing the essential adaptation of facilities in the various regions—through population-responsive measures—will give rise to problems. In fact, by means of population-influencing measures, spatial policy aims at increasing the opportunities for making use of existing facilities, thus avoiding the destruction of capital.

14.3. Application of models

14.3.1. Models used in regional planning in the Netherlands

To what extent have we, in the Netherlands, already succeeded in developing models which can provide answers to the questions with which regional planning, as stated above, is being confronted?

As in other countries, demographers in the Netherlands have long been working on and with models for the forecasting of population growth and population distribution (Eichperger, 1984). National population forecasts are drawn up by the Central Bureau of Statistics. For this purpose a model is used in which the development of births, deaths, and external migration is taken into account. To distribute these forecasts across the provinces, the National Physical Planning Agency in co-operation with the Central (Economic) Planning Bureau has drawn up the Regional Population Forecasting Model (RBPM). In order to estimate the migration component, this model makes use of regression equations which relate provincial net migration to economic and social factors (Eichperger, 1984; Van Delft and Suyker, 1984). An advantage of RBPM is that regional estimates are consistent with national forecasts (the top-down effect). A disadvantage, however, is that no account is taken of region-specific demographic processes.

For this reason a multiregional model has been developed (Willekens and Drewe, 1984) which may be viewed as an attempt to combine the advantages of both the top-down approach (consistency) and the bottom-up approach (regional idiosyncracies). This multiregional model is known as MUDEA. It has three dimensions, namely age, sex, and province of residence. It is, moreover, an open system, since it takes account of emigration and immigration. With the aid of a system of equations, the transitions between and within the various dimensions are described (from age cohort 1 to age cohort 2, but also from age cohort 1 in region i to age cohort 2 in region j). The age cohorts are at the same time subjected to birth, mortality, and emigration probabilities. The transitions between the regions are also determined with the aid of probabilities. The model is an elaboration of the multiregional model developed by Rogers (1975) and Willekens and Rogers (1978).

In its present form, MUDEA is a purely demographic model. If it is to be used for planning, estimates of migration probabilities will have to be incorporated. In 1978 a migration study was started, called AMIRES (*A*nalysis of *M*igration on a *R*egional *S*cale). By the end of 1982, the AMIRES project had resulted in a coherent set of explanatory migration models. These models take explicit account of the role played by households in migration processes. Ten household types are distinguished as migratory units, and for each of these household types the migration propensity (the generation factor) and the choice of destination (the distribution factor) are separately modelled. On the basis of migration theory a number of explanatory variables are chosen and the related parameters are calculated for each of the specific models. Testing of the models has shown, *inter alia*, that different types of households indeed have different types of migration behaviour (Op 't Veld *et al.*, 1984).

On the basis of AMIRES, a projection model (PROMIRES) is being developed. In order to create a link with the multiregional model, the results of AMIRES must be converted into sex- and age-specific migration probabilities, since population disaggregated by sex and age constitutes the basic unit for demographic projection. Inversely, for the purpose of regional planning, the results of the multiregional model must be translated into numbers and types of households.

For the conversion of population into households, a model has been developed which calculates the number of households by size per province (Bureau for Strategic Marketing Research, 1982). This model, which we can refer to as HUGROM, proceeds from population projections and external estimates of expected family size. With the aid of the average family size, the population can be converted into the number of heads of household and the number of members of households. The number of members is subsequently distributed over the heads of household classified by age by means of a Poisson distribution.

The need to convert the population into households clearly comes to the fore when planning housing construction. For the purpose of determining the number of dwellings required, the PRIMOS regional projection model (which should not be confused with the PRIMOS household projection model discussed by Brouwer in chapter 15) is employed to calculate the population per municipality. Again, the migration probabilities require detailed study. The probabilities must be related to period-specific exogenous factors. By employing variables to define these factors, which are sensitive to government policies, a simulation model is generated which is suitable for policy makers. This is achieved by differentiating the migration component into structural migration and migration resulting from residential construction. Structural migration leads to a demand for dwellings, since, when migration is directed toward a specific municipality due to such factors as employment opportunities, attractiveness of residential environment, public facilities, and so on, the household will require a dwelling in the direct vicinity. By contrast, migration resulting from residential construction is determined by the construction programme. Households move into a given municipality because dwellings become available there. Translated into spatial terms, one could say that structural migration is predominantly long-distance migration, whereas migration resulting from residential construction is mainly short-distance migration within a housing market area. For a detailed description of the PRIMOS regional projection model, see Brouwer *et al.* (1984).

Though above we speak of households, the model deals only with numbers of persons disaggregated by sex and age. Only in the final conversion of the population into units in need of dwellings is the number of households calculated by means of the headship rate method. The headship rates used are age-, year-, and municipality-specific.

Scholten (1984) elaborates further on the PRIMOS regional projection model and its application in regional planning in the Netherlands. He also examines the qualitative aspects of the housing market. Qualitative differentiation of the demand for housing calls for insight into more aspects than merely the number of households. To be able to draw up a usable demand profile, further disaggregation by size and income is necessary.

In the last model to be discussed here, the Double Allocation Model, household development plays a secondary role. DAM (see Verster, 1984, for a detailed description) may be described as a spatial interaction model. Contrary to the PRIMOS regional projection model, this model considers not only changes in region of residence but also changes in region of employment and relates them to each other. The explanatory variables in the model relate to housing stock and employment and to the development of these factors. The results obtained from DAM are the relocations of workers who in a given year change place of residence and/or work. This model also yields commuter flows between the regions, after incorporation of the relocations. The input needed for DAM includes data such as the number of 'withdrawers' and 'starters' on the labour market and the number of workers per dwelling. Precisely these variables are closely related to the formation of households, since not only has there been a sharp increase in the number of two-person households, but the increase in the number of households in which both partners have an income and, more generally, the increase in the participation of women on the labour market constitutes one of the most striking changes of recent years.

14.3.2. Further modelling requirements

The fact that we were able to refer to no less than seven models in section 14.3.1 might give the impression that Dutch regional planning is amply supplied with models. Up to a point this is indeed the case, but there are a number of (related) objections to the models. Each model is only concerned with specific components of the demographic–spatial system; only one model (HUGROM) focuses on household formation, all the others focus on migration or population trends; they can only be linked to one another to a limited degree; to some extent they are based on outdated parameter values since external input is required which, though known for the past, cannot be independently extrapolated; with the exception of one model (MUDEA), they are comparative–static rather than dynamic models.

A few examples will serve to illustrate these objections. The projection models RBPM and MUDEA are disaggregated by age, but not by type of household. As a consequence, not only do they fail to yield results per type of household, which are of vital importance for population-responsive policies, but they also fail to take account of the influence of changes in household structure on migration, though such an influence has been demonstrated by AMIRES. The simulation model DAM, as was explained above, calls for inputs which are dependent on the development of households, even though this dependency is not expressed in the model. PRIMOS makes use of age, year, and municipality-specific headship rates, which can, of course, be chosen on the basis of assumptions regarding household formation, but the interdependency between household formation and migration is not taken into account. As a result of this shortcoming, it has proven to be extremely difficult to arrive at satisfactory estimates for headship rates of migrants.

The only household model, HUGROM, calls for input from previous population forecasts. This means that HUGROM takes no account of the interdependency between migration and the formation of households. Moreover, HUGROM ascribes the development of the number of households into various size classes almost exclusively to demographic variables (box A, Figure 14.1). In reality, social factors (box B) are of greater importance, and their significance does not remain constant. This is evident if one traces the extent to which the increase in the number of households can be explained on the basis of demographic variables (marriage, divorce, and mortality). In the period 1960–70 this was possible for 93.3 per cent, in 1971–6 for 83.4 per cent, and in 1977–81 for only 42.8 per cent. Variables other than vital events thus play an increasingly important role (Ploegmakers and Van Leeuwen, 1984).

This reference to an actual trend in the Netherlands in the past twenty-five years introduces the central problem in model development: the fact that models reveal theoretical shortcomings does not disturb planners greatly, provided they give a reliable estimate of shifts in the relevant variables, namely population distribution and household structure. It is precisely the shifts in the development of these variables which interest the planner, on the one hand because he must adapt facilities to these shifts with the aid of population-responsive measures, and on the other hand because it is precisely his job to try to bring about (or prevent) such shifts with the aid of population-influencing measures.

In section 14.2 we saw that migration in particular has shown a number of shifts in the Netherlands in the past decade. In view of this, the practical utility of the available models is less than planners could wish for. Not only do these shifts undermine faith in forecasting models such as RBPM, which are dependent on parameters measured in the past, but the fact that migratory developments, together with regionally divergent processes in household formation, have resulted in differences in population composition between regions creates problems which are practically impossible to solve with the aid of existing models. Over a long period of time, the unequal distribution of different cohorts across the regions (for example, many children in suburbs, and single young adults in the cities) will lead to processes of household formation which, as may be expected on the basis of the information taken from AMIRES regarding the location preferences of various types of households, will be accompanied by migration flows which deviate from the present ones. It is, however, impossible to calculate these migration flows, since it is not known precisely what will be the patterns of household formation in the various regions. To acquire such information, it would first be necessary to apply HUGROM, but for this we must have at our disposal a population forecast, thus also migration estimates. We are now in a vicious circle. We could perhaps work iteratively, but in that case we would at least need estimates of the migration propensity per type of household. However, in view of the altered distribution of households across the regions and the sharp decrease in the overall migration propensity, it is highly questionable whether the values measured in the past with A M I R E S could be used for this purpose.

The problem becomes even more complicated if policy principles are taken into account. In the framework of a population-responsive policy, local facilities should be adapted to the changes in household structure. For instance, dwellings should be made available for households which come into being in the suburbs as the children living there leave the parental home. As is shown by P R I M O S, however, this housing supply would also stimulate migration, which would be at odds with the population-influencing policy of the Dutch government. This policy is aimed at promoting equilibrium in the urban labour markets, counteracting commuting, and making optimal use of existing facilities. For the time being, these objectives are being met by striving after a zero migration balance for all regions. P R I M O S can be employed to calculate iteratively which supply of dwellings would have this effect; but the impact of this housing supply on the formation of households would not be known. The same objection applies to the D A M, when used to test whether the objectives regarding the labour market and commuting are being achieved, since D A M does not take account of household development either.

14.3.3. Toward solutions

Our analysis of the Dutch situation shows that, for the purpose of regional planning, it is at present very important to gain more insight into household formation and dissolution in relation to population distribution and migration (boxes C and D, Figure 14.1).

To achieve this, better household models are indispensable, since the development of models in the field of household formation is in a less advanced stage than that of migration models. The model described by Brouwer in chapter 15 of this book and the N I D I model referred to by Keilman in chapter 9 (both not mentioned in section 14.3.1 since they were not yet operational) do provide improvements, but only at the national level. For the purpose of regional research and regional planning, it would be especially desirable to subject the relationship between migration and house-hold formation to specific research. We are of the opinion that this research should focus partly on the microlevel. In fact, we still know little about individual behaviour with respect to migration and household formation, in spite of the—in themselves satisfactory—theories on which our behavioura' migration models are based (see, for example, Speare *et al.*, 1975; Varady, 1983).

Next, for the purpose of regional planning, it might be well worth while to focus on those components of migration and household development which show the greatest variation over time. These are the components which call for the greatest adaptation in population-responsive policies and which offer the largest number of openings for population-influencing policies. In the Netherlands it has, for instance, been found that the overall level of migration shows much less temporal stability than does the relative generation of migration per region (Baydar, 1984). Policy makers could make use of data of this nature.

The most important strategy for the improvement of methods for explaining and projecting household development and population distribution appears to be the development of techniques which will make it possible to link the existing models. Both from the point of view of usability, and to promote clarity for the policy maker, the linking of partial models would be preferable to the integration into one super-model. We expect that multidimensional demography may in two ways play an important role in linking the models. Firstly, the existing multiregional model, MUDEA, may be given a central position in the system of models, since it represents in a consistent manner the central demographic relationships which under no circumstances may be overlooked. Secondly, multistate methodology may be applied to make the other models more dynamic and more suitable for linkage.

We feel confident that the strategies indicated in this section will, in the coming years, make it possible to improve the models available for regional planning purposes. However, two warnings are due here. Firstly, the disappointing experiences in the 1960s and 1970s with large-scale models in planning (Lee, 1973) show that models need to be as clear and concise as possible if policy makers are to use them. Secondly, shortcomings of models such as those pointed out in this paper should not be viewed too absolutely. Despite these shortcomings, the models yield more insight than would be obtained if one worked purely intuitively. Policy is always made amidst uncertainty. Reduction of this uncertainty, however small, with the imperfect models at our disposal, is better than nothing.

References

BAYDAR, N. (1984). Issues in multiregional demographic forecasting (Interuniversity Programme in Demography, Brussels).

BROUWER, J., H. E. GORDIJN, AND H. R. HEIDA (1984). Toward unravelling the interdependency between migration and housing stock development: a policy model, in: Ter Heide and Willekens (1984), 287–308.

BUREAU VOOR STRATEGISCH MARKTONDERZOEK—BSM (BUREAU FOR STRATEGIC MARKETING RESEARCH—BSM) (1983). Trendrapport volkshuisvesting 1982 (Trend report on housing 1982) (BSM, Delft).

CLARK, W. A. V. (1982). Recent research in migration: a review and interpretation, *Progress in Planning* 18, 1–56.

—— AND J. ONAKA (1983). Life cycle and housing adjustment as explanations of residential mobility, *Urban Studies* 20, 47–57.

DELFT, A. VAN AND W. B. C. SUYKER (1984). Interregional migration in a multi-regional labour market model for the Netherlands, in: Ter Heide and Willekens (1984), 253–70.

EICHPERGER, C. L. (1984). Regional population forecasts: approaches and issues, in: Ter Heide and Willekens (1984), 235–52.

FOLMER, H. (1983). Measurement of effects of regional economic policy: some methodological aspects (Rijksuniversiteit Groningen).

FUCHS, R. J. AND G. J. DEMKO (1983). Rethinking population distribution policies, *Population Research and Policy Review* 2, 161–87.

HÄRSMAN, B. AND F. SNICKARS (1983). A method for disaggregate household forecasts, *Tijdschrift voor economische en sociale geografie* 74(4), 282–90.

HEIDE, H. TER (1979). Implications of current demographic trends for population redistribution policies (National Physical Planning Agency, The Hague).

—— (1984). The use of demographic research in physical planning, in: Ter Heide and Willekens (1984), 337–54.

—— AND C. L. EICHPERGER (1978). Dynamic interrelations between population redistribution policies and demographic developments (National Physical Planning Agency, The Hague).

—— AND F. J. WILLEKENS (eds.) (1984). *Demographic Research and Spatial Policy* (Academic Press, London, New York).

HOEKVELD, G. A. (1981). Stedelijk wonen (Urban living) (Free University, Amsterdam).

LEE, D. B. (1973). Requiem for large-scale models, *Journal of the American Institute of Planners* 39, 163–78.

OP 'T VELD, A., E. BIJLSMA, AND J. STARMANS (1984). Explanatory analysis of interregional migration in the nineteen-seventies, in: Ter Heide and Willekens (1984), 171–200.

PAELINCK, J. M. P. (1971). Techniques of regional plan formulation: problems of interregional consistency, in: D. M. Dunham and J. G. M. Hilhorst (eds.), *Issues in Regional Planning* (Nijhoff, The Hague).

PLOEGMAKERS, M. J. H. AND L. T. VAN LEEUWEN (1984). Huishoudens in Nederland: twee decennia verandering (Households in the Netherlands: two decades of change) (Agricultural University, Wageningen).

RICHARDSON, H. W. (1969). *Regional Economics* (Weidenfeld and Nicolson, London).

ROGERS, A. (1975). *Introduction to Multiregional Mathematical Demography* (Wiley, New York).

SCHOLTEN, H. J. (1984). Planning for housing construction and population distribution in the Netherlands: the use of forecasting models, *Town Planning Review* 55, no. 4.

SPEARE A., S. GOLDSTEIN, AND W. H. FREY (1975). *Residential Mobility, Migration and Metropolitan Change* (Ballinger, Cambridge, Mass.).

STAPLETON, C. N. (1980). Reformulation of the family life cycle concept: implications for residential mobility, *Environment and Planning* 13, 1103–18.

VARADY, D. P. (1983). Determinants of residential mobility decisions, *Journal of the American Planning Association* 49, 184–99.

VERGOOSSEN, T. W. M. (1983). Pensioenmigratie in Nederland (Retirement migration in the Netherlands) (Katholieke Universiteit, Nijmegen).

VERSTER, A. C. P. (1984). A double allocation model for interregional residential and job mobility, in: Ter Heide and Willekens (1984), 201–34.

WEBB, J. W., A. NAUKKARINEN, AND L. A. KOSIŃSKI (eds.) (1981). *Policies of Population Redistribution* (Geographical Society of Northern Finland, Oulu).

WILLEKENS, F. J. (1984a). Approaches and innovations in policy-oriented migration and population distribution research, in: Ter Heide and Willekens (1984), 21–43.

—— (1984b). Spatial policy and demographic research opportunities, in: Ter Heide and Willekens (1984), 355–401.

—— AND P. DREWE (1984). A multiregional model for regional demographic projection, in: Ter Heide and Willekens (1984), 309–34.

—— AND A. ROGERS (1978). Spatial population analysis: methods and computer programs, Research Report RR-78-18, IIASA, Laxenburg, Austria.

YUILL, D., K. ALLEN, AND C. HULL (eds.) (1980). *Regional Policy in the European Community* (Croom Helm, London).

15

Application of household models in housing policy

J. Brouwer

ABSTRACT

This paper describes the model used today by the Ministry of Housing of the Netherlands for the estimation of numbers of households. The model is a macrosimulation model, describing changes in the positions of individuals within households by 1-year age groups and sex. The positions are: child living with its parents, person living alone, living together (including married couples), having lived together (including divorced persons), and those not living in households (namely, old people's homes, nursing homes, and other institutions). From this, the number of households can be derived. The estimates are based on the assumption that the trend toward individualization will continue in the coming years. This assumption is based on an analysis of household trends during this century, which led to the conclusion that an increase in the number of households became possible due to an increase in the number of sources of income; in particular due to industrialization and the introduction of the welfare state.

The trend toward individualization is only possible if each source of income increases sufficiently. In the event of too restricted a growth, however, this trend, if it has already set in, will only be reversed very slowly. The outcome of the calculations was that in the Netherlands the number of households will increase by another 1.5 per cent per year up to 1990 and by 0.8 per cent after 1990; it was 2.4 per cent in the 1970s. The housing demand has been deduced on the basis of the expected economic growth.

15.1. Introduction

15.1.1. The Dutch housing situation compared with other European countries

To this day, there has been considerable pressure to build a large number of new dwellings in the Netherlands. In comparison with neighbouring countries, a large number of new houses has been built in the past ten years. This is due to the continuous population growth and the growing number of households since World War II, even as late as the 1970s. The population of the

225

Netherlands is relatively young compared with other West European countries, and the number of dwellings per inhabitant is relatively low. In 1982 for instance, there were 354 dwellings per 1,000 inhabitants in the Netherlands, 388 in Great Britain, 450 in Belgium, 423 in Germany, and 441 per 1,000 inhabitants in Sweden.

The housing supply in the Netherlands is controlled almost entirely by private institutions. Roughly speaking, there are three forms of housing administration. In the first place, corporations which let houses on a non-profit basis, secondly, commercial lessors, and lastly owner-occupiers. But there are differences in the share of each sector within the housing market. The non-profit sector is relatively large in the Netherlands; 75 per cent of all rental dwellings are managed on a non-profit basis. In 1982 the percentage of owner-occupied houses was 43 per cent in the Netherlands, 38 per cent in the Federal Republic of Germany (1980), 61 per cent in Belgium (1982), 41 per cent in Sweden (1980), 61 per cent in Great Britain (1982), and 48 per cent in France (1982).

The realization of sufficient, payable, and qualitatively well-built houses is an important political goal in almost every West European country. Governments try to realize this by setting certain standards for the quality of new houses, and by supplying loans and subsidies or by granting tax facilities. Such ways of supporting the housing market are known in all West European countries. However, in one respect the Dutch situation is special. The National Budget finances almost 100 per cent of the non-profit housing sector. Other countries provide only interest subsidies and the private sector supplies the capital.

Because of the aforementioned factors the building programme has become an important political, as well as budgetary, issue.

15.1.2. General approach to household models

Each year, the Ministry of Housing works with a long-term housing programme. In drawing up these long-term programmes, household models play an important role. It is, after all, the growing number of households which, to a large extent, determines the increase in the housing demand. The Ministry of Housing pays much attention to household estimates through its own research department, as well as through research agencies working for the Ministry.

Two approaches have been chosen. Firstly, the demographic approach. Starting from known methods of estimating population growth (cohort-component), we tried to develop an approach which would enable us to simulate household formation. This new method is a considerable improvement on the traditional 'headship rate' model. Secondly, the macroeconomic approach. Research has been carried out to explore the relation between household formation and economic development. Over the last one hundred years both processes have gained momentum. This suggests that they must be related although we do not know exactly *how* they are related. Both approaches will be dealt with in this chapter. The methods and their assumptions will be described, and some results will be given (sections 15.2, 15.3, and 15.4). The application of the estimates will be dealt with in section 15.5 and finally some possible improvements upon the method will be indicated in section 15.6.

15.2. Demographic approach to household models

15.2.1. The PRIMOS household model

A household can be considered a biological unit especially aimed at producing and raising children. Therefore, matters such as birth, growing-up, pairing, ageing, and death will be stressed in studies of household formation.

The method most used to describe household trends is the headship rate method. The headship rate is the percentage of heads of household within a certain sex and age group. This method, however, has a number of drawbacks (see chapter 8 by Linke). This is the reason why this method has been discarded. By order of the Ministry of Housing, the Netherlands Centre for the Study of Physical Planning developed a method which made it possible to simulate household formation and dissolution (Heida and Gordijn, 1985). This so-called PRIMOS household model was recently completed and some of the results of the study will be presented here. Its methodology is reviewed in chapter 9.

In order to make it possible carefully to describe household dynamics, the population is decomposed by:

- age (1-year age groups);
- sex;
- member of a private household or not.

The persons living in private households are further divided into four categories:

- child living at home;
- person living alone;
- living together (including married persons);
- having lived together.

The idea underlying this classification is that it must be based on a concept of households closely related to views of the household members themselves. Thus, the concept of a household is defined neither financially nor judicially. For this reason, marital status is not explicitly included. Many adults live together without being married, so marital status cannot be a relevant characteristic to describe the actual household situation, which is much more interesting to the Ministry of Housing. Furthermore, persons who have left the parental home and are not living together are placed in the category of persons living alone or of persons now living alone, but having lived together. In this context 'living alone' refers to a person living without a steady partner. Persons with children can, therefore, also be considered as living alone.

The population not living in private households has been divided into the following categories:

- living in an old people's home;
- living in a nursing home;
- living in another institution or home.

This division has been made because it yields a better picture of developments in the past, and in order to meet the users' requirements. There are great differences in the age structure of each separate group and government interference in housing of each group is entirely different.

For each individual group (about 1,300 in number), size and transitions can be determined by censuses or by surveys. The distribution of individuals over these household classes was taken from the 1982 Housing Demand Survey with about 70,000 respondents (Figure 15.1).

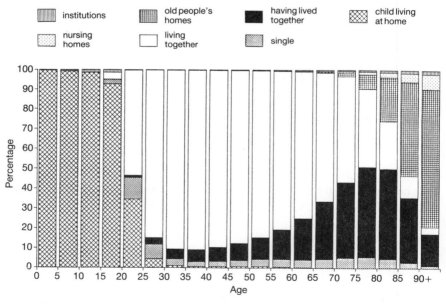

FIG. 15.1. Division of females by household situation, by age, the Netherlands, 1982

Figure 15.1 shows the percentage distribution over the different household groups among women of each age class. The picture for men is similar. With the aid of this division a table can be constructed which indicates the transitions between the different household categories (see Table 15.1).

TABLE 15.1. Transitions between household situations

	Situation after transition					death	emigration
	child living at home	living alone	living together	having lived together	old people's/ nursing home/ institution		
Initial situation							
child living at home	—	1	2	0	3	4	5
living alone	*	—	6	0	7	8	9
living together	0	0	—	10	11	12	13
having lived together	0	0	14	—	15	16	17
old people's/ nursing home/ institution	*	*	*	*	—	18	*
immigration	19	20	21	22	*		
birth	23	0	0	0	0		

0 = (direct) transition impossible.
— = no transition.
* = transitions quantitatively negligible.
Numbers refer to types of events, see chapter 9 by Keilman.

The inner part of the table describes the possible transitions between the different categories of households. The two right-hand columns show the possible population decrease by death and emigration, and the two bottom rows show the possible accessions by birth and immigration. Each cell must be split up by age and sex, and indicates the relative importance of the transitions. Dashes indicate persons who experience no transition. The transitions among *different* categories are indicative of the dynamics in the system. The most important transitions are transitions 1, 2, 6, 10, 14, 15, 16, 18, and 23. They include:

- living at home to living alone;
- living at home to living together;
- living alone to living together;
- having lived together to living together;
- having lived together to living in an old people's home or nursing home.

Some transitions occur only sporadically (an asterisk) and some transitions are impossible by definition. These transitions are indicated by a zero.

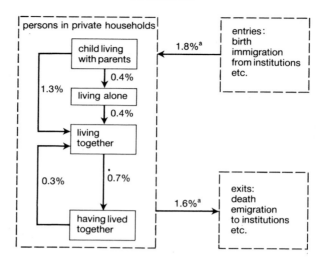

[a] As a percentage of the population in private households.

FIG. 15.2. A rough outline of the life cycle

Figure 15.2 represents the average one-year transition probabilities for all age groups and for both sexes. In principle, each age group and each sex has a different diagram. The transition probability in relation to age shows a regular pattern which has been estimated by means of mathematical functions. It is possible to determine the parameters of these functions using data from censuses and surveys. The nature of the mathematical functions and the graduation methods used will not be described. It is a rather complicated procedure, since the estimation must be done simultaneously on a non-linear basis. Furthermore, changes in population size through birth, death, and migration must be taken into account. It is important to note that it is possible to find a set of parameter values by means of which household processes can be satisfactorily described. Figure 15.3 shows the household pattern for women as observed and simulated in 1982. It is clear that deviations are small.

15.2.2. Developments in the past

The available data and the simulation give an idea of household developments in the past. Generally speaking, this leads to the following.

- The number of heads of household has increased both relatively (per age group) and absolutely during the past century.
- Among other things, this was the result of the continuous decrease in the age at which children left their parental home. This decrease continued up to about 1970, after which, on average, it remained constant.

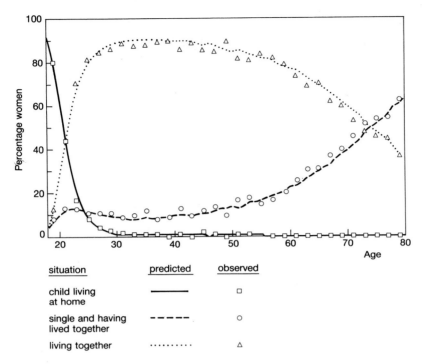

situation	predicted	observed
child living at home	——	□
single and having lived together	– – –	○
living together	··········	△

FIG. 15.3. The household patterns of women, 1 January 1982, observed and predicted by the model

- Nevertheless, there was an increase per age group in the relative number of households, even after 1970. This is the result of the fact that an increasing number of people live alone, and for longer periods of time.
- Another important development is a strong increase in the number of divorces during the past 20 years, causing a considerable increase in the category of persons having lived together.
- The number of old people living with relatives (especially with their own children) started to decrease more than 20 years ago. Nowadays, most old people live independently.
- The number of old people's homes and nursing homes is known to have increased drastically during the 1960s and 1970s. Today, this increase is hardly noticeable.

On the whole, the developments described indicate a continuous individualization. The question arises as to whether these developments will continue in the future and, if so, in what way and to what extent. However, it is very difficult to explain this process from a demographic point of view. Possible explanations lie in the socio-economic field. For this reason, household formation is studied from an economic point of view.

15.3. Macroeconomic approach to household formation

Apart from being a biological unit, a household is also a consumption unit.
The members of a household commonly consume a great number of goods,
such as a house, for example. A study of the household as a consumption unit
should, therefore, not be omitted. In a recent study by the Bureau for
Strategic Marketing Research, by order of the Ministry of Housing, an
attempt was made to analyse household development from a macroeconomic
point of view (BSM, 1983; 1985). The results of this study have been used in
the following.

For some hundred years now economic growth has been almost continuous.
During the present century, economic growth in the Netherlands averaged
2.8 per cent a year. The number of households increased more or less simultaneously, averaging some 1.9 per cent a year. One may assume that these
developments are related.

When prosperity increases, the extra growth can be spent on higher consumption by the members of society, or on immaterial matters. For a household, these are primarily social security and individualization. The needs
underlying this premises will not be enlarged upon here. It is clear that these
immaterial matters, too, have their economic price.

The social existence of a household must be guaranteed by at least one
source of income. The price of economic individualization is that the
economies of scale of a larger household are nullified. The overhead expenses
related to the formation of a household, such as the house itself, furniture,
heating, and the like, are usually higher for a member of a small household
than for a member of a large household.

Which priority is given to these immaterial matters? It is assumed that
society distributes prosperity according to a hierarchy of social needs:

- the need for social security;
- the need for individualization;
- the need for consumption.

The need for social security has been operationalized as the number of
sources of income per household. The need for individualization has been
operationalized as the number of heads of household per 1,000 inhabitants,
and the need for consumption as the average income per household.

It is difficult to determine the exact causal relationship between the social
processes mentioned since many feedbacks are involved. On the one hand,
economic growth creates new possibilities; on the other hand, the existing
socio-cultural situation imposes demands upon economic growth and its distribution. The analysis yields the following results.

The number of sources of income per household has remained remarkably
constant during this century (Table 15.2). The ratio fluctuated around 1.6. So
the increase in the number of households was parallel to the increase in the

TABLE 15.2. Sources of income and the number of households in the Netherlands, 1899–1982

	Labour force (000s)	Social benefits (000s)	Study allowance (000s)	Total (000s)	Households (000s)	Sources of income per household
1899	1,787	—	5	1,792	1,113	1.61
1909	2,102	6	9	2,117	1,306	1.62
1920	2,530	13	15	2,558	1,579	1.62
1930	2,950	68	21	3,039	1,957	1.55
1947	3,648	420	46	4,014	2,514	1.60
1960	4,182	1,206	81	5,469	3,204	1.68
1971	4,724	1,912	191	6,827	4,056	1.68
1978	4,680	2,535	261	7,476	4,706	1.59
1982	4,742	2,997	286	8,025	5,055	1.59

number of sources of income. This increase was possible because of a considerable increase in the number of jobs in industry following the industrial revolution. After World War II, due to the rise of the welfare state, non-active persons also saw an increase in their sources of income.

On calculating the elasticity between economic growth and social security as defined here, over the period examined, we find it to be practically equal to zero. The elasticity between the increase in the National Income and individualization appeared to be 0.16 during the same period, and that of consumption appeared to be 0.33.

In economics elasticities are often used to divide goods into 'luxury' and 'essential' goods. When the elasticity is higher than one, it concerns luxury goods; for essential goods the elasticity is below one. The smaller the elasticity, the more basic the need. The above results, therefore, affirm the assumption concerning the hierarchy of social needs.

We can try to clarify the results in yet another way. On average, the annual growth of the National Income in the Netherlands during this century was about 2.8 per cent. Of this, 1.9 per cent was used to supply new households with a source of income and to effect a certain individualization, while the ratio between sources of income and households remained constant. The remaining 0.9 per cent actually led to a rise in income per household. If individualization had not occurred, there would have been room for a 1.5 per cent rise in annual income.

15.4. Some projection results

In section 15.2, some trends were pointed out with regard to household formation. Considering the explanation given in the previous section, a number of specific assumptions are now plausible.

- The age at which young people leave the parental home will not change, which means that it will remain at about 24 years for men and about 21 years for women.
- However, more often young people will live alone after leaving the parental home and the length of time during which they live alone will increase slightly. This increase will probably level off.
- The number of household dissolutions (through divorce, among other things) will continue to rise. The increase will slow down gradually, as has been the case in recent years.
- The supply of accommodation in old people's homes will not continue to rise, causing a rising average age at which old people enter these homes.

We also used the assumptions employed in the low variant of the 1980-based national population forecast of the Netherlands Central Bureau of Statistics (CBS, 1982).

- The average number of children per woman will decrease to 1.65.
- The life expectancy for men will increase slightly; for women it will remain constant.
- Net foreign migration will be zero in the coming years.

The assumptions have been expressed in the parameters of the PRIMOS household model, enabling us to determine the transitions for all age groups and sexes in Table 15.1. The outcome of the simulation is shown in Table 15.3.

TABLE 15.3. Population and households in the Netherlands, 1960–2000

	Population		Households	
	Absolute (m.)	Annual growth rate (%)	Absolute (m.)	Annual growth rate (%)
1960	11.5	1.3	3.13	2.2
1971	13.1	0.8	3.97	2.4
1982	14.3	0.5	5.13	1.5
1990	14.9	0.3	5.78	0.8
2000	15.3		6.31	

The number of households is determined by adding up the numbers of persons living alone, those having lived together, and slightly less than half of those living together. In the category of persons living together there is also a small number of households of more than 2 adults which makes correction necessary. Table 15.4 gives the distribution of individuals over the various household positions.

Table 15.4 shows that the relative decrease in the number of children living at home is considerable, merely as a result of the falling birth rate. In spite of

TABLE 15.4. Percentage distribution of persons over households in the Netherlands, 1971–2000

	Children living at home	Living alone	Persons having lived together	Living together	Old people's homes/ institutions/ nursing homes
1971	40.9	3.1	4.0	50.0	2.0
1982	35.1	3.6	6.3	53.2	1.9
1990	30.6	3.9	7.7	56.0	1.9
2000	27.8	4.2	9.1	57.1	1.9

the fact that, per age group, fewer persons are living together, the number of shared households still appears to be increasing. Because of the age structure of the Dutch population, a considerable increase in the 35–55 age group is to be expected. The development of the number of persons living alone and of the number of persons having lived together is in conformity with general expectations.

15.5. Application of the results

As was stated in the introduction, household estimates are the basis of new building programmes. However, some adjustments are necessary with regard to the following.

- The future number of households indicates how many households need to be housed. Whether this should be a house for one or for more households depends primarily on income developments. On the one hand, medium-term developments of the National Income have a restricted influence on household formation; on the other hand, they have a direct influence on the household budget.

Table 15.3 shows that until 1990 households will increase by 1.5 per cent a year and after 1990 by 0.8 per cent a year. If economic growth up to 1990 should be lower than 1.5 per cent, as is now assumed, it will have direct consequences for housing consumption. A study of this subject has shown to what extent the housing demand will decrease in such a case, and to what extent the demand for smaller and cheaper houses will increase (BSM, 1983; 1985).

- In the period 1930–47 the number of households continued to increase, while the National Income remained almost constant. As a result, there was hardly any increase in the housing supply, since the housing market was relatively free in those days. The Dutch government did not stimulate the housing supply—nor the demand—through either subsidies or loan facilities.

- In the second period of economic stagnation (in the mid-1970s and early 1980s), the government supported public housing. In those days, the housing supply increased even faster than the number of households, since there was still a considerable housing shortage. The supply then increased by 2.0 per cent and the number of households by 1.8 per cent a year. Research has shown that, with the present subsidy system in the Netherlands, the elasticity between the growth of the National Income and the demand for houses is about 0.08, given the increase in the number of households (BSM, 1985). In the short and medium term, the elasticity between the National Income and the housing demand consists of a fixed part and a variable part, for income changes. With zero growth of the National Income, a 1.5 per cent increase in the housing demand can be expected. For each additional 1 per cent growth of the National Income, there will be an additional 0.3 per cent increase in the housing demand.

- Apart from the adaptations of the household estimates mentioned before, a number of corrections are still necessary in order to arrive at an estimate of the housing demand. For instance, 2.5 per cent of the houses in the Netherlands have been reserved to guarantee adequate turnover on the housing market. Furthermore, the number of withdrawals from the supply is to be taken into account.

The adaptations mentioned above yield an estimate of the housing demand in the years to come. As an example, we take the priod of 1985–99, at an assumed National Income growth of 1 per cent a year, which is considered to be the most likely situation (see Table 15.5).

We then find that, up to 1990, economic growth will not be sufficient to supply all households with the same average income. Consequently, the increase in the demand for houses will be smaller. But after 1990, the increase in the number of households will slow down considerably as a result of demographic factors, so that the assumed economic growth will be sufficient to maintain the average income per household. After 1995, even a 1 per cent

TABLE 15.5. Necessary production of houses per year during the period 1985–1999, assuming a yearly economic growth of 1 per cent in the Netherlands

	Necessary production (000s)				
	Increase in households (000s)	Increase in the demand for houses	Withdrawals	Growth to guarantee turnover	Changes in shortage or surplus	Total
1985–1989	80	74	15	2	11	102
1990–1994	66	65	18	2	—	85
1995–1999	41	47	21	1	—	69

annual growth of the National Income will be more than sufficient. Consequently, the demand for houses will increase slightly. It is expected that the number of withdrawals will increase, because of the relatively outdated housing stock. On balance, however, the number of houses to be built could decrease considerably up to the year 2000.

The estimates of the housing demand presented here, which can also be specified according to type, size, and ownership, have been used within government, in parliament, and with interest groups for debates about the housing programmes for coming years (up to 1990). The programme chosen provides for about 100,000 houses; practically all will be subsidized, and the Dutch government will finance 30 per cent of the costs.

This should be seen against the backdrop of a 1 per cent growth per year,

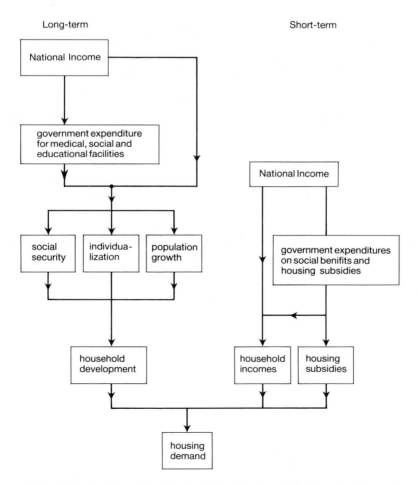

FIG. 15.4. Rough outline for the determination of the housing demand

which for the present is considered to be the most realistic assumption and which means a decrease in the income per household up to 1990. Therefore, a considerable financial contribution by government is necessary, so that houses will remain payable for future households.

The previous sections clearly indicate that there are short-term as well as long-term relations between National Income, household formation, household income, government expenditures, and housing demand.

In conclusion, we have tried to combine the major relations in one diagram (see Figure 15.4).

15.6. Future improvements

The household model as described in sections 15.2, 15.3, and 15.4 forms the basis of the method to determine the size, as well as the nature, of the future housing demand. The model is presently being put to practice, and lives up to expectations. Household formation has been looked at from a demographic and a macroeconomic point of view, which is sufficient for practical purposes. The developments outlined here seem plausible, but there are still some question marks. For example, individualization was considered to be a positive result of the increase in welfare. This process, however, also has its drawbacks. Increasing solitude and isolation may have repercussions which are unforeseeable at present.

Another point concerns the price of individualization. Section 15.3 roughly indicates its actual existence ('economies of scale'). The exact price is still an open question. Since a growing number of households consist of one or two persons, this price could well be higher than it used to be. Besides the decreasing growth of welfare since the 1960s, both developments mentioned could be an additional cause of the decreasing trend towards individualization. Further research is needed to determine whether this is actually the case, and where possible limits lie.

References

BUREAU VOOR STRATEGISCH MARKTONDERZOEK—BSM (BUREAU FOR STRATEGIC MARKETING RESEARCH—BSM) (1983). Trendrapport volkshuisvesting 1982 (Trend report on housing 1982) (BSM, Delft).

—— (1985). Toetsing en actualisering trendrapport volkshuisvesting (Additions to the trend report on housing) (Ministerie van Volkshuisvesting, Ruimtelijke Ordening en Milieubeheer, The Hague).

HEIDA, H. AND H. GORDIJN (1985). Het PRIMOS-huishoudensmodel: analyse en prognose van de huishoudensontwikkeling in Nederland (The PRIMOS household model: analysis and forecasts of household trends in the Netherlands) (Ministerie van Volkshuisvesting, Ruimtelijke Ordening en Milieubeheer, The Hague).

THE NETHERLANDS CENTRAL BUREAU OF STATISTICS (CBS) (1982). Prognose van de bevolking van Nederland na 1980 (Forecast of the population of the Netherlands after 1980) (Staatsuitgeverij, The Hague).

PART V

Conclusions

16

Reflections on household modelling

J. Bartlema and A. Vossen

ABSTRACT

*Household modelling is considered an abstract representation of the out-
come of behavioural processes in the field of formation and dissolution of
relationships. In order to be adequate, such a model must be rooted in an
understanding of the behavioural phenomena involved; it should be fed with
input which contains valid information on social reality and provide output
which is close enough to reality to be useful. The body of this chapter
attempts to contribute to an understanding of the underlying social processes. Model output and structure are discussed in this perspective. In view
of the fact that current developments in the institutional structure of society
give rise to an unprecedented degree of pluriformity, it is argued that
atheoretical, strictly demographic, modelling cannot perform adequately. A
reorientation towards the social determinants of the process is advocated.*

16.1. Introduction

THE point of departure in the discussion is an analysis of the two most recent
population projections carried out in the Netherlands. Particular attention
will be given to 'what went wrong, and why?'. The conclusion will be drawn
that the self-contained demographic projection procedure works rather well
for some variables, but less so for others. The term self-contained refers to
the sole inclusion of demographic variables in the model. The closer the
phenomenon in question is to being structurally determined, as in the case of
mortality where a near universal intention to avoid it may be taken as given,
the better the results.

Contrarily, the more individuals intervene in the decision-making process,
the larger the likelihood of discrepancies between forecast and reality. This is
the case for fertility, marriage, divorce, migration, and so forth.

We assume that successful aspects of current household forecasting should
be maintained, while those aspects which lead to serious discrepancies
between forecast and reality deserve reconsideration, especially upon
transposing the general approach to an area where behavioural transitions
are predominant. Moreover, household projections apply a variety of

243

approaches, but (when compared to national population projections) they do not provide such an authoritative tradition of research that it would be natural to take it as the basis for analysis.

An attempt will be made to look into the possible causes of the shortcomings of national population forecasts, and implications for remedial action will be indicated. The level of abstraction and scope of argument will be different at various points in the discussion, since the objective of this chapter is to place the task of forecasting institutions in the societal context in which it is being carried out in Western societies in the mid-1980s.

The conclusion is reached that it is inadvisable to apply an approach to modelling which has proven to be incapable of predicting the course of behaviourally determined variables to a new field of demographic endeavour—household modelling—in which trends are predominantly determined by precisely such factors.

16.2. Recent population forecasts in the Netherlands: How far off?

In the Netherlands, national population forecasts are carried out by the Netherlands Central Bureau of Statistics (CBS). During the last ten years, the CBS compiled forecasts in 1975, in 1980, in 1984, and, as from that year, annually. In Table 16.1 we present the per cent deviations of forecasted versus observed values for the basic demographic components of live births (marital and extra-marital), deaths, net migrations, marriages, and divorces since 1975. The forecasted values refer to the most recent projection for the date in question. The 1975–9 figures are thus related to the 1975 forecast and those for dates after 1980 to the forecast carried out in that year. In both cases two variants are given: for the first forecast the high (H) and the low (L) variants, and for the second forecast the low and the medium (M) variants, chosen because they were closest to reality.

Recent experience shows a tendency for the forecast to deviate from reality with a margin of plus or minus 10 per cent or more within a period of five years from the date the projection was carried out. Mortality estimates were quite close to reality, especially in the last projection. The discrepancies between observed and predicted values are largest for variables in which the component of personal decision-making intervenes most strongly: migration, marriage, divorce, and fertility. If we had not taken events, that is, total flows, as the yardstick, but rather the stocks of married people, divorced people, and so on, the picture would, of course, have been much less striking, though by no means wholly reliable. This once again poses the implicit question as to whether the results of the models used justify their internal refinement. The fact that the flows presented are themselves subtotals of more

TABLE 16.1. Observed minus projected numbers of basic demographic components in percentages of the observed values for 1975 to 1983, the Netherlands

		Total births	Marital births	Extra-marital births	Deaths	Net migrations	Marriages	Divorces
1975	H	0	0	3	−1	0	0	3
	L	0	0	3	−1	0	0	3
1976	H	−1	−2	20	−3	3	−5	−1
	L	2	1	23	−2	86	−5	−1
1977	H	−4	−5	26	−9	32	−16	−5
	L	2	2	30	−8	120	−16	−5
1978	H	−4	−5	26	−9	32	−16	−5
	L	6	5	40	−7	124	−28	−9
1979	H	−6	−8	40	−10	63	−41	−7
	L	7	5	47	−9	114	−41	−7
1980	M	0	0	0	0	0	0	0
	L	0	0	0	0	0	0	0
1981	M	0	1	0	0	0	0	9
	L	−1	−1	0	0	−18	−2	9
1982	M	−6	−7	0	0	−400	−5	13
	L	−8	−9	0	0	−525	−9	13
1983	M	−8	−9	8	−2	−117	−11	17
	L	−11	−12	8	−2	−217	−16	17

Computed from: CBS (1976), CBS (1982), and various issues of 'Maandstatistiek van de Bevolking', Netherlands Central Bureau of Statistics.

refined transitions—for example the marriages presented are the sums of first marriages, remarriages by widowed persons, and remarriages by divorced persons, totalled over all ages—underlines this point.

After it became evident that the differences between forecasted and observed values for aggregate behavioural phenomena over as short a period as a quinquennium (1975-9) were not negligible, the obsolete results of the 1975-based calculations were replaced by a new projection. Then, in late 1984, the 1980 projection was in turn replaced by a new one. In both instances alterations in the projection model were introduced. Particular problems were the validity of the model with respect to changes in marital status, the interdependence between fertility and nuptiality, and marriage market mechanisms. Attention was focused on the fact that the model was incapable of adequately replicating the past, especially with respect to divorce and remarriage. Given the observed values of exogenous variables, the self-contained demographic model should be able to simulate observed population trends accurately, unless of course the model structure is incorrect.

In the face of unsuccessful attempts to replicate demographic behaviour which causes changes in population size and composition, the axiom that the future is knowable and can be modelled by self-contained demographic instruments has led official forecasters to believe that the model is incomplete and/or that the procedures for generating hypotheses about trends are deficient.

However, we believe it is highly unlikely that discrepancies as large as those presented in Table 16.1 are primarily due to the imprecision of estimation procedures. Roughly speaking, a useful forecasting model is an abstract representation of the actual system which strikes a balance between clarity and detail. Model validation should incorporate enquiries into the logic of the model, but also into the requirements with respect to data input and its output, that is, whether it satisfactorily predicts the behaviour of the system. Fascination with the tool, rather than an interest in the behavioural phenomena to be predicted, leads to models which are over-accurate in structure, over-taxing on data, and under-precise in output.

16.3. Sociological interlude

The starting-point of this section will be two existential observations, namely that human beings are social creatures and that they have needs. The justification for rushing through the corollaries of these two axioms is to be able to sketch the backdrop against which our diagnosis of the problem with population projections will take place.

Certain tasks must be carried out in groups in order to fulfil individual needs and to guarantee group-survival. Such tasks are the production and distribution of goods, distribution of power, reproduction, socialization, and the maintenance of a cultural apparatus capable of legitimizing the social structure to parties whose interests are least served by it. Since these tasks are necessary for the well-being of society, they may be considered to be basic functions. Societies differ greatly in the structural solutions they adopt to fulfil these functions, that is to say, in their institutions, their kinship, economic, political, legal, and legitimation structures.

We shall follow Zijderveld's (1974) general line of reasoning in defining institutionalization as the fundamental anthropological process, in which individual human actions are transformed into objective, stable, and normative patterns which acquire and maintain their own existence, regardless of the actors. These structures define more or less rigidly roles and rules which are enforced more or less formally through social sanctions and therewith create a certain degree of social stability. Institutions are endowed by the legitimizing procedures of culture with status, respectability, and credibility, in order to promote their efficiency.

When sociology as a discipline was still in its infancy, a conception of the development of institutions which accompany industrialization awoke: this process carries the name of structural differentiation and outlines a process of change from few relatively simple multifunctional structures to the generation of increasing numbers of more specialized institutions. It was soon realized that structural differentiation raises the problem of reintegration. Authors describing the process customarily use the example of the development of the family from a combined production–consumption unit which fulfils reproductive and sexual functions, is the major focus of socialization, and is a crucial determinant of the position of its members—by sex and age—in the status hierarchy to a proliferation of institutions. An important driving force behind the process is allegedly the distribution of labour which alters the nature of the workforce, transforming self-employed workers into wage labourers, generating a demand for skilled labour, causing concentration of population in production centres, creating new needs for public housing, creating dependence on wages and hence liability to unemployment, sickness, employment injury, retirement in the absence of an extended family, and a familiar benevolent 'Umwelt' to fall back upon in case of need, and hence the generation of a myriad of welfare agencies.

We shall be as brief as possible and pick up the strand of the integrative mechanisms we left dangling in the section above. The expanding sphere of state interference is in accordance with the concept of structural differentiation. The increasing scale and complexity of society increasingly requires an all-encompassing integrative mechanism, placing ever higher demands on government and generating the Moloch of the modern state. A universal trend toward state-organized collective provisioning has accompanied the process of structural differentiation and industrialization, so that the entire process may be summarized as a development from a kinship-dominated to a state-dominated social system. These two institutions lie at the opposite extremes of a continuum of primary versus secondary groups, informal versus formal organization, private versus public spheres, the individual versus the collectivity, particularistic versus universalistic norms, mechanical versus organic solidarity, and so on; and it is clear at which extreme of the continuum the individual's most immediate loyalties lie.

The state is the ultimate institution in the sense that it is very 'objective' and 'external', undeniably 'normative' and 'coercive', the champion of internal and external order and stability. The state is organized around the central functions defined above, as materialized into ministries of Economic Affairs, Justice, Education, departments of family policies, welfare, and so on. To ensure adequate planning and control, these interrelated administrative entities need information and, since policy making implies foreseeing alternatives and taking appropriate measures, they also need forecasts, projections, and scenarios of various degrees of conditionality. In order to generate this kind of aggregate information, industrializing countries, of course, create an institution and call it the National Statistical Institute, the Census Bureau, the Central Bureau of Statistics, or something of the sort. This administrative machinery gathers, orders, and processes information on other institutions in society. What, for example, is left of the family now that the state has taken over so many of its original tasks? We shall concentrate on the family since it is most germane to the topic under consideration, namely population forecasting in the Netherlands.

The state nowadays does all kinds of things which individuals used to do themselves or together with family and friends. The individual—rational and economical as he is—will attempt to maximize his personal gain; that is, he will contribute as little as possible to acquire as much as possible from the abstract, external agent he refers to as 'the system'. The externalization that takes place in institutionalization does not go hand in hand with a mirror process of internalization. Hence the individual does not identify with the instruments of the state, he does not personally accept their authority, and he does not feel responsible toward the state as he did toward his family and his friends. He or she may comply with the rules, but will not support them; may play roles, but does not believe in them; but then again, he or she may not. In the newly created situation of non-scarcity, in the direct sense of fulfilment of physical needs, the individual who is aware of his rights may disagree with the legitimacy of his obligations. This is also a fundamental right, perhaps the most fundamental one: the right to disagree. Since the welfare state guarantees a minimum state of well-being to all its citizens, the risk involved is relative. Intermediate institutions such as the kinship structure, the church, the job environment, and so on have lost their compelling normative power, heralding the age of individual autonomy, the me-myself- and-I era.

The concentration of institutional traits in the state is effectively synonymous with the de-institutionalization of society. Also in this respect, we may consider the state as being the ultimate institution; for the time being it is the last one. Whether the 'unfrozen' and 'liquid' stages of the social change process will be followed by a 'refreezing' of altered structures is an open question. From what we know today, we can only observe that the stability previously derived from the institutional build-up of society is being replaced by an opportunistic, or if you wish creative, situational adaptation to changing circumstances by autonomous actors with a broad and, in the process, expanding range of alternatives.

If institutions are by definition conservative, our ultimate specimen is the more so because of its sheer size, and the formal, bureaucratic nature of its problem solving. This is inevitable, considering the diversity of situations it must handle through classification, regulation, and administration, and in view of the social distance between policies and individuals who have a problem to be solved or an income to be taxed. While individuals are increasingly opting for a growing variety of ways to live their personal lives, which were previously ordered through institutions, the administrative machinery is losing its grip. If reality is indeed a social construction—to use a term coined by Peter Berger—there may be many realities in a pluralistic, multicultural society, but there are undeniably at least two: the reality of the administrative registration system and the compound social reality of everyday life.

The family is still an important institution, judging by the attention it receives from the legitimation machinery of our culture; do we not have family law, family sociology, family counselling, family planning, and so on, and do our churches not regularly issue declarations on appropriate rules of conduct? However, nowhere is the gap between the official registration system and social reality more obvious. Terms such as 'incomplete' families, 'unmarried' cohabitation, one-person households, 'non-family' households, and so on indicate that atypical constructions are arising which confront statisticians with problems of classification and which are dealt with by some kind of reference to familiar concepts. The numerical proportions or processes covered by such hybrid institutions are anything but negligible. Losing grip of the process one is supposed to control is disagreeable and necessitates remedial action, such as research.

The truth is that the overlap between the categorization of the registration system and the group solutions sought by actors to satisfy their needs is diminishing in all realms where intermediate institutions were previously dominant, but particularly in the domain where the traditional nuclear family reigned until quite recently. In contemporary society, registered marriages are no longer a valid operationalization of the formation of stable sexual unions. What such a 'sanctioned' marriage means to those involved is also often questionable in the eyes of the individual. Many prefer to marry or separate—or not—because benefits can be obtained or because costs can be avoided by the couple with respect to the collective welfare system, not in relation to each other. This is a specific version of the legitimation crisis referred to in more general terms above. Similarly, the validity of divorce, widowhood, and so on is also at stake, since the dissolution or termination of an unknown proportion of unions is not included, and the meaning of the registered transitions is not self-evident. The interpretation of the term 'validity' in this context, it is understood, refers to the classical problem of asking ourselves whether we are measuring what we want to measure. It is also taken for granted that what we want to measure is social reality and that our interest in statistics is only instrumental, in the sense that it provides the material with which we can operationalize the object of our study.

However obvious the last statement may be, its consequences are not—as far as we know—drawn by many demographers. We continue to rely on the petrified categories of nuclear family as a reliable representation of social behaviour, and we devise ever more sophisticated techniques to replicate trends in these figures, and unsuccessfully at that. Should a model finally succeed in replicating nuptial behaviour over, say, a period of three years, what of it? It would be of limited use to us as an index of phenomena we are really interested in, such as the formation of sexual and reproductive unions and their consumption patterns (housing, manufactured goods, and so on).

The sociological detour we made brings us to the theorems that the deinstitutionalization of primary groups focusing on sexual, reproductive, and affective needs makes the future unknowable, and that self-contained atheoretical demographic modelling is not capable of reliably representing our object of interest, because civil registration data are invalid for this purpose and, more fundamentally, because we lack an appropriate classification structure. The answer to the question whether resignation to such a limited set of variables as those traditionally covered under the heading 'demographic' is the best we can do, as suggested in the illuminating article by Keyfitz (1982) on whether knowledge can improve forecasts, is negative, because we cannot but be disappointed in the degree of accuracy attained. The diagnosis is that the pluralization of social reality has outgrown our capacity to grasp it and measure it, let alone forecast it, within the narrow limits of curve-fitting and extrapolation.

A satisfactory strategy in such a situation will strive to avoid overbidding one's hand and to steer clear of rigidity and standard procedures during the game. As far as the government's official estimating machinery is concerned, it is not incomplete but overcomplete with respect to modelling the process at the aggregate level. The most appropriate thing to do would be to eradicate unnecessary detail, to trim down the complexity, and carefully to monitor strong and weak points, paying specific attention to the input in first instance and gradually restoring sophistication when results justify such refinements. Any modifications should be preceded by a sound sensitivity analysis—for instance, as Cruijsen and Van Hoorn (1983) did for the Netherlands—to warrant the investment with respect to the difference it might possibly make to the results. It would also most positively entail not applying a methodological approach akin to those in the behavioural sector, such as household modelling, even if, for example, the Ministry of Housing offers a handsome reward for such an undertaking. If our analysis is correct, the processes that underlie the willingness to spend money on the topic also exclude the possibility of doing a good job on it within the restricted framework of self-contained demographic modelling.

The topic of household modelling is of undeniable interest and cannot be brushed off with a mere 'impossible'. The next section will outline our ideas on how to proceed from here with respect to the subject of this chapter: modelling households.

16.4. Implications for household modelling

We have suggested that refinement of detailed flow models in which the transitions are behaviourally determined is not very promising if the model is to be used for forecasting, since not only do people move between states, but the states themselves are in transition too. The use of discrete-state models, whether continuous or discrete in the time dimension, is bound to be unsatisfactory, because persons are no longer inside or outside 'states', they are always somewhere in between and may be on their way to creating new 'states'. Those 'states' are devoid of sociological meaning: refined measures of household type in terms of kin, pseudo-kin, ex-kin, or non-kin, for example, will not provide a satisfactory classification scheme, since they no longer reflect social reality. Neutral, abstract typologies in terms of characteristics such as age–sex composition, household size, in which nothing is said about types of relationships, will do fine. A modest stance should be adopted with respect to the reliability of the results of forecasting operations on more than a short-term basis.

If it is true that demographers are inclined to rely heavily on large bodies of administrative data, and if demographers are willing to undertake household modelling, it appears that the crudeness of the data available to them for the purpose constrains the complexity of the model, perhaps to such an extent as to make it devoid of intellectual challenge. If, on the other hand, household modellers do not restrict themselves to strictly demographic methods, nor to conventional demographic data, then (besides the question why we speak of household demography at all, rather than of something like mathematical sociology) we may ask ourselves which data, and which methods they should use.

Trying to find useful answers to these questions should involve looking for elements with which to construct a model that fulfils a number of conditions with respect to its theoretical basis, its input, and its output:

1. The model should be rooted in behavioural theory.
2. The mathematical description of relationships between elements of the model should be in agreement with reasonable hypotheses about (collective) human behaviour.
3. The structure of the model should be as simple as possible, given available input and required output.
4. The input should be a valid operationalization of the social behaviour it attempts to model.
5. The input of the model should include manipulable variables, that is, variables amenable to policy intervention.
6. The output of the model should be within pre-defined margins of reality.
7. In order to warrant that forecasting remains within acceptable margins,

it should be limited to the near future and be updated annually as a standard procedure.

8. No forecasts will be carried out beyond a pre-defined horizon of, say, five years. Any projections of households which transcend such a horizon should bear the stamp of conditionality and be called 'scenarios' rather than any term suggesting an element of prediction. Scenario-building should place particular emphasis on working out the model's implications of strategies in terms of the manipulable variable, under various combinations of the non-manipulable factors that the model incorporates.

9. The model should be as flexible as possible, containing few predetermined categories, but permitting, through a combination of traits, the construction of novel pluriform typologies.

These criteria are to be considered as objectives one should strive to achieve; as demands they are too strenuous. It will seldom be possible to live up to all of them. Notwithstanding these noble intentions and our wise suggestions as to where to look for answers to the two straightforward questions asked above, we cannot disguise the fact that 'We don't know' is their equally straightforward answer. It is our conviction that new (survey) data will have to be collected and new methods developed if the task of modelling households is to be successful in advanced societies.

16.5. Conclusions

The conclusions reached are:

1. A characteristic which households share with other contemporary institutions in society is instability. The de-institutionalization of society has diminished the degree of order and predictability to such an extent that household formation can no longer be modelled by atheoretical relations. The structure of household models has received disproportional attention, to the detriment of their theoretical basis.

2. Official registration systems containing information with respect to marital status do not provide valid information for the operationalization of the flows between different 'types' of households. Survey data must form the empirical content of models of the formation of the relations that create households.

3. The basic attitude of the household forecaster should be one of modesty and pragmatism. Unfortunately, the execution of household forecasts is inevitable. Given this situation, the margin of error in previous forecasts should receive ample coverage. The time period over which forecasts are carried out should not exceed five years. Any attempt to foresee the implications of particular courses of action on household formation should be phrased in terms of 'scenario-building', therewith explicitly underlining the

fact that the results are not to be qualified as predictions.

4. Household modelling can fulfil the needs of a wide variety of users, ranging from the marketing of consumer goods to housing construction. Different users have different demands. A common market-place where social scientists and planning agencies can meet to agree on what is possible on the supply side and what is desirable on the demand side of estimates and forecasts is often lacking. If the output produced by household modellers is to match the needs of public and private organizations, the creation of such a market-place is advisable.

5. If intended as more than a case-study representation, the structure of a household model should be as flexible as possible to enable it to follow the pluriformity of configurations that are arising in society. Rigid pre-established typologies should be avoided, and the level of aggregation should be as low as possible, thus making it possible to combine elements in the categories that the data themselves suggest are most appropriate.

References

CRUIJSEN, H. G. J. M. AND W. D. VAN HOORN (1983). Prognose 1980, gevoeligheidsanalyse van het rekenmodel, *Maandstatistiek van de Bevolking* 31(12), 20–30.

KEYFITZ, N. (1982). Can knowledge improve forecasts?, *Population and Development Review* 8(4), 729–51.

THE NETHERLANDS CENTRAL BUREAU OF STATISTICS (CBS) (1976). *De toekomstige demografische ontwikkeling in Nederland na 1975* (Staatsuitgeverij, The Hague).

—— (1982, 1984). *Prognose van de Bevolking van Nederland na 1980*, vols. 1 and 2 (Staatsuitgeverij, The Hague).

ZIJDERVELD, A. C. (1974). *Institutionalisering* (Boom, Meppel).

17

Recurrent issues in dynamic household modelling

N. Keilman and N. Keyfitz

ABSTRACT

This final chapter attempts to synthesize the most important issues arising from the previous chapters. We concentrate on seven topics: the household concept; new trends in household formation and dissolution; the link between household theory, household modelling, and household forecasting; micro- versus macromodels; modelling household dynamics; the individual versus the household as a unit of analysis and modelling, and the related two-sex problem; and finally the prospects for data collection and parameter estimation techniques.

17.1. Introduction

IN contrast to *qualitative* studies of household behaviour, whose history starts shortly after World War II (Glick, 1947), *quantitative* household studies which attempt to model household dynamics are quite recent. Not only has the subject of modelling household processes only recently gained interest, it is also confronted with a number of difficulties that prevent rapid progress in this field: standard definitions and typologies are lacking, and not much agreement exists with respect to appropriate procedures for analysis and model-building (Bongaarts, 1983, p. 38; see also chapter 2 by Schmid and chapter 6 by Schwarz for difficulties with definitions and typologies).

Notwithstanding the differences of opinion that emerge in this volume regarding the best research approach to modelling household dynamics, we want to make an attempt to synthesize the findings of the authors of the previous chapters and to place them in a wider perspective. Common findings as well as conflicting opinions are listed. In this way we hope to contribute to the formulation of a research strategy which should ultimately lead to a better performance and therefore a greater usefulness of household models. Our discussions concentrate on seven issues which seem to be present in most studies that model household processes: the concept of a household (section 17.2), new trends in household formation and dissolution (section 17.3), theories of household development and their relation to model-building and forecasting (section 17.4), macro- and micromodels (section 17.5), modelling household dynamics (section 17.6), the individual versus the household as the unit of analysis, and the related two-sex problem (section 17.7), and finally prospects for data collection and for methods of estimating the parameters of household models (section 17.8). The selection of these seven issues entails that we focus on theories and models (parts I and III of this volume) and that data and applications (parts II and IV) will receive somewhat less explicit attention.

17.2. Household definitions

Schmid and Schwarz complain about the lack of uniformity in definitions of what a household is (see also Wall, 1984, p. 75). It is not easy to apply one single definition across cultures; those cultures in which privacy is important are likely to have more stringent requirements for a living space to be considered a separate household than those in which less privacy is desired or can be afforded.

The complexity of the subject of household demography begins with the elaborate and subtle definitions required for the sheer counting of numbers. The boundaries of the household require more detailed specification than the boundaries either of the population—usually a simple configuration on a map—or of the individual within its skin. Moreover, the household cannot always be defined and classified according to legal definitions. A married couple has made up a contract, so that marriage can be regarded as an administrative institution. But a household often lacks such a legal base, as the relationship between many of its members is based upon companionship and/or informal agreements.

To see what quasi-scholastic distinctions have to be made in the definition of households, let us look at the first of the three possibilities which the United Nations recently recommended for population and housing censuses.

1. The 'housekeeping unit' concept: a private household is either (i) a one-person household, that is, a person who lives alone in a separate housing unit or who occupies, as a lodger, a separate room of a housing unit but does not join with any of the other occupants of the housing unit to form part of a multi-person household; or (ii) a multi-person household, that is, a group of two or more persons who combine to occupy a whole or part of a housing unit and to provide themselves with food and possibly other necessities of life. This is the housekeeping unit concept employed by Ermisch (section 3.1) and by Linke (chapter 8, Appendix).
2. The 'household-dwelling' concept: a private household is the aggregate number of persons occupying a housing unit. Schmid (section 2.2) denotes this concept as the 'co-resident domestic group'.
3. Institutional households and other communal relationships: an institutional household is comprised of groups of persons living together, who

usually share their meals and are bound by a common objective and generally subject to common rules, for example, groups of persons living together in dormitories of schools and universities, hospitals, old-age homes and other welfare institutions, religious institutions, and so on.

Concentrating on the first two definitions, it will be clear that for an analysis of economic household characteristics (for example, household income, household consumption) the housekeeping unit is appropriate. For some other special purposes (for example, analysis of dwelling conditions, studies on energy consumption) the household dwelling concept is more suitable. We should note, however, that it is not always possible to collect data according to a given household concept—the definition to be applied depends heavily on the constraints imposed by the method of data collection. Therefore, some differences exist in the concepts and definitions used within countries as well as between countries. The Conference of European Statisticians recently compiled a useful overview of the type of household definitions used by national statistical bureaux in Europe and their sources of data for household statistics; see Table 17.1.

About two-thirds of the nineteen countries listed in Table 17.1 employ the housekeeping unit concept in their data collection, irrespective of the type of survey. Also, about two-thirds of these countries use (approximately) the same definitions in *all* the sources.

This diversity of the household concept makes a precise comparative analysis for different regions and/or periods rather difficult. Moreover, as Schwarz (section 6.1) points out, uniformity is lacking in the classification of persons within the household: he notes difficulties for persons with more than one dwelling (see also Linke, chapter 8, Appendix), for persons who are not related to the family (subtenants, service personnel) and so on. Schmid argues that the scoring of non-related persons present in the household has a considerable effect on the enumeration of people in households. This, together with the effect of other definitional difficulties, would then suggest that it is not easy to reveal consistent patterns and trends in household developments. Therefore, one is surprised to note that many authors in this volume and in other studies observe a clear tendency in Western society: a continuous decrease of household size and a steady increase in the number of non-traditional households (one-parent households and cohabiting persons) as well as in the number of one-parent families. In other words, in spite of the lack of uniformity in household definitions and classifications for different regions and/or different periods, some consistent trends can be observed. Then why do many demographers strongly emphasize the importance of uniform definitions? One might think that this is caused by the fact that they are used to the excellent quality of population statistics derived from censuses, surveys, and population registration systems in the developed countries. When studying households, it might be useful, therefore, to learn from the experience of demographers who deal with migration statistics based upon the vague concept of 'residence', or with deficient statistics in Third World countries; or we could learn from the experience of labour market statisticians or students of personal income distribution. They do not get stuck in problems created by vague definitions or the low quality of their data and they *do* reveal important patterns and trends. Although we are well aware of the problems that are possibly caused by definitions and classifications varying in time and space, we think that these difficulties should not be overemphasized.

17.3. New trends in household formation and dissolution

There is much debate on whether the classical nuclear family household is here to stay or on its way out. Both have been argued, and often using the same data. Divorce is high, and rising: this proves, say some, that marriage is no longer the sacred covenant that it was, but only a passing convenience to both parties. No, say others, it does not prove that, since most divorces are followed by subsequent remarriage for at least one of the partners. The high divorce rate shows that people will not let one mistake saddle them with an unsatisfactory partnership for life, that is, marriage is taken more seriously than ever. In the past, marriage could only be meaningful when the partners engaged in complementary activities, and so were fully and truly dependent on one another. No, it is said now, since the wife is not totally dependent on her husband as she once was, the partner is a voluntary choice; it is no longer a matter of desperately accepting any man who comes along; so marriage can be truly democratic, and the family is bound together by affection rather than by sheer necessity. The change from institution to companionship, as Burgess and Locke point out, can hardly be reckoned a step backward.

The argument carries over to fertility. How can the family be important if its purpose is no longer to have children? But just as with divorce, the fact that women are no longer tied down in continual childbearing makes the family better, not worse.

17.3.1. New forms of family life

Forms of joint living that would have been scandalous two or three decades ago now pass without comment. Unmarried couples can now live together without arousing their neighbours, friends, or employers. This change in attitude towards the formality of marriage, an indicator of deep changes in the family in advanced countries, appeared early in Europe, most noticeably in Sweden, and from there it spread through the Western World. The socialist countries are more conservative in this respect, and so is much of the Third World. But the situation in the Third World varies from one place to the next;

TABLE 17.1. Sources of data on households in selected ECE countries, and type of definition used[a]

	Population Register	Population and Housing Census	Microcensus or Multi-purpose Sample Survey	Labour Force Survey	Budget Survey	Income Survey	Housing or Living Conditions Survey	Same Definitions used in all Sources?[b]
Austria		A, B, C	A					Yes
Belgium		A, C		A, C	A, C		A, C	Yes
Bulgaria		A, C	A			A	A	Yes
Canada		B, C		(B), (c)	(B)	(B), (c)	B	No
Cyprus		A	A		A			Yes
Czechoslovakia		a, B, c	a, B		a			Yes
Denmark	B[c]	(B)[d]	B		a	a		No
Finland		B			a	a	a	No
France		B, C		b, c	b	b	B	Yes
Germany, Federal Republic of		A	A	A	A	A	A	Yes
Hungary		A, C	A, C	A	A	A	A	Yes
Netherlands		A, C		A, C	A	A, C	A	Yes
Poland		A	A		a	a	a	No

Romania	A			A		No
Sweden	B, C			a	a, b	No
Switzerland	A, C			a		No
Turkey	A		A	A	A	Yes
United Kingdom	A, C	A	A	A	A	Yes
United States	B, C	A, B, C	B, C	B, C	B, C	Yes

Meaning of Codes A: Housekeeping unit concept
  B: Household dwelling concept
  C: Institutional households
  Uncapitalized letters: some variation from the census recommended definition
  Letters between parentheses: largely consistent with the definition in the ECE 1980 census recommendations

[a] Based on response to ECE questionnaire of November 1981.
[b] It was not always clear from the responses submitted by countries whether the same definition of households was used consistently in the different data sources. Therefore, the information provided in this column should be viewed only as being tentatively correct.
[c] The household dwelling concept is also used for institutional households. It is, however, possible to differentiate between private and institutional households.
[d] The data on households and families in the Danish population and housing censuses are derived from administrative registers, see also Petersen (1985).

Source. Adapted from 'Sources of data on and definitions of households and families in countries in the ECE-region', Working Paper no. 2 prepared by the Secretariat of the Conference of European Statisticians, on the occasion of the Informal Meeting on the co-ordination of Statistics of Households and Families, January 1983.

Latin America had informal types of marriage long before they started to appear in Europe.

Morality can adapt to such changes more easily than can statistical collection. Whatever other purposes were served by formal marriage, it yielded durable and hence countable family groups. A married couple could be properly enumerated in only one way until they got divorced or one member died; mistakes might be made, but the legal status was unambiguous. In the new situation ambiguity is rife; one does not even know for sure, in the light of all the facts, whether a couple have a durable relationship and can so be called effectively married, or whether the relationship is transitory enough to be disregarded.

17.3.2. Patterns of remarriage

One of the numerous patterns within the range of formal marriage is the formation of a couple when both are in their early or mid-twenties, remaining married and perhaps having one or two children until their thirties or early forties, then divorcing, the husband remarrying, perhaps someone 5 to 15 years younger than himself, and the wife remaining single.

To say that such a pattern could become universal is to become embroiled in self-contradiction, for under ordinary conditions there are not enough young women to supply wives both to men of their own age and to older divorced men. But a certain fraction of the population could follow this pattern, and a simple model would tell what fraction.

Such a pattern is hardly consistent with equality of women, given the relative attractiveness of younger partners over older ones. We discuss age and sex roles of household members in the overview of theories explaining household behaviour in section 17.4. Here we quote a popular Canadian columnist, Doris Anderson, who writes of it ironically, in what might have been a commencement address (see Dalhousie Alumni Magazine, Autumn, 1984):

To the young women I should have said: delay marriage as long as possible and concentrate on getting established in a lifelong career . . . And what advice for the men . . .? I should have said to them: grab the most promising and energetic woman you can find. Marriage is the best bargain you will ever get. Today a wife will help you in your career and help you build up equity in a home, car, etc. While you live with her, she will do almost all of the work in the home for free, manage your social life, raise your children and look after your sex life. Then, if you find marriage palls and children don't suit your lifestyle, you can walk away from it all, with half the house, car, etc., and all of the stocks, bonds and pension, and start all over with a younger, more energetic woman. You can even get out of the tiny support the law requires you to pay to help raise your children—if you have no conscience.

17.4. The link between household theory, household modelling, and household forecasting

Household models should be based on household theories, as Bartlema and Vossen emphasized correctly in section 16.4. In this volume, Schmid and Bartlema and Vossen consider the household from a sociological point of view. Both point out that household developments in the Western world are to be understood from broad general tendencies in these societies, in particular the process of weakening norms and institutions. In fact, they adhere to lines of thinking presented by Max Weber, who views changes in the family and the household as a function of its changing economic position which, in turn, is a function of the changes in the total society stemming from the urban–industrial revolution. The dominant sociological hypothesis relating technology and social organization postulates a functional interdependence between industrialization and urbanization, and the small nuclear family as the unit of social organization. But many more explanations exist.

Ermisch adopts an *economic* perspective: utilities in the household are maximized under certain restrictions. The minimal household unit forms the unit where these economic decisions are made. This theory can, in fact, be considered an adaptation of the theory of *new home economics*, as presented by Becker (1981). In his theory, Becker states that women have a comparative advantage by their work in the home because they have to bear and raise the children, and at the same time they can do the housework. Marriage is necessary for women to protect themselves against being abandoned with children whom they would not be able to support. Within the family a degree of altruism exists: each person's utility function depends positively on the utility of others, and so the family as a whole can be thought of as having a collective utility function.

An alternative economic interpretation of marriage and divorce behaviour is supplied by Easterlin's (1980) *relative income hypothesis*. Couples compare their material aspirations with their earning potential. The income-earnings prospects of today's young adults are unfavourable as compared with their aspirations, which were created some years earlier when they lived with their parents. Therefore, marriage is deferred. After the occurrence of marriage, wives may feel they have to work to help support the family, the couple may not have as many children as they would like to have, and these factors produce marital tensions that lead to marital dissolution. On the other hand, high relative income leads to an optimistic attitude toward marriage and childbearing, and it makes divorce less probable.

Unlike the new home economics and the relative income hypothesis, the *transaction cost approach* considers the internal organization and structure of families and households. It focuses on the role of institutions in structuring complex, long-term relationships. It views marriage as a 'governance structure' and recognizes the dual role of family- or marriage-specific capital. Marriage-specific capital is defined by two characteristics (Pollak, 1985, p. 601): it increases productivity in the household and it is worthless if the marriage dissolves. Satisfaction with one's relationship is an example of marriage-specific capital, to which Becker, Landes, and Michael (1977, p. 1142, p. 1152) have added 'working exclusively in the household' and 'children'. The theory predicts that an increase in marriage-specific capital will widen the gap between remaining in a particular marriage and leaving it.

A very different approach is the *political* theory of the family, by which indeed there is a division of labour, but it is determined by the power and solidarity of males, which define culture both within the family and in society as a whole. The fact that women remain subservient in the classical family lies ultimately not in the more efficient division of labour, nor in altruism, but in their having no choice. In exchange for protection for life, they must be sheltered from (or kept out of) the world and in effect be domestic servants to males. Traditional societies could impose an acceptance of this by suitable training of girls from a very early age.

Alongside the sociological, economic, and political views is a *biological* view (Wilson, 1975). In all times and places, women remained in the residential area all day long while men went out to forage. The greater mobility of men and the relatively sedentary character of women are presumably built into human genes, the result of long evolution. It is not hard to see that some such division of characteristics, and consequently of labour, has its evolutionary advantages. The degree to which it applies under conditions of civilization is debatable. Plainly we need some other explanation of the rapid changes since World War II, with women now foraging almost as much as men.

Bargaining models are more persuasive. Marriage is treated as a cooperative game, in which the players have complete freedom of preplay communication to make joint binding agreements (Luce and Raiffa, 1957). These models, developed by Manser and Brown (1980) and by McElroy and Horney (1981), do not require that either spouse be altruistic, although one or both may be. Spouses favour different activities. That alone would cause them to separate, but this is only a 'next-best' alternative for each party. Agreement is reached by some explicit bargaining rule (see also Pollak, 1985, p. 599).

The *social–psychological theory*, related to the bargaining model, explains formation and dissolution of couples by sex ratio imbalances on the marriage market. Guttentag and Secord (1983) state that when sex ratios are high, men are in excess supply. Young adult women are scarce and traditional sex roles are common. But any shortage of eligible males (such as the present situation in the United States, for instance), would give bargaining power to men and lead to a reduced commitment to marriage and family life. The reason is that in times when there is an oversupply of women, society would not emphasize love and commitment of men to the same woman throughout her childbearing years. Instead, women would seek their economic independence outside of marriage.

Burch (1985) argues that there has been a *change in age and sex roles*. Women's liberation and an increasing freedom for children have led to a situation in which household members are more or less autonomous, and all tend to have similar skills and activities. There is thus less room for a division of labour. This means less differentiation and so less solidarity which flows from the division of labour among individuals; there is consequently less to be gained from living together.

On the other hand, 'The young, the old, women, the unmarried, servants, boarders—all have been accorded more nearly equal "rights" to various household goods previously reserved to the patriárch or breadwinner'. This in effect makes the household more 'crowded' in the sense that there is more competition for scarce, space-related goods. It is as though the democratization of the family has deprived its members of a separate niche which each could occupy in the past. Thus on the one hand they compete with one another for the scarce good of space; on the other hand, they hardly depend on one another, so they might as well live separately.

The liberation to which our age testifies so amply has roots that go back to the Enlightenment, to ideas of individual worth, as Lesthaeghe (1983) points out; built into this idea is the liberation from the need to live with others. Pampel (1983) attempts to find out to what degree living alone as we observe it can be explained by compositional variables, including age, income, and so on. If the increase is fully accounted for by the fact that there are more old people, that incomes are higher, and so on, then we do not need to search any further. However, he finds that these compositional variables go only part of the way to explaining the observed increase in living alone.

It goes without saying that searching for *the* universally valid theory is a futile attempt. Moreover, the choice of a particular theory will be based on intuition, taste, tradition, and other subjective factors, since empirical tests often remain inconclusive. Therefore we may expect that some elements of one theory will be accepted by the majority of the demographic forum, and some other elements will be taken from other theories. This points to the need for a consistent framework to synthesize these parts of theoretical explanation. The life course perspective provides such a framework, as Willekens suggests in chapter 7. The life of an individual consists of several careers. At the individual level we may distinguish the educational career, the health career, the labour market career, the housing career, the fertility career, and so on. At the group level one may have household and family careers, for example, the marriage career. A career contains a sequence of events signalling the transition from one status to another. In life course analysis one is interested in the relationship between two or more events within and across careers. Hence, the life course perspective is not a theory explaining behaviour;

rather, it is a set of concepts in which behavioural aspects can consistently be brought together. Modelling of norms, values, and attitudes, then, still remains a challenge.

How do all these and other theories contribute to household modelling and household forecasting?

Household models can be constructed on the basis of specific elements of household theories when the relevant concepts can be formalized: we need variables and functional relations for such a model. This is what Bartlema and Vossen must have had in mind when they formulated their second criterion in section 16.4: 'The mathematical description of relations between elements of the model should be in agreement with reasonable hypotheses about . . . human behaviour'. The economic theory of household behaviour provides a good example. An essential part of that analysis is the household production function, which indicates how, for instance, the time which the individual spends on household activities results in household production. Here we see that economic theory leads to a set of equations, relating some exogenous economic factors to variables describing household behaviour. It is this set of behavioural equations which is denoted in chapter 1 as 'econometric' models, either of the static ('equilibrium') or of the dynamic type.

It is not always possible to operationalize a theory of human behaviour and to base the construction of a formal model on it. Yet such a theory may help us to identify groups of persons with more or less similar behaviour. The sort of considerations given by Schmid and Bartlema and Vossen open up the possibility of categorizing individuals in different household classes. The use of fixed household categories in such a model is criticized by the latter two authors, who write that '. . . not only are people moving between [household] states, but the states themselves are in transition'. This then would suggest that household status is a continuous dimensions, rather than a discrete one with bounded classes: although we have an intuitive notion of 'household status', it is not that of a strict division of some set in smaller subsets—rather, the boundaries are fuzzy in our mind. In fact, our intuitive notion of such a classification is a mixture of a discrete and a continuous household dimension. However, the statistics with which we will study the household situation will not conform to this intuition. Alonso (1986, p. 262) argues that the reasons for this lie in the nature of mathematics and bureaucracies. The data are usually gathered by bureaucratic institutions, which must produce them by a set of definable and well-specified procedures of identification and measurement. And the nature of set theory tells us that an element is or is not a member of a set; and the set is bounded. Therefore, our mathematical models, which use functions and equations ultimately based on set theory, have harder edges than reality has, just as data do.

Do these fuzzy functional boundaries between household categories then imply that we should use 'fuzzy set theory' in household demography? For instance, a researcher may have difficulties, when considering a couple having an affectional relationship, in deciding whether they are cohabiting or not. The boundaries between the statuses 'cohabiting' and 'not-cohabiting' are, in general, not sharply defined. The concept of the membership function, which plays an important role in the theory of fuzzy sets, may effectively deal with this imprecision (Zadeh, 1982, p. 29; compare also Sekita and Tabata, 1979, p. 40). Consider the fuzzy set cohabiting/not cohabiting. The membership function expresses for each person in a certain group the grade or degree of membership (expressed by a number between zero and one) with respect to this fuzzy set. Hence one person may have been given a grade of membership of cohabiting/not-cohabiting status of 0.87, indicating a strong degree of cohabitation, whereas another person may have been given a grade of membership of 0.19, when the relation with the partner is only weak. Ideally, two cohabiting partners would have the same grade of membership, although any differences between them might capture differences in subjective experience of the relationship. Given the inexactitude of household behaviour, it appears worthwhile exploring the application of fuzzy set theory in household demography (for an earlier suggestion, see Paelinck, 1983, p. 77).

Now let us discuss the link between household theory and household forecasting. It has been argued that theories of population growth cannot be usefully incorporated in forecasts (Keyfitz, 1982, p. 144). Several reasons account for that; for instance, many theories provide only conditional results, different theories predict different demographic trends, exogenous variables cannot be forecasted, empirical evidence may change, or reliable predictions can only be given for the very short term. These arguments seem to apply not only to fertility, but also to household behaviour. Does that mean that household theories are useless if one wants to predict household trends? In order to answer this question, one should focus on exogenous variables in the model and distinguish between qualitative and quantitative trends in those variables. This refers to different levels of forecast assumptions, and qualitative trends (increase, levelling off, cyclic behaviour, and so on) are assessed on what Pittenger (1977, p. 365) calls the 'scenario' level. Household theories may provide useful information for these general trends, although different theories may point in different directions (see for instance Espenshade, 1985, pp. 236–8). However, they will be of little use when assumptions formulated on the 'scenario' level have to be quantified. It is here that the extrapolation of observed regularities has to be applied, since a truly behavioural way of estimating future household trends is impossible. The situation in household demography is perhaps similar to that in other disciplines. Consider, for instance, the opinion of Openshaw (1986, p. 145) regarding regional science, that '. . . theory-based models . . . will probably move asymptotically to a level of predictive performance not much better than can be achieved by theoryless black-box methods of today'. And in econometric model building some scholars doubt the effectiveness of including behavioural equations in models. Our understanding of economic behaviour is so inadequate that a particular value for the independent variables in a behavioural relation will in many cases enable the value of the dependent variable to be specified over a comparatively large range only (Van Driel *et al.*, 1980, p. 37). Instead, a 'core' model could be used, in which the behavioural equations are replaced by inequalities, which vary from inevitable limitations (for example, actual production does not exceed available capacity) to requirements (for example, no decrease of available capacity in some sectors), to avowed political desiderata (for example, unemployment decreases by at least *x* per cent). The mathematical consequence of working with inequalities is that one transfers from the world of difference equations to that of optimization models. The freedom of movement of the 'dependent' variables is much larger in such a model, since there are usually a number of feasible solutions, instead of just one as in the model with equalities. This neatly expresses our ignorance about the exact course the model variables will take.

One is inclined to think that the formal modelling in household demography (or perhaps in demography in general) should be generalized into composite modelling in which quantitative as well as qualitative features are incorporated. This task involves mostly the development of a comprehensive language within a formal system which is adequate for describing models that are both qualitative and quantitative (Lewis, 1985). Quantitative models express mathematical relationships between the model objects, as do the existing household models. On the other hand, qualitative models characterize logical relationships that are specific to the particular context in which the phenomenon occurs. They could include the qualitative relationships between exogenous and endogenous objects (or model variables) referred to above.

Obviously, all this introduces uncertainty and forecasting errors into household forecasts. Given the poor record of demographic theories as an aid to making quantified predictions it would be appropriate to spend more effort on the study of these errors, rather than merely trying to discover causal mechanisms. In other words, one should not only try to *reduce* uncertainty (by understanding the demographic process), but also, and perhaps more so than in the past, try to *understand* uncertainty and quantify it. The evaluation of past forecasts helps us to improve the quality of future forecasts, because it gives us the possibility of adjusting our judgemental forecasts by using extrapolated regularities in observed forecast errors.

17.5. Microsimulation and macrosimulation

When the household model is too complicated to carry out deductive analyses, we can experiment with the model using specified numerical values for its values and thus simulate the behaviour of the system. Simulation can handle very complex hypotheses. Whatever time sequence of births, whatever age-specific rates of marriage and of childbearing, whatever rates of dissolution are fed into the model, a 'census' can be taken periodically (in the internals of the computer—the only place where the exact count of a population is possible!) to see to what cross-sectional distribution the input rates have led. This is what Heida and Gordijn did when they validated the PRIMOS household model (see section 9.2.4).

Simulators are too frequently confused with models; however, by a simulator we mean a (computer) programme that transforms input data into output data by means of a procedure that itself is based on some prior nonprocedural information: the model. The confusion between a simulator and its underlying formal model is often harmful, because the assumptions that underlie a given model are obscured beyond the point of recognition within the computer programmes that simulate the model: '. . . It is the model, and the analysis thereof, that provides understanding by way of . . . law-like . . . explanations [,] not the simulation of the model [that provides understanding] . . .' (Lewis, 1985, pp. 212, 213).

Analytic solutions contribute more to an understanding of the important factors in the overall process than simulation does, but simulation is needed to obtain any numbers at all when analytic equations prove intractable. The simulation approach has proved its success in kinship modelling in particular, but in formal demography of households it is valuable too.

As was pointed out by Kuijsten and Vossen in chapter 1, two types of simulation approaches may be distinguished: microsimulation and macrosimulation. In a microsimulation programme, each individual (or group of homogeneous individuals) has a record in which the values of a number of relevant attributes are contained: sex, age, household status, marital status, number of children, working status, and so on. These attributes are updated according to the assumed behaviour of the individual. This behaviour is, ideally, expressed in the form of behavioural relationships derived from theory and empirical data, but in practice it is often merely assumed. On the other hand, macrosimulation programmes break the population down by relevant categories (or, alternatively, they assign probabilities for an individual to occupy certain states) and groups of individuals may experience transitions from one category to another during a certain time period.

Many modellers of social phenomena are confronted with the choice between a microsimulation programme and a macrosimulation programme.

However, it appears that most scholars make this choice based on arguments of tradition, convenience, and taste (Wachter, 1986). Therefore, Galler's contribution to this volume is particularly useful, as it describes both the advantages and the disadvantages of microsimulation programmes. They are often very complex and expensive to run (see also Caldwell, 1983, pp. 368, 369). On the other hand, they facilitate a highly detailed description of individuals and households, they create life histories for individuals and households, and they are capable of addressing the role of individual *and* household behaviour (for the latter point, see section 17.7). In general, the pros and cons of microsimulation and macrosimulation balance each other out and thus, as Wachter (1986) states, it is unjustified to claim that any method is intrinsically best. He expects that the joint use of these techniques will be the pattern of the future.

One major advantage of microsimulation is the possibility of introducing several explanatory variables in a relatively easy way, provided that reliable behavioural knowledge is available. Macroprogrammes are based on the concept of a state space, and their size is proportional to the product of the numbers of categories of each explanatory variable. On the other hand, the size of microprogrammes is proportional to the number of these variables, irrespective of the number of classes they contain. Now, for most applications where a relatively large number of explanatory variables is used, the corresponding microsimulation programme would be much smaller than the corresponding macrosimulation programme. This advantage, also mentioned by Galler, is certainly true when only the programmes are considered. But both types require transition probabilities as input parameters, describing the passing of individuals (or groups of individuals) from one state to another. These probabilities can be derived from a data set with the relevant events. Calculation of these probabilities, however, requires numerators and denominators of sufficient size in a multidimensional cross-table set-up. Therefore, in the microsimulation approach, problems related to programme size are shifted towards the data set which produces the input parameters. Problems of this sort may be avoided if one is willing to drop the multidimensional input table for microprogrammes or the state space for macroprogrammes as an appropriate device to include additional explanatory variables. Instead, one could adopt the hazard modelling approach in which transition probabilities or rates are expressed as a function of covariates. An illuminating example of this approach is provided by Courgeau and Lelièvre in section 11.3. Even fairly small data sets permit fitting such hazard models, and transition probabilities dependent on covariates may be included in both approaches.

Nevertheless, any one of the many kinds of transition matrices that can be devised according to the macrosimulation approach has a corresponding way of projecting population. Recognizing age and sex gives the familiar Leslie matrix, very commonly used in forecasting population.

One can go on to incorporate marital status (say single, married, widowed, and divorced), using formulae similar to those of the Leslie matrix, but now with a much larger matrix. Some countries in the Western World thus include marital status in their official population forecasts (Keilman, 1985a). Alternatively, one could recognize household classes and so generate future estimates of persons distributed by age, sex, and household status. Since a useful classification of households requires more than four classes (which is as far as we usually have to go with marital status) this merely means enlarging the matrices once again.

Thus one arrives at household status projection models and runs them by macrosimulation (see the models contained in chapter 9). Simplifying assumptions often have to be made to keep those models manageable. For instance, in the NIDI household model it is assumed that the future household of children leaving their parents is independent of the size of the parental household (Keilman and Van Dam, 1987). This assumption turns out to be necessary because household size is not included in the state space of that model. Also, Kuijsten (section 12.4) reports that model simplifications are necessary but this is caused by data limitations.

If the sometimes strong assumptions could be accepted with impunity and if a certain minimal accuracy could be attained, the usefulness of household projections would not be doubted by anyone. The most obvious practical application is in determining the housing supply needed to accommodate the population, and the types of new dwellings required. Any study of household expenditures and the projection of household expenditures into the future will be aided by knowledge of the future household composition of the population.

17.6. Modelling household dynamics

Many of the purely demographic models in this book can be considered to describe the outcome of a stochastic process in which individuals 'move' from one household situation to another. The choice of these household classes is, of course, of crucial importance for analysis. This choice should be based on insights derived from household theory, although the user's requirements and data restrictions frequently interfere. But once the household classes have been chosen, we may adopt mathematical–statistical theory to describe the processes behind household developments.

To simplify matters, the Markov assumption is commonly used, which states that the probabilities of transition in each duration interval (say year of age, or calendar year) depend only on the distribution of states with which the last interval ended, and in no way on the path through which that last condition was reached. Then, with this Markov assumption, the essentials of the stochastic process are described by the Kolmogorov equation:

$$d\ \mathbf{l}(x)/dx = -\mu(x)\ \mathbf{l}(x), \tag{17.1}$$

where $\mu(x)$ is the matrix of transition intensities at successive ages among whatever states are recognized, and $\mathbf{l}(x)$ is a vertical array (column vector) in which the ith element is the number of the population in the ith category at age x. In general, where people enter and leave the various categories, we are interested in probabilities for the transitions between pairs of categories. Then, with one additional assumption, we can solve expression (17.1) for $\mathbf{l}(x)$ and write it as a function of $\mu(x)$.

If, within the interval $(x, x + h)$, the quantity $\mu_{ij}(x)$ is constant, say M_{ij}, for all i and j, and $\mathbf{M}_x$ is the array of the M_{ij}, then we can write

$$\mathbf{l}(x + h) = \exp\{-h\mathbf{M}_x\}\ \mathbf{l}(x). \tag{17.2}$$

With an arbitrary radix $\mathbf{l}(0)$, equation (17.2) permits the construction of $\mathbf{l}(x)$ step by step at intervals of h all the way to the end of life. Alternatively, expanding the exponential in (17.2) to its first two terms gives

$$\mathbf{l}(x + h) = (\mathbf{I} - h\mathbf{M}_x)\mathbf{l}(x). \tag{17.3}$$

This linear approximation was used by Heida and Gordijn in the PRIMOS household model (see section 9.3). The approximation can be improved by first premultiplying equation (17.2) on both sides by $\exp(\frac{1}{2}h\mathbf{M}_x)$ and then expanding to linear terms to obtain the more symmetric

$$(\mathbf{I} + \tfrac{1}{2}h\mathbf{M}_x)\mathbf{l}(x + h) = (\mathbf{I} - \tfrac{1}{2}h\mathbf{M}_x)\mathbf{l}(x) \tag{17.4}$$

or, on multiplying by $(\mathbf{I} + \frac{1}{2}h\mathbf{M}_x)^{-1}$ on the left,

$$\mathbf{l}(x + h) = (\mathbf{I} + \tfrac{1}{2}h\mathbf{M}_x)^{-1}(\mathbf{I} - \tfrac{1}{2}h\mathbf{M}_x)\mathbf{l}(x). \tag{17.5}$$

Thus equation (17.5) is an approximation close enough for many kinds of data with intervals of one year or even five years.

An alternative approach is due to Schoen (1975) and Rogers and Ledent (1976). They obtain flow equations, the multidimensional analog to $l_{x+h} = l_x - {}_hd_x$, representing relations within the life table. Alongside these are orientation equations, analogous to ${}_hM_x = {}_hd_x/{}_hL_x$, where ${}_hM_x$ is the observed rate. Finally the set is completed with numerical integration equations analogous to ${}_hL_x = (\frac{1}{2}h)(l_x + l_{x+h})$. As in the single-region case, the solution can be given explicitly if one is satisfied with a straight-line integration formula. The result is then

$$\mathbf{l}(x + h) = (\mathbf{I} + \tfrac{1}{2}h\mathbf{M}_x)^{-1}(\mathbf{I} - \tfrac{1}{2}h\mathbf{M}_x)\ \mathbf{l}(x). \tag{17.6}$$

The interpretation of this formula is different from that of equation (17.5). Expression (17.5) should be seen as a linear approximation of (17.2), which satisfies the Kolmogorov equation when transition intensities $\mu(x)$ are constant during $(x, x + h)$. In order to arrive at (17.6) it is assumed that the survival function $\mathbf{l}(x)$ is linear in x during $(x, x + h)$. In that case, (17.6) is considered to be the exact solution of the Kolmogorov equation, in which the intensities are a hyperbolic function of time. Meanwhile, it should be noted that any state vector $\mathbf{l}(x + h)$ obtained by expression (17.6) is numerically very close to its counterpart obtained by the corresponding exponential formula. When the same $\mathbf{M}_x$ is used in both cases, a Taylor series approximation shows that they are equivalent when terms in $\mathbf{M}_x$ of powers three and higher may be disregarded.

There are, however, some difficulties when expression (17.6) is used. Under certain conditions, the matrix

$$\mathbf{P}(x, x + h) = (\mathbf{I} + \tfrac{1}{2}h\mathbf{M}_x)^{-1}(\mathbf{I} - \tfrac{1}{2}h\mathbf{M}_x) \qquad (17.7)$$

contains elements outside the (0,1)-range and cannot be considered a transition probability matrix (Hoem and Funck Jensen, 1982). This is the case when at least one diagonal element of the matrix $\mathbf{M}_x$ exceeds the value $2/h$. Moreover, it can be demonstrated that the linear integration model in expression (17.6) is not compatible with the Markov assumption (Keilman and Gill, 1986). Projection by multiplication of the matrix in (17.7) for successive ages is therefore aesthetically unsatisfactory, and the model with constant intensities could be used instead. However, we want to stress the fact that the linear integration model as well as the constant intensities model should often be seen as no more than a rough approximation of reality. This is particularly true when the events and their accompanying intensities show considerable fluctuations, for example, with infant mortality or with seasonal patterns in marriage behaviour when the interval length is one year.

It should be noted that both the macrosimulation *and* the microsimulation approach require an expression for the probability of making a transition from one state to another, to be derived from the parameters of the stochastic process. But in the microsimulation approach, as opposed to macrosimulation, not much attention seems to be paid to such a derivation. As an illustration of the difficulties arising as a consequence of this, consider the phenomena mortality and nuptiality that Galler's microsimulation model describes. In section 10.3 he informs us about priorities in the sequence of events. Individuals are subject first to the risks of mortality and the survivors next to those of nuptiality. But mortality first, followed by divorce, will produce different results from those obtained if divorce comes first and mortality next. This is so because mortality shows considerable differences for persons of various marital states. Clarke (1986, p. 251) even lists the problem of sequential ordering of events as one of the drawbacks of microsimulation.

In general one could say that the priority in two or more events is important when these events are correlated. Courgeau and Lelièvre provide us with examples from the competing risks theory (their 'bivariate' problem, section 11.2.1) illustrating the usefulness of a stochastic process framework, and which could be applied fruitfully in microsimulation, thus avoiding the need to choose a particular priority. In that case, one does not evaluate the possible occurrences of two or more events one by one (event A: yes/no; event B: yes/no, . . .). Rather, the possible occurrences of those events are considered simultaneously (event A/event B/no event). This may be achieved by drawing two or more uniformly distributed numbers and comparing them with the probabilities of occurrence of the event in question which are calculated in the model. To account for the competing risks nature of this model, the event may be chosen for which the computed probability is closest to the drawn number, as measured by some distance function.

17.7. Unit of analysis: The individual or the household?

Household demography deals with groups consisting of several individuals. Dynamic household models, therefore, may describe the behaviour of households or the behaviour of individuals belonging to households. But the problem of choosing between the individual and the household as a unit of analysis is an unresolved issue in household demography, unless, of course, one studies one-person households.

Modelling individual behaviour has at least four advantages:

   (i) the methodology is well-known from conventional analysis of population dynamics, as was argued by Kuijsten and Vossen in the introductory chapter;

  (ii) data on individual events are produced more often than those for household processes. This argument has, among others, been brought forward by Kamarás in chapter 14, where he discusses possibilities of modelling household dynamics among the aged;

 (iii) it is much easier to define and classify individual persons than households, as we argued in section 17.2;

 (iv) an individual experiences birth and death only once, whereas a household may 'be born' and may 'die' more than once.

On the other hand, taking the individual as the unit of analysis has two important drawbacks, as compared to analysing the household:

   (i) many decisions (migration, housing choice, saving, consumption) that influence household behaviour are taken by the household (see, for instance, Castro and Rogers, 1983), or at least by some smaller group within the household, as Ermisch argues in chapter 3;

  (ii) the behaviour of individual household members is often interrelated. For instance, when a partner leaves the household, this changes the household situation of the remaining members.

These arguments show that the issue of selecting a proper unit for analysing and modelling households is particularly important when dynamic behaviour, that is, household formation and dissolution, is studied. In a static analysis, simple grouping rules may be sufficient to retain consistency between individual and household aspects. When household dynamics are studied, we need a different approach.

The issue of a proper unit of analysis is present throughout this book. For example, Ermisch introduces the minimal household unit (MHU) as an intermediate unit between the individual and the household. He argues that the MHU, and not each (adult) member forms the economic decision-making unit. He takes one utility function for the entire MHU and assumes restrictions upon its budget. Hence he implicitly supposes a total harmony of interests between MHU members. Others argue that this may be appropriate for certain decisions, but that it seems unlikely in general (Renaud and Siegers, 1984). Therefore, one might prefer to specify a separate utility function for each MHU member and consider the individual as the decision-making unit.

The issue is not new in family economics. Samuelson (1956) formulates his family consensus model which postulates a family social welfare function, and he gives an early discussion of this problem. Becker's use of the concept 'altruism' implies that individual differences of preference between family members can be submerged and that the family can be treated as a single harmonious unit with consistent preferences (see for instance Becker, 1981, p. 192).

A second example of the individual/household issue is provided by Galler who demonstrates that one may describe household behaviour on *both* levels when a microsimulation approach is used. Each person has an individual record, containing the relevant attributes, including position in the household. This creates the possibility of assembling personal records in household records and of describing the relationships between household members. Thus individual behaviour may induce changes in the characteristics of the particular household, including some attributes of other household members. This is similar to what was done in the Japanese household microsimulation model for health and welfare administration (Hanada, 1984, p. 32; Kono, 1986). Thus, in a microsimulation approach, consistency between individual behaviour and household behaviour is automatically guaranteed.

The interdependency of the individual behaviour of members of one household brings us to an important methodological issue in household modelling. One may prefer the individual as a unit of analysis and introduce a classification not only by individual characteristics (sex, age, marital status, and so on), but also by household characteristics such as household size and type of household. But, as was noted above, this approach requires that one deals adequately with interdependencies between household members.

The problem of interdependency of the behaviour of members belonging to a family or a household was first recognized in the forties, and was then known as the 'two-sex problem'. Authors like Vincent, Karmel, and Hajnal studied fertility using models which were no longer female-dominant, as were the familiar models of Lotka and Leslie. Instead, they related births to females *and* males, thus ensuring that the number of births in a certain period depends on the availability of adults of both sexes. Karmel, Kendall, and Goodman established the relationship with marriage. During the seventies, divorce and transition to widowhood were introduced, mainly due to the fact that some countries (Denmark, Sweden, Norway, Great Britain, the Netherlands) produced official population forecasts in which individuals were classified by sex, age, and marital status as well. For instance, the two-sex requirement applied to widowhood states that the number of new widows in a certain period is equal to the number of married males dying, and vice versa. When the unit of analysis is the individual, rather than the married couple, any realistic nuptiality model should fulfil these and other two-sex requirements.

Relationships between the behaviour of the sexes should be formulated for household models, too. For example, when 'cohabiting' is one of the household states that an individual can occupy, the numbers of new female cohabitors and new male cohabitors in a certain period should be equal (assuming equal numbers of males and female homosexual couples). But in household modelling the problem is of a more general nature than that of the two sexes. Therefore, one might speak of a 'consistency problem' or an 'interdependency problem'. An illustration taken from the NIDI household model may clarify this (see Keilman and Van Dam, 1987).

In the NIDI household model, individuals are classified into seven household states. Among these seven we have 'cohabiting' (two adults, not married to each other, having an affectional relationship, no children present), 'other family' (two cohabiting adults and one or more dependent children), and 'dependent child'. Suppose one such child is the only child in an 'other family'. When it leaves the parental home to form a household of its own, the two adults make a transition from 'other family' to 'cohabiting'. Therefore, the NIDI model contains an algorithm to ensure consistency between the number of only children who belong to an 'other family' and who leave the parental household on the one hand and, on the other hand, the number of adults who experience a change in household status induced by this event.

Depending upon the particular classification of individuals by household status, one or more consistency requirements have to be formulated. Any projection model on the sub-household level (including one which applies Ermisch's MHU-concept) would necessitate an algorithm to ensure consistency. The NIDI model contains such an algorithm with ten relations, seven because of consistency in behaviour between males and females, and three describing the relation between adults and dependent children. The algorithm which ensures consistency in these ten relations is the same as the one applied earlier for the official population forecasts of the Netherlands in the context of nuptiality (Keilman, 1985a, pp. 216, 217):

   (i) formulate, for each age and sex, initial values of the occurrence/ exposure rates that describe changes in household status. These rates are assembled in the matrices M_x given in expressions (17.2)–(17.7);

   (ii) check the resulting absolute numbers of events and adjust them for consistency;

   (iii) translate consistent absolute numbers of events into adjusted occurrence/exposure rates.

This algorithm is applied for each (five-year) projection interval.

Step (iii) deserves special attention. If *all* events described by the model were influenced by the consistency algorithm, adjusted occurrence/exposure rates would follow in a straightforward manner from adjusted numbers of *all* events. In practice, however, some events do not show up in the consistency algorithm, and occurrence/exposure rates for these events have to remain unchanged (mortality of individuals in one-person households, for instance). This means that one has to employ a projection formula which contains absolute numbers for some events and occurrence/exposure rates for others. When the projection model is of the linear type as in expression (17.6), step (iii) can be carried out easily with closed form formulae (Keilman, 1985b, p. 1488). However, if one employs the exponential model given in (17.2), iterations are required to derive the occurrence/exposure rates from the corresponding events, keeping rates for other events constant (Keilman and Gill, 1986, pp. 17–20).

The considerations given here demonstrate that rather complicated algorithms are necessary to cope with consistency problems that arise when the individual is chosen as the unit of analysis. One could, in principle, model the behaviour of households, instead of that of individuals. But this creates other difficulties, as will be shown below. An important one is the problem of a longitudinal definition of a household and, related to that, transitions of households from one type to another. We will not discuss here quasi-longitudinal household definitions which characterize the household by variable(s) of one member, such as age and/or marital status of the head or of the wife (for example, Pitkin and Masnick, 1980).

    McMillan and Herriot (1985) give a thorough discussion of the possibility of developing a proper longitudinal household definition. The core of this problem is that a set of continuity rules or accounting principles must be developed which identify cases of household formation, household dissolution, and cases where two households at two points in time are identified as the same household. In other words, it must be decided what will be defined as being the same and what will be defined as a change.

The discussion by McMillan and Herriot shows that all possible dynamic household definitions contain one or more decision rules which are arbitrary to a certain extent. For instance, one possibility they list involves the rule that two households, at two separate points in time, which have the same head of household, are the same household. This approach is analogous to the concept of a 'marker', proposed by Brass (1983). These ideas may be criticized because of the somewhat arbitrary way in which the head of household is defined, and because it may create what some consider an unreasonable change within a continuing household (McMillan and Herriot, 1985, p. 52). Another example of arbitrariness is the rule adopted by the authors in their own definition of a longitudinal household: they consider a household to be a continuous one as long as the head of household and 50 per cent or more of the members are the same at two points in time (McMillan and Herriot, 1985, p. 53). Also, Muhsam (1984, p. 42), in his discussion of a transition probability matrix of family structure, reports difficulties in accounting for the creation of new families, leading to arbitrary decision rules.

Arbitrariness alone is not a sufficient reason to criticize the approach discussed above. More important is the fact that different continuity rules produce different findings for the same situation. Ernst *et al.* (1985) give a methodological discussion of the impact that different longitudinal household definitions may have upon the estimation of such household variables as income and labour force participation. Citro (1985) assesses the implications of measuring poverty and income, on an annual basis, on different ways of defining longitudinal households. Using data from the 1979 Research Panel of the Income Survey Development Program in the United States, she finds household counts corresponding with six alternative definitions, where the maximum count exceeds the minimum number by 26 per cent. McMillan and Herriot (1985, p. 53) analyse households facing divorce, and they assume that the female half of these households will be poor after divorce. On the basis of one definition, 20 per cent of the households would be below the poverty line during a particular period of time, whereas, with another definition, the corresponding figure is 50 per cent. This is caused by the fact that some definitions create a much larger number of households of a certain type (and much less of another type) than do other definitions.

This section has shown that the choice between the individual and the household as a unit of analysis is by no means an easy one. Both approaches have major drawbacks. It is our impression that choosing the individual may be preferred (although one may maintain that we are not dealing with household demography in that case, but rather with some extended form of the traditional individual-based demography, see Kuijsten, 1987, and chapter 12 by the same author). *Modelling* individual household behaviour requires a proper solution to the problem of interdependence between household members. Although, from a theoretical point of view, Ryder (1985, p. 209) correctly states that the latter problem has so far proven resistant to technical ingenuity, the solutions recently suggested in the context of projection models may be considered to be good working approximations. As for *analysing* the data collected at the individual level, these reveal an unambiguous picture of reality, once a household classification is chosen. When the unit of a household is adopted for analysis, observations on historical trends will contain a certain (sometimes large) degree of bias due to arbitrary dynamic household definitions. Building a household model based on such problematic data is a hazardous task.

Duncan and Hill (1985, pp. 368–72) list various types of objections that have been raised against their assertion that the longitudinal household approach should be abandoned in favour of an individual-based approach. Two important problems are that a longitudinal household definition is needed if data are to be comparable, since so much work has been done with cross-sectional data using the household as the unit of analysis; and that behavioural theories dictate that the household, rather than the individual, is the decision-making unit. But Duncan and Hill respond to these objections that no longitudinal definition of a household produces a truly comparable analogue to a cross-sectional household; and that few theories based at the household level have adequately handled compositional changes.

Our final point with respect to the individual/household issue is of a more philosophical nature. Our preference for the individual as a unit of observation, analysis, and modelling implies that we believe that the properties of the whole (the household) can be understood through the dynamics of the parts (the individual household members). But in quantum theory, the relationship was reversed at the beginning of this century: physicists now believe that the parts (atoms, particles) show different properties depending on the experimental context. They interpret nature not as a mechanical universe composed of fundamental building blocks but rather as a network of relations: and they think that, ultimately, there are no parts at all in this interconnected web. Whatever we call a part is merely a pattern that has some stability and therefore captures our attention. Thus, the whole is primary and, once you understand its dynamics, you can then derive the properties and interactions of the parts. Capra (1985) believes that this new paradigm applies to all sciences where systems thinking is used, not just to physics. If this is true for demography, too, then our preference for analysing the individual might be outdated sooner or later. Of course, no one will argue that individual persons (the parts) do not exist. But it is certainly true that they behave differently depending on the context. Applying Capra's thesis to household demography might therefore imply that one should study the network of relations between individuals inside (and outside?) the household, in order to understand the behaviour of the individual—and many sociologists will wholeheartedly agree. Is our present preference for the individual as the object of analysis mainly due to the attention the individual receives in Western society and to the trends of increasing individualization in our era?

17.8. Data, models, and parameter estimation techniques: Some prospects

Most students of household demography only deal with one particular issue. They develop theories of household behaviour or improve existing ones, they construct household models or extend others, or they are responsible for data collection. This focus on selected aspects of household demography may be the reason for the fact that, according to some scholars, they can only report marginal improvements over earlier results because progress in other areas is very slow. For instance, there is a shortage of statistical household data, and this is sometimes attributed to the lack of theoretical study of the household. Others complain about the opposite—that the lack of theory is due to the lack of statistical information. Certainly, theory and data influence each other and the absence of one may be a handicap to the other. In addition to that, the complexity of the subject of household demography makes it difficult both to gather data and to develop rational understanding (Keyfitz, 1985, p. 371; Bongaarts, 1983, p. 27). However, we strongly believe that prospects for further improvements in the field of household demography are better than the pessimistic assertions above suggest.

First, there are data. Wall (1984, p. 75) notes that there are three difficulties: lack of comparability between one country and another in their definitions of household and family; a failure to record the full variety of household and family types; and amendments to table design and to definitions between censuses which destroy the temporal sequence. Therefore, the United Nations give high priority to the systematic collection of internationally comparable statistics on households and families. As a consequence, the programme of work of the Conference of European Statisticians (CES) includes a project 'Statistics of household and families'. Work to be undertaken in this project involves not only a review of definitions of households and a further study of criteria used in applying these definitions in different data sources, as was discussed in section 17.2. Also, the CES plans to analyse classifications used in tabulating household statistics, to collect and tabulate data on special types of households (for example, lone-parent families, consensual unions), to co-ordinate and integrate data on households and families obtained from different sources, and finally to study methodological and technical problems in measuring household and family formation and dissolution (United Nations, 1983a).

In some countries, the statistical bureau devotes much effort to a systematic collection of household data. For instance, in Denmark work is well under way to construct register-based annual household and family statistics (Petersen, 1985). One striking point in this project carried out by the Statistical Bureau of Denmark is that the general structure of the register is very similar to the computer files used in microsimulation models. Each person's family and household characteristics are established, following cer-. tain classification rules. Reference numbers define for each individual his or her ties to other members of the family, and a household consists of all persons living at the same address, irrespective of family relationship.

In the United States, the Bureau of the Census started a major panel survey of 20,000 households and their members in 1983–4. To this so-called Survey of Income and Program Participation (SIPP) a second panel of 15,000 households was added in 1985 and a third of 15,000 households in 1986. SIPP follows individuals with periodic measurements at intervals of four months during a period of 32 months. It collects a wide range of information on family characteristics, fertility, health, employment history, and, in particular, socio-economic characteristics. Many methodological issues arising in the context of such a complex survey have been discussed in the annual meetings of the American Statistical Association in 1984 and 1985.

These recent developments show that there is considerable scope for improved collection of household data and that many promising attempts have been undertaken already. However, we think that these new data should be available in such a form that one is able to carry out *longitudinal* household analyses.

While a great deal of what we know about the family, as about mortality and other elements of individual demography, is by means of cross-sectional analysis, in which it is assumed that the reports on successive ages at a given moment in time are valid for successive ages of the same cohort, one would like to get rid of the assumption wherever there is a suspicion that significant changes have taken place among cohorts. That is the reason why so much effort has been put into longitudinal analysis. The longitudinal analysis is sometimes based on successive interviews, say one a year, of the same households (panel survey), and sometimes on interviews that attempt to pick up the history of the household retrospectively.

Many of the data sources in this book enable one to take a longitudinal perspective. The Bielefeld project in Klijzing's chapter and the OPCS 1% Longitudinal Study discussed by Murphy, Sullivan, and Brown are panel surveys. The Belgian NEGO-project, the General Household Survey in Great Britain, the Norwegian WFS-survey, the Dutch ORIN-survey (see Klijzing in chapter 4), as well as the French BBB-project (see Courgeau and Lelièvre, chapter 11) contain retrospective elements.

Because of the way in which household composition changes so drastically during the course of the life cycle, longitudinal analysis is particularly appropriate for household demography.

With successive cross-sections that do not follow individual households one can indeed ascertain net changes: fractions of households that are below the poverty line in successive points in time (but it is also of value to have the gross figures)—how many households rose above the poverty line in the time interval, and how many fell below it? What kinds of households move in each direction across the poverty line?

One would also like to know something about the relationship of variables applying at one age to the circumstances of the household at a later stage. How does a woman's employment experience prior to marriage affect her employment prospects when she re-enters the labour market after the children have left home (Parnes, 1972, p. 13)? Cross-sectional studies cannot deal with such questions.

Given the scope for improved collection of household data, it is not unreasonable to expect that this will lead to better theories and more realistic models, following the usual sequence of model-building laid down by Kuijsten and Vossen in their introduction. Then, still, it may be the case that there is insufficient data to estimate the parameters of the model (a situation which is, of course, currently observed, too). Openshaw calls this the *ultimate dilemma for theory-based models*: better theory leads to models for which there are either no data or only partial data. On the other hand, '. . . attempts to simplify the theoretical content of models to match available data tend to result in such butchery that any pretence of a theoretical basis becomes impossible to sustain' (Openshaw, 1986, p. 145). But special techniques of parameter estimation may partly remedy the severe problems caused by scarce data. Therefore, we think that a *second* area for improvement of household demography is the application of modern techniques of parameter estimation. Two examples may illustrate this: indirect estimation techniques and mathematical–statistical estimation techniques.

Indirect estimation techniques attempt to measure values of basic demographic parameters, such as the birth rate, the death rate, or the level of total fertility, under less than perfect conditions. These techniques depend upon models, use consistency checks, or indeed use conventional data in an unconventional way (United Nations, 1983b, p. 2). However, indirect estimation techniques do not have to be restricted to vital events. The field of household demography, for which either data-collection systems do not exist or their performance is poor relative to the models, may benefit from these techniques. For instance, Preston (1986) provides useful techniques for estimating parameters in household demography using data from two censuses. He starts with a well-known cohort relation and then, by assuming local stability, he moves to a contemporary or period relation. It so happens that there are plentiful data from pairs of censuses and, with no (or no calculable) outside flow, the observed counts at age x give the $r(x,t)$, the rates of increase, specific to the particular age, obtained from the pair of censuses. As Preston says, the merit of this approach is that it substitutes a second census for the flow data—registered deaths—that would be used in a more convential calculation.

A formula designed for mortality can be used for any other decrement—in particular for the decrement of marriage dissolution. Formally there is no difference between the survivorship of an individual in the face of death and the survival of a marriage in the face of any other contingency that terminates marriage—specially divorce. A test, by comparison with the marriage table of the US National Center for Health Statistics relating to 1975, comes out well. For example, the probability that a marriage will survive 10 years is 0.670 on the Preston method and 0.673 on the official NCHS calculation using flow data.

Preston goes on to analyse age at marriage if the decrement of mortality were eliminated. He is able to improve on the Hajnal (1953) results in which a single census was used, and which have the disadvantage of combining marriage and mortality rates of a mix of past periods. The Preston method requires no assumption relating to any period prior to the first of the two censuses on which it is based.

Recent developments in *mathematical statistics* have produced estimation techniques that are especially suitable when the data are incomplete in some sense. For instance, Partial Likelihood methods (Cox, 1975; Gill, 1984) may effectively deal with the estimation of model parameters from censored data. Courgeau and Lelièvre used this method for their semiparametric model in section 11.3.1. Another promising method which was recently developed in mathematical statistics is the EM-algorithm, which we shall discuss below.

The EM-algorithm is a method for Maximum Likelihood estimation of model parameters from incomplete data (Dempster *et al.*, 1977). The iterative algorithm may be applied to various situations, including the cases of missing values, of grouped, censored, or truncated data, of models with a finite mixture of probability density functions, and many others. Each iteration of the algorithms consists of an expectation step followed by a maximization step—hence the name EM-algorithm. The expectation step gives an estimation of the *complete* data, given the *observed* data and the model. The maximization step then takes the estimated complete data as if they were the observed data and estimates the unknown parameters by Maximum Likelihood.

In their paper, Dempster *et al.* derive theory showing that successive iterations always increase the likelihood function, and that convergence implies a stationary point of this function. They also give sufficient conditions for convergence and they describe the rate of convergence of the algorithm close to a stationary point.

We must be well aware of the drawbacks of the EM-algorithm—for instance, it does not readily provide estimates of standard errors, and in some applications it is computationally worse in performance than other algorithms (see the discussion following the article by Dempster *et al.*). But the algorithm is simple to implement and its numerical stability is very good. It should be regarded as a powerful candidate for Maximum Likelihood estimation procedures in the situation where data to estimate the parameters of a household model are scarce or incomplete. Demographers have traditionally fitted their models by what statisticians call 'the method of moments', that is, they equated model moments with corresponding observed values. Hence difficulties arise when we have more model parameters than data points. In those situations, modern estimation techniques proposed in mathematical statistics may fruitfully be applied.

Thus, we have argued that both data collection and theory are handicapped by the complexity of the field of household demography but that modern estimation techniques may help to find a way out of the difficulties that arise.

References

ALONSO, W. (1986). Intuition, science and the application of regional models, in: A. M. Isserman (ed.), *Population Change and the Economy: Social Science Theory and Models* (Kluwer-Nijhoff, Boston), 261–9.

BECKER, G. S. (1981). *A Treatise on the Family* (Harvard University Press, Cambridge, Mass.).

—— E. M. LANDES, AND R. T. MICHAEL (1977). An economic analysis of marital instability, *Journal of Political Economy* 85(6), 1141–87.

BONGAARTS, J. (1983). The formal demography of families and households: an overview, *IUSSP Newsletter* 17, 27–42.

—— T. K. BURCH, AND K. W. WACHTER (eds.) (1986). *Family Demography: Methods and their Application* (Oxford University Press, Oxford).

BRASS, W. (1983). The formal demography of the family: an overview of the proximate determinants, in: The family, Proceedings of the British Society for Population Studies Conference, 1983, Office of Population Censuses and Surveys Occasional Paper no. 31 (OPCS, London), 37–49.

BURCH, T. K. (1985). Changing age-sex roles and household crowding: a theoretical note, in: *International Population Conference, Florence 1985*, vol. 3 (IUSSP, Liège), 253–61.

CALDWELL, S. B. (1983). Modelling demographic–economic interactions: micro, macro and linked micro/macro strategies, *Socio-Economic Planning Science* 17(5–6), 365–72.

CAPRA, F. (1986). Criteria of systems thinking, *Futures*, Oct. 1985, 475–8.

CASTRO, L. J. AND A. ROGERS (1983). Patterns of family migration: two methodological approaches, *Environment and Planning A* 15, 237–54.

CITRO, C. F. (1985). Alternative definitions of longitudinal households in the Income Survey Development Program: implications for annual statistics, in: *Survey of Income and Program Participation 1985*, compiled by D. Frankel (US Bureau of the Census, Washington, DC), 21–6.

CLARKE, M. (1986). Demographic processes and household dynamics: a micro-simulation approach, in: R. Woods and Ph. Rees (eds.), *Population Structures and Models: Developments in Spatial Demography* (Allen and Unwin, London), 245–72.

COX, D. R. (1975). Partial likelihood, *Biometrika* 62, 269–76.

DEMPSTER, A. P., N. M. LAIRD, AND D. R. RUBIN (1977). Maximum Likelihood from incomplete data via the EM algorithm, *Journal of the Royal Statistical Society B* 39, 1–38 (with discussion).

DUNCAN, G. J. AND M. S. HILL (1985). Conceptions of longitudinal households: fertile or futile? *Journal of Economic and Social Measurement* 13(3/4), 361–75.

EASTERLIN, R. A. (1980). *Birth and Fortune: The Impact of Numbers on Personal Welfare* (Basic Books, New York).

ERNST, L. R., D. L. HUBBLE, AND D. R. JUDKINS (1985). Longitudinal family and household estimation in SIPP, in: *Survey of Income and Program Participation and Related Longitudinal Surveys 1984*, compiled by D. Kasprzyk and D. Frankel (US Bureau of the Census, Washington, DC), 105–10.

ESPENSHADE, TH. J. (1985). Marriage trends in America: estimates, implications and underlying causes, *Population and Development Review* 11(2), 193–245.

GILL, R. D. (1984). Understanding Cox's regression model: a martingale approach, *Journal of the American Statistical Association* 79(386), 441–7.

GLICK, P. C. (1947). The family life cycle, *American Sociological Review* 12, 164–74.

GUTTENTAG, M. AND P. F. SECORD (1983). *Too Many Women? The Sex Ratio Question* (Sage, Beverly Hills, Calif.).

HAJNAL, J. (1953). Age at marriage and proportions marrying, *Population Studies* 7(2), 111–36.

HANADA, K. (1984). A household micro-simulation model for health and welfare administration, in: *Demography of the Family* (CICRED, Paris), 31–2.

HOEM, J. M. AND U. FUNCK JENSEN (1982). Multistate life table methodology: a probabilist critique, in: K. C. Land and A. Rogers (eds.), *Multidimensional Mathematical Demography* (Academic Press, New York), 155–264.

KEILMAN, N. W. (1985a). Nuptiality models and the two-sex problem in national population forecasts, *European Journal of Population* 1(2/3), 207–35.

—— (1985b). Internal and external consistency in multidimensional population projection models, *Environment and Planning A* 17, 1473–98.

—— AND R. D. GILL (1986). On the estimation of multidimensional demographic models with population registration data, Working Paper no. 68 (Netherlands Interuniversity Demographic Institute, The Hague).

—— AND J. VAN DAM (1987). A dynamic household model: an application of multidimensional demography to life styles in the Netherlands (Netherlands Interuniversity Demographic Institute, The Hague).

KEYFITZ, N. (1982). Can knowledge improve forecasts?, *Population and Development Review* 8(4), 729–51.

—— (1985). *Applied Mathematical Demography* (Springer Verlag, New York), 2nd edn.

KONO, S. (1986). The headship rate method for projecting households, in: Bongaarts, Burch, and Wachter (1986).

KUIJSTEN, A. (1987). Has family demography something to contribute to urban planning? in: *Population and Family in the Low Countries V* (Netherlands Interuniversity Demographic Institute, The Hague).

LESTHAEGHE, R. (1983). A century of demographic and cultural change in Western Europe, *Population and Development Review* 9, 411–36.

LEWIS, A. A. (1985). Complex structures and composite models: an essay on methodology, *Mathematical Social Sciences* 10(3), 211–46.

LUCE, R. D. AND H. RAIFFA (1957). *Games and Decisions: Introduction and Critical Survey* (Wiley, New York).

MCELROY, M. B. AND M. J. HORNEY (1981). Nash-bargained household decisions: towards a generalization of the theory of demand, *International Economic Review* 22(2), 333–49.

MCMILLAN, D. B. AND R. HERRIOT (1985). Toward a longitudinal definition of households, *Journal of Economic and Social Measurement* 13(3/4), 349–60.

MANSER, M. AND M. BROWN (1980). Marriage and household-decision making: a bargaining analysis, *International Economic Review* 21(1), 31–44.

MUHSAM, H. (1984). The transition probabilities in the demography of the family, in: *Demography of the Family* (CICRED, Paris), 37–43.

OPENSHAW, S. (1986). Modelling relevance, *Environment and Planning A* 18(2), 143–7.

PAELINCK, J. H. P. (1983). Bevolkingsstructuur en sociaal economische aspecten (Population structure and socio-economic aspects), in: *Demografisch onderzoek en praktijk* (Demographic research and practice) (Nationaal Programma Demografisch Onderzoek, Voorburg, The Netherlands), 66–88.

PAMPEL, F. C. (1983). Changes in the propensity to live alone: evidence from consecutive cross-sectional surveys, 1960–1976, *Demography* 20, 433–47.

PARNES, H. S. (1972). Longitudinal surveys: prospects and problems, *Monthly Labor Review*, Feb. 1972, 11–15.

PETERSEN, O. K. (1985). Register-based family and household statistics, in: *The Seventh Nordic Demographic Symposium* (The Scandinavian Demographic Society, Helsinki) (Scandinavian Population Studies 7), 74–87.

PITKIN, J. R. AND G. S. MASNICK (1980). Projections of housing consumption in the U.S. 1980–2000 by a cohort method (US Department of Housing and Urban Development, Washington, DC).

PITTENGER, D. B. (1977). Population forecasting standards: some considerations concerning their necessity and content, *Demography* 14(3), 363–8.

POLLAK, R. A. (1985). A transition cost approach to families and households, *Journal of Economic Literature* 23, 581–608.

PRESTON, S. H. (1986). Estimation of certain measures in family demography based upon generalized stable population relations, in: Bongaarts, Burch, and Wachter (1986).

RENAUD, P. S. A. AND J. J. SIEGERS (1984). Income and substitution effects in family labour supply, *De Economist* 132(3), 350–66.

ROGERS, A. AND J. LEDENT (1976). Increment–decrement life tables: a comment, *Demography* 13(2), 287–90.

RYDER, N. B. (1985). Recent developments in the formal demography of the family, in: *International Population Conference, Florence 1985*, vol. 3 (IUSSP, Liège), 207–20.

SAMUELSON, P. A. (1956). Social indifference curves, *Quarterly Journal of Economics* 70(1), 1–22.

SCHOEN, R. (1975). Constructing increment–decrement life tables, *Demography* 12, 313–24.

SEKITA, Y. AND Y. TABATA (1979). A health status index model using a fuzzy approach, *European Journal of Operations Research* 3, 40–9.

UNITED NATIONS (1983a). Statistics of households and families, note by the secretariat no. CES/494 (Statistical Commission and Economic Commission for Europe, Conference of European Statisticans, 31st plenary session, 13–17 June 1983, Geneva).

—— (1983b). Manual X: indirect techniques for demographic estimation, Population Studies no. 81 (United Nations, New York).

VAN DRIEL, G. J., J. A. HARTOG, AND C. VAN RAVENZWAAIJ (1980). *Limits to the Welfare State* (Martinus Nijhoff, Boston).

WACHTER, K. W. (1986). Microsimulation of household cycles, in: Bongaarts, Burch, and Wachter (1986).

WALL, R. (1984). Beyond the nuclear family, in: *Demography of the Family* (CICRED, Paris), 72-5.

WILSON, E. O. (1975). *Sociobiology: The New Synthesis* (Harvard University Press, Cambridge, Mass.).

ZADEH, L. A. (1982). Fuzzy systems theory: a framework for the analysis of humanistic systems, in: R. Cavallo (ed.), *Systems Methodology in Social Science Research: Recent Developments* (Kluwer-Nijhoff, Boston), 25-41.

Author index

Subject index